D0981946

PETER MANSBRIDGE ONE ON ONE

PETER MANSBRIDGE

ONE ON ONE

FAVOURITE CONVERSATIONS AND THE STORIES BEHIND THEM

RETIRÉ DE LA COLLECTION UNIVERSELLE
Bibliothèque et Archives nationales du Québec

RANDOM HOUSE CANADA

Copyright in the Work © 2009 Peter Mansbridge
Interview Material © Canadian Broadcasting Corporation

All rights reserved under International and Pan-American Copyright Conventions.
No part of this book may be reproduced in any form or by any electronic or mechanical
means, including information storage and retrieval systems, without permission in
writing from the publisher, except by a reviewer, who may quote brief passages in a
review. Published in 2009 by Random House Canada, a division of Random House of
Canada Limited, Toronto. Distributed in Canada by Random House of Canada Limited.

www.randomhouse.ca

Random House Canada and colophon are registered trademarks.

Library and Archives Canada Cataloguing in Publication

Mansbridge, Peter
        Peter Mansbridge one on one : favourite conversations and the stories
behind them / Peter Mansbridge.

Interviews first aired during the first 10 years of the television show
     Mansbridge: one on one.

ISBN 978-0-307-35784-7

1. Interviews—Canada. 2. Interviews. I. Title. II. Title: Mansbridge
one on one (Television program).

CT120.M353 2009   920.071   C2009-901749-0

Design by Jennifer Lum

Printed in the United States of America

2 4 6 8 9 7 5 3 1

For Jennifer, Pamela and Will

CONTENTS

ACKNOWLEDGEMENTS

A BOOK LIKE THIS OBVIOUSLY INVOLVES the work of more than just one person, and this is my opportunity to acknowledge those who truly made it happen.

Cynthia Dale and Will Mansbridge allowed me the time to write what I needed to write, and both were never shy about what they thought worked and what didn't.

Leslie Stojsic is the producer of *Mansbridge One on One*, and from the first hint of this project she has been all over it, chasing down the transcripts and supervising their editing, looking for matching photographs and video images, and always bouncing new ideas off my head (and yes, some of them hurt).

Tony Burman, my former boss at CBC TV News and now the managing director of Al Jazeera English, deserves thanks for allowing me the opportunity to host a program like *One on One.*

Karen Bower stickhandled the delicate issue of rights at the CBC for both the transcripts and the CBC images that are found on these pages. John Rahme helped with stills and video.

Mark Bulgutch has been by my side on many of the great stories of our time, from the fall of the Berlin Wall to 9/11 and beyond. When I've needed help with a thought or a word, Mark has always been there, and he didn't let me down on this "story" either.

Chanel Grist Algie was incredibly patient in dealing with a subject who hates posing for pictures.

Perry Zimel has handled negotiations for my written work in the past and handled this, my first book, and I am greatly appreciative of that.

Anthony Wilson-Smith, a former editor of *Maclean's*, encouraged me to start writing down my experiences and gave me the confidence to believe that a lifelong television journalist can actually wade—a tiny bit, anyway—into the waters of print.

And finally, thanks to Michael Schellenberg and Louise Dennys at Random House Canada. Michael cracked the whip and made sure things came in on time and was always ready with an idea or smart criticism. This book was Louise's idea: she pitched it to me and was the one who took the gamble on it. The fact that she is now sitting in her office asking "What did I do?" should not be held against her.

To all, my sincere thanks.

INTRODUCTION

RON FINCH WAS THE FIRST PERSON I ever interviewed. He was a nice fellow: funny, smart and happy in his job. It was the summer of 1969 in Churchill, Manitoba. The summers there are short but there's always lots of action at the grain terminals in the harbour. Finch was the Canada Customs agent monitoring the arrival and departure of foreign ships feverishly taking part in the grain trade. Time was always ticking down on Hudson Bay's ice-free days. When the ice returned, the Port of Churchill was shut down—there was no negotiating that fact.

Customs agent Finch had become a friend during that northern summer forty years ago, and our interview was probably one of the worst I've ever done. And I've done a lot. I've lost track of how many there have been since then, and I certainly couldn't name all the people involved (most of them probably can't remember me either). But in my career as a reporter and correspondent for two decades, and as a nightly news anchor for two more, it is probably safe to assume I've done an average of one interview a day. That begins to approach fifteen thousand interviews. So let's be ultra-conservative and say I've done around ten thousand. Remembering the first one may sound impressive—something like an NHL veteran recounting, years after the fact, his every move as he potted his first career goal. But I remember this interview for one simple reason: I was scared silly. As I lugged my heavy, briefcase-sized 1960s "portable" Nagra tape recorder down to the customs office, I had no idea how to do an interview.

By happy coincidence, it turned out that Finch had no idea how to be interviewed. Thinking back, it was a hilarious scene. We had talked for days about what questions I'd ask, what answers he'd give, how I'd refer to him in my comments, how he'd refer to me, how long he should talk, how I'd thank him at the end. If that sounds like questionable journalism to you, you're right. It's not supposed to happen that way. But the story had its complications, and in fairness to all, let's step back a bit for some context.

I had arrived in Churchill the year before to work as a ticket agent for Transair, one of the country's leading regional airlines. I was nineteen and a high-school dropout, and I had just recently left an exciting but relatively unsuccessful stint in the Royal Canadian Navy. The Transair job looked like fun, and it quickly became just that. I was travelling around the West and the North, doing anything and everything that needed doing. I loaded planes and sold tickets. I was once even responsible for keeping the engines warm on an old but pretty reliable four-engine DC-4 that ran supply missions to isolated weather and defence stations in the High Arctic.

Then one day in September, just a few months after I arrived, with a crowded passenger terminal filled with ticket holders anxious to head south, someone asked me to "announce" the flight. In Churchill that meant heading over to a microphone at the ticket counter, pushing down the Talk button, and rolling out these words: "Transair Flight 106 for Thompson, The Pas and Winnipeg is now ready for boarding at Gate One. Passengers travelling with small children and those requiring boarding assistance, please check with the agent at the gate."

Then I was supposed to dash to the gate to be that agent, but before I could get there, someone who had been standing in the crowd cut in front of me. "You've got a great voice," he said. "Have you ever thought of being in radio?"

And that is how I started working for the CBC. The man in the crowd was Gaston Charpentier, the station manager of CHFC, the tiny CBC Northern Service station in Churchill. The very next night he had me doing the late-night two-hour music show at CHFC. A one-hour training course, a quick tour through the station's selection of 45s and LPs (for younger readers, those were vinyl discs of recorded music that spun around on . . . oh, never mind) and that was that—my career in broadcasting had begun.

Could that happen today? Sure, just like the Leafs could win the Stanley Cup. When I tell this story to journalism students, they are not amused. These young people have spent thousands of their (or their parents') hard-earned dollars on years of classes hoping, just hoping, to get a shot at the short list for such a job. I explain that, back in those Churchill days, getting someone to move north to be a broadcaster was almost impossible, and if I hadn't said yes Charpentier would almost certainly have moved to the next voice he heard. And so today it might be a former taxi dispatcher or bank teller or telephone operator anchoring *The National* and writing this book.

Those early months of broadcasting were hit-and-miss for me. Mostly miss. I was no music buff and possessed no sense of what was needed to make a song a hit. During my high school years, in 1963 and 1964, the early years of the British invasion, all my friends insisted that the best British band was the Beatles and that John, Paul, George and Ringo would last forever. I disagreed, and made the case instead for the Dave Clark Five by mimicking their foot-stomping rendition of "Glad All Over." (To this day I confess total humiliation about my Beatles myopia. Had I been born in another era I might have thought that Shakespeare was an "okay" writer, or that that guy Rembrandt could paint some.)

It took me only a few days to realize that I loved broadcasting and that I wanted to do it for the rest of my life. But if being a music expert was required, I knew I was going to hit the wall pretty quickly. And this is where I thank my parents, who always encouraged my sister, my brother and me to discuss the events of the day around the breakfast and dinner table. We did it all the time—with relish.

So news came naturally to me, as it does to many who end up with a career in journalism. We are fascinated by and curious about what goes on around us. We like asking questions and challenging assumptions, and we like telling others what we've learned. To me, that's the news business in a nutshell. Find out what's happening, then tell everyone. But there are basic skills attached to all this, and in 1969 I had none of them. What was worse, there was no one at the station to train me. In fact there was no local newscast when I joined, so I suggested we start one, and management thought it a fine idea. Of course I didn't have the first clue about how exactly to put a newscast on the radio—good thing it wasn't surgery.

Enter Ron Finch, my first interview assignment. He was dead scared of saying something wrong and ruining his Canada Customs career. I was dead scared of saying anything at all. It's one thing not to know how to do something, but it's infinitely worse to know you don't know; there's no blissful ignorance going in. If there is still a copy of the interview in the CBC Radio archives I can't find it. I do remember what my colleagues said after they heard it: "Sounds a bit wooden, Peter." Or "Were you reading those questions?" Or even worse, "Was he reading his answers?" I was determined never to let that happen again, and so I began right then and there to try to figure out the art of the interview.

When there's no one to teach you how to do something, you have to improvise. In Churchill in 1969, that meant listening to the short-wave. I spent hours and hours listening to how other broadcasters in North America and around the world did interviews, how they wrote newscasts, and of course, how they sounded. I listened to anything and everything I could tune in on the station's receiver: short-wave broadcasts from the BBC, the internal CBC feed, and whatever commercial radio from southern Canada could be picked up at night. Some nights I'd even drive just out of town and try to find some high ground on the tundra (not much of that in Churchill!) to try to pull in a Winnipeg, Saskatoon or Regina station so I could hear how the "professionals" did it.

That helped get me started and effectively launched me into my career as a journalist at the CBC, a career that has taken me through both radio and television, to postings in Winnipeg, Regina, Ottawa and Toronto, temporary stints in Washington and London, and assignments in every province and territory and almost every corner of the world. I've been incredibly lucky, of that there is no doubt, but I've also never forgotten where and how it started.

———

I'VE BEEN ESPECIALLY FORTUNATE to have worked with some of the best interviewers in the business. Barbara Frum, Peter Gzowski and Pamela Wallin are at the top for me. Barbara and Peter were very different from each other, but they had a magical touch that made an interview come alive. Barbara knew her subject cold and you knew she knew it. She would spend hours prepping for every interview, arriving for the task with dozens, sometimes hundreds of pages of scribbled notes along with her producer's research and suggested questions. Her interviews with Pierre Trudeau when he was prime minister were classic—Barbara draped in notes, Trudeau trying to challenge her assumptions, Barbara battling back.

Peter was much more subtle; he knew the topic but he often sounded like it was a "first time" for him. When I first heard him in 1969 it was on a CBC radio program called *Radio Free Friday*, one of the first of the brilliant radio productions that erupted from the mind of Mark Starowicz. I'd sit there on the floor of the CBC studio in Churchill, marvelling at this guy and how he could make an interview into a conversation. He'd stumble and bumble his way through it just as we do when we talk with friends or family around the dinner table or in a pub. He was like that: natural, and so good at just being himself. What you heard was who he was.

Barbara's and Peter's different styles worked perfectly for them and for those of us listening or watching. We got to know their guests as if they were sitting in our homes. Pamela's specialty was the round table or panel. She was a true maestro, juggling the egos and strengths of her guests, asking just the right question at the right time to leave you, the viewer, better informed for having been in attendance.

There are others whom I find especially skilled and whom I have admired over the years: Brian Stewart for the depth of knowledge he displays as he questions others, and Wendy Mesley, Neil Macdonald and Linden MacIntyre for their accountability interviews—they can leave subjects wondering why, instead of agreeing to the interview, they hadn't chosen to spend the day standing naked on a street corner asking passersby to poke a stick in their eye.

Running through all those very different styles should underline the fact that there is no single way to interview. When journalism students ask me, "What's the secret to a good interview?" I respond by telling them to find their own comfort zone and develop their own technique. While I've always felt you can learn from others, copying them is not the way to go. In my view it rarely works and it can often come off as phony and staged. I think most viewers can tell when someone is copying another broadcaster; if that's the style they want they'll go to the original.

But some techniques are common to all good interviewers. First, they do their homework. They don't sit down in a studio across from someone and just wing it. They do the research. The guest obviously knows the subject matter much better, and the interviewer can't become an expert overnight, but it is possible to at least understand the big picture, get the facts straight and know where the controversies are or where the most human stories might be found. The guest will always be more animated, more forthcoming, more invested in the discussion, if the person talking to them is actually informed and interested.

The next secret? Good interviewers listen. It sounds simple, but you've probably watched interviews where it seemed like the interviewer wasn't hearing the answer. A question is asked; an answer is provided. The next question should follow up on the answer, but instead there's a question from out of the twilight zone. Sometimes there's a legitimate reason for that. Someone in the control room might be communicating through the interviewer's earpiece, overriding the words of the guest. It's happened to me—rarely, but it has happened. I've been questioning someone and a producer has relayed important information while the guest was answering and all I could see was the guest's lips flapping. It's a very uncomfortable feeling as you venture your next question, terrified that the answer may just have been given without your knowledge. But most of the time, questions from nowhere happen for a very different reason: the interviewer isn't listening; instead he or she is trying to figure out what to say next or searching through notes looking for another question, mind racing, fearful that the person across the way will stop talking at any second, and if another question isn't ready there will be an uncomfortable silence or embarrassing hemming and hawing. That can be disastrous, and it results in nothing that could ever be described as a normal conversation.

One of the ways I force myself to listen is to do most interviews without notes. That way the subject matter is in my brain, and while the guest is speaking I don't have my nose buried in a clipboard, searching for another question. I'm listening carefully, hoping the answer will open the door to the next question, but confident that if no door opens on its own, I can kick one down based on what I learned when I did my homework. It is funny how often I get messages from others in the business along the lines of "I can't believe you went into that interview without notes." I've become entirely comfortable with the concept, although I'll admit that confidence was tested a bit when I interviewed President Obama in the White House in early 2009. I wondered whether I should go into what was probably the biggest news interview of my life without a single note. What would happen if I blanked? But in the end I stayed the course and didn't use notes. There is an added advantage to this tactic: it often seems to leave the guest a bit uneasy. "Where are his notes and questions?" the guest seems to be wondering. I like that as it sometimes gives me an edge, especially in accountability interviews.

Some major television networks hire consultants to work with interviewers on their technique, and those consultants have lots of good tips. For example, it's a good idea to ask open-ended questions that start with *how*, *what* or *why* or to use phrases such as "Tell me about" or "Explain that to me." That way a guest is forced to come up with fuller, more rounded answers. The right way, then, might be as follows. Question: "Why was that so difficult?" Answer: "Well, I had never been in that situation before and I just couldn't find a way to get past that poisonous snake without endangering the lives of all the children." And here's the wrong way. Question: "Was that difficult?" Answer: "Yes."

The consultants' tips are useful and shouldn't be ignored, but in the end a broadcast conversation will probably be good for the same reasons that any conversation is good. The two people are engaged in a lively back-and-forth. There's a flow and logic to it all. There's energy, perhaps even tension in the talk. And information is exchanged. Just as you handle dozens of conversations every day without worrying about structure or what you're going to say next, a good broadcaster will have confidence in the questions rolling out naturally.

Sometimes, of course, no matter how well you're prepared, the interview just doesn't work. I've had my share of those, and one stands out more than the rest. I'd interviewed Margaret Thatcher twice during her time at 10 Downing Street, but those were remote interviews. In other words, she was at a different location than I was and we were hooked up through technology. That's never the preferred option, but circumstances often dictate that the interview be done that way. I always want a face-to-face encounter, and I finally got my opportunity to sit across from her in 1993.

Thatcher was out of office by then and flogging her memoirs, *The Downing Street Years*. I had read the book, and I was especially keen to talk about the 1982 Falklands War. I've always been fascinated by wartime leadership—how choices are made and how a leader handles the burden of decision-making that can cost people's lives. When I'm asked what historical figure I'd most like to have interviewed, there's no hesitation in my answer: Winston

Churchill. Margaret Thatcher's war was in no way comparable to Churchill's, but the Iron Lady seemed to have some of the same character traits as her predecessor. So I was genuinely excited as the interview approached.

There I was pacing the floor in a suite in Toronto's King Edward Hotel waiting for Lady Thatcher to arrive. Eventually I sat down and used the time to reread the Falklands sections of her book, just to be sure of what had been written. Finally she arrived, and right away I could tell she wasn't in a good mood. She didn't like the chair; she didn't like the lighting; she didn't even like the room. I wasn't sure if she liked me either, but I had my doubts. "Ah," I thought. "Maybe this is all part of her leadership style, setting an unpleasant, no-nonsense tone and establishing who is in charge." So I ignored the grumpiness and plowed ahead, into the minefield of Thatcherism.

Peter Mansbridge: During those periods in the early days of the Falklands, when the fleet was on its way through the South Atlantic—twenty-five thousand men covering eight thousand miles—when your head hit the pillow at night, were there ever moments when you thought, "Am I absolutely sure this was right?"

Margaret Thatcher: I really don't think you could have read the full book. You are complaining that I really knew what I wanted, and what I wanted was right. I would have been culpable if I hadn't gone for that. And what is more, the Falkland Islands were the first case when any country decided that an aggressor should not succeed. It was the first case of upholding international law. And, if I might gently remind you, it's probably because of that Argentina has democracy today.

PM: Lady Thatcher, I really—I'm not complaining, and—

MT: Good.

PM: —and I did read the section in the book on the Falklands very carefully. Let me try it again. You once said—I think you might have been joking, but perhaps you were very serious— that you wanted to open a business called "Rent-a-Spine."

MT: That's right.

PM: And that, I guess, is striking at the heart of what I'm asking. The ability to have that laser focus on a target that you obviously feel is missing in many people, and many leaders of our day.

MT: I think it is. I think that a lot of people would do just exactly as you wish, compromise because they had no prin- ciple, and therefore they regarded pragmatism as the thing. And as I say, it's like starting on an ocean journey without stars to steer by.

That was just the start, and things never got any better. Almost every time I ventured into a new question area—and for the most part these were pretty friendly questions—I got the same response: "You obviously never read the book." I must have been intimidated, because though I told her, "Actually I have," there was a mischievous voice inside me screaming that I should really be saying, "Actually I have. Did you write it?" This might have put the Iron Lady on the defensive, as there had been mur- murings in the British media that Thatcher had commissioned three different writers to script her memoirs. Perhaps she would have admired my wit and my cheekiness. Or it might have been enough to make Lady T. pick up the nearby tea tray, hot water and all, and pitch it into my lap. Either way it would have been better television than this was turning out to be. But I wimped out; I just couldn't bring myself to fire the shot. She, of course, felt completely free to dish it out, passing summary judgment on my journalistic efforts.

PM: Could Margaret Thatcher have served under a Margaret Thatcher?

MT: I don't know. I think it's a silly question to ask.

The interview staggered to its conclusion, but there was still one more twist of the Thatcherian knife. As we were taking off our microphones and the camera crew began putting away the equipment, the former British prime minister leaned forward, smiled for the first time since we had laid eyes on each other, and purred, "Peter, would you like me to sign your copy of my book?" What could I say? I was actually thinking of something else she could do with the book, but instead I babbled something like, "Oh, thank you, Lady Thatcher." Sixteen years later my edition of Margaret Thatcher's *The Downing Street Years* sits in my library at home, unopened since the day she scribbled her signature in it.

It's the interviews with the big names like Margaret Thatcher, prime ministers, presidents, celebrities from sports, theatre or music that people assume are my most memorable. And while many are right up there on my list, it's often talking to ordinary people caught in extraordinary circumstances that I find has affected me most. As a young correspondent in the late 1970s I covered the exodus of "boat people" from Vietnam. It was an incredibly compelling story that captured the attention of the world. Thousands of ethnic Chinese, persecuted in Vietnam, were doing anything they could to get out of the country. They were so desperate they were taking wild risks, piling by the hundreds onto tiny fishing boats made to hold no more than a few dozen. Many of the vessels sank. Others were attacked by pirates. Women were raped, children were crushed, men were murdered. I talked with some of these amazing people. Barely having to ask anything, I simply held out the microphone and their stories of courage and determination tumbled out. They were all convinced that no matter what hell and uncertainty they had faced during their exodus, anything was better for the future of their families than staying where they had been. Tens of thousands survived the crossing and then crowded into refugee camps sprinkled across Southeast Asia. I remember standing in one such camp in Hong Kong, watching a twenty-two-year-old Canadian immigration officer make life-altering decisions about who would be allowed into Canada and who simply didn't have the government-designated "credentials." He did it with emotion and humanity, but it seemed like such an overwhelming responsibility I couldn't imagine how anyone could handle such a role.

Now, years later, I occasionally meet one of the almost sixty thousand boat people who were welcomed by Canada, and I marvel at how well they've done. Just last year I was handing out my annual Junior Achievement–Peter Mansbridge Award for Leadership, a ten-thousand-dollar scholarship, to a young girl from Ontario who had excelled in entrepreneurship at her high school. When she introduced me to her parents, she made a point of explaining that her mother had arrived in Canada as a boat person. It immediately took me back to the waters of the South China Sea and to some of the most remarkable people I've ever met. They had a deep conviction that there were better days ahead, and I saw those better days in the eyes of that young girl and her parents.

Because of the nature of my anchoring job, the majority of my interviews are done in the studio, not the field. So these days it's more common to see me challenging politicians and business and labour leaders rather than interviewing the kind of people I found in the South China Sea. My interviewing style is normally non-confrontational because I hate interrupting people; I generally like to allow them to finish their thoughts before either challenging them or moving on with the conversation. But there are times, especially in political accountability interviews, where that can't happen. Interviewing Canadian prime ministers is always a challenge. They're just people like the rest of us, but as heads of government they're almost symbols of the nation, and they have to be afforded a certain deference. However, that doesn't mean they should get a pass on tough questions or on follow-up questions when they appear to be dissembling.

But when and how to interrupt is always an issue. Doing so can make the guest unnecessarily hostile, which may not make the answers any clearer. And it can also make the audience think you're being a bully, which makes them sympathize with the guest no matter how indefensible the position.

I could cite a dozen examples, but let me give you one of the most recent. In late 2008, Ottawa was brought to a standstill by parliamentary chaos so great that Stephen Harper had to ask the Governor General to prorogue Parliament. Most analysts, most opposition members and, quite frankly, many Conservatives felt Harper had called down the problem upon himself. He'd pushed certain initiatives in Parliament that were highly partisan and he'd followed that up by making inflammatory comments about the opposition in the House of Commons. A few days after Parliament had been shut down, the Prime Minister sat down with me in a studio at the CBC in Toronto for an interview. Here's an edited portion of our conversation:

> Peter Mansbridge: Are you saying that you have no regrets about anything you either did or said over these past two weeks?

> Stephen Harper: You pick out the political subsidy issue. Let's be very clear. The public firmly supports the government's position on that, firmly supports the government. And that position, in our judgment, is in the public interest. But what I say to you is—

> PM: Was that the place to put it?

> SH: But what I say to you is this, Peter. The government has shown that it is willing to make changes to accommodate the opposition. Smart people in the Liberal Party realize we've got significant economic problems, and in a minority Parliament we're only going to deal with them if we sit down and work together. We can't do that, Peter. We cannot do that if the

three opposition parties are committed only to working with each other.

PM: It seems that Mr. Ignatieff, who appears about to be the interim Liberal leader, is not firm on the coalition idea. But let's leave all of that aside just for a minute, because I want to understand clearly that what you're telling me is you don't feel that you either did or said anything in the heat of battle last week, and there were a lot of things said on the floor of the House of Commons—you don't think you said anything that you regret?

SH: Peter, the main thing I said last week is that I believe that parties forming a coalition government that would give the Bloc Québécois a veto over the governing affairs of the country, that is not in the interests of this country—

PM: Mr. Duceppe said you talked to him about what he'd like to see in a Throne Speech in 2004 in an attempt to defeat the Martin government.

SH: Peter, first of all, let me finish my sentence. I believe that's not in the interests of the country and I believe that anyone who wants to do that, they have an obligation to go to the people, because certainly everybody denied they would ever do anything like that, including, by the way, the separatist party. We have listened to Mr. Duceppe and the Bloc on issues. We have accommodated them on issues. But I have never as prime minister, nor would I ever, put myself in a position where I cannot govern the country except by the veto of the Bloc Québécois.

Now that kind of back-and-forth is pretty normal, but the fact that I'd pushed for a direct answer to a direct question still met with competing reactions. Those who sided with the Prime Minister felt I had been disrespectful, and they made their case forcefully. Those who felt the Prime Minister was deliberately hiding the truth argued that I was too soft on him and should have pursued him with far more vigour. I got hundreds of emails in just a few hours. Here are a couple of them showing, as they say, "sharply divided" opinions.

> *Mr. Mansbridge: I watched with interest your interview with Mr. Harper and was quite amused to see that no matter how hard you tried to corner him into saying something you wanted to hear in order to make him look the fool, he would not allow you to do it. He is a very intelligent man, he really knows his stuff and I was so proud of him. You surely are over rated as a top notch newsman.*

> *Stephen Harper is a megalomaniac. Thank you Peter for showing the Prime Minister as he really is. Every question you gave him was answered in hyperbole as a paranoid megalomaniac. No apology, no contrition, only he is correct. Good Job Peter.*

I always love it when both sides respond with such passion. I figure it means we must have done something right.

———

IN THE EARLY SUMMER OF 1999 the CBC's then managing editor of news, Tony Burman, came to me with an idea. He wanted to know whether I'd be interested in doing an interview program for CBC Newsworld. It would explore some of the issues of the day and involve panels, individual guests and special reports. Then he added, as is often added at the CBC these days, "Of course, we have no budget." He was exaggerating, but not by much. The program was going to have to be done with about as much money as a big American network would spend on coffee and doughnuts for a staff meeting. Nevertheless, I was flattered and intrigued. But I knew that my time was already limited, given my duties as chief correspondent and anchor of *The National*. I was also about to become a father again, with the birth of our son, Will, due at the end of July that year.

But if there was one thing I'd always wanted, it was to have more time for my interviews. On *The National* it was rare to get feature-length time for an interview. Instead you found yourself cramming interesting people into three- or four-minute slots. Or even worse, bright, articulate, thoughtful, sincere people who had lots to say were reduced to eight- or ten-second clips within the body of a news item. So I countered Tony's proposal by suggesting that instead of doing a series of interviews every week, I would do just one, and I would have the final say on who appeared as a guest. That way every interview would be one I wanted to do. Tony started thinking about it. Then I told him that this format would obviously be much cheaper than his original proposal— that seemed to clinch the deal.

It has been ten years now since *Mansbridge One on One* went to air. The first guest was Conrad Black. There have been a couple of hundred interviews since and they have taken me across the country and around the world. It's been a wonderful experience and I feel richer for having done it. I've been lucky because my role on the program is the easiest: I just sit down and ask questions. With few exceptions, these are not accountability interviews. We rarely put the guest on the hot seat, instead aiming to understand an issue, a situation, a person. And that's what has made it so much fun for me.

Not so much fun perhaps for the producers I've worked alongside. Sian Jones, Angela Naus, Harry Schachter, Jasmin Tuffaha and Leslie Stojsic have each taken a turn filling the one producer's role assigned to the program. They have done the heavy lifting, along with Fred Parker, who's been my director since I started anchoring *The National* in 1988, and floor director Paul Mounsteven, who has also worked on *One on One* from the beginning.

I'm sure you've had the experience of looking through an old photo album. You see the snapshots taken ten years ago and you have several reactions. *Has it really been that long? On the other hand, it seems like yesterday. How could I ever have allowed that picture to be taken? Good to see Aunt Dorothy looking so well.* It was like that when I started going through the *One on One* album. Was I really in the same room with so and so? Never thought that interview would end. How could I have asked such a stupid question? Look where he is ten years later.

We don't do much editing on *One on One*. We know how long our program is, and that's how long we try to talk; we don't record twice as much as we need and then hack it down. Most weeks it is live-to-tape, which leaves no room for mistakes. Which isn't to say that I don't make mistakes—we just live with them, just as we live with imperfections in the rest of our lives. Anyway, there's probably no such thing as the perfect interview. And it's just as well, since I haven't come all that close.

We have done some editing for this book. First we selected only relatively few interviews from all the ones we've done. Then we chose only parts of those interviews. That's how you arrive at the best of the best. But it's a subjective exercise, and it wasn't always easy to choose what to leave out.

The final lineup is pretty impressive, I think. The people you'll meet represent at least one way to look at the first decade of the new century. They aren't necessarily the biggest news-makers, the megastars of stage, screen or music, the giants of sport or the richest captains of business. We have some of those, but we also have people who leave more than a footprint on the beach. No matter how deep that footprint, the waves will wash it away. But some people have lasting power. They're more than celebrities, more than just flavours of the week, and that's usually because they stand for something. They can't be replaced by the next thing that comes along; they've led lives that really mean something. They may have contributed to better science, better literature, better education. They may have led political move-ments that put most practitioners of politics to shame. They may speak to the better instincts in all of us.

When I asked my questions of Ron Finch in Churchill, Manitoba, so long ago, I thought that an interview was like a grenade with the pin already pulled—the best I could hope for was to escape before it blew up. Now I see interviews as wonderful opportunities. I talk to people I couldn't ever hope to meet without a television program bringing us together. Oh sure, my anchoring job allows me to meet plenty of A-list types, but that's a handshake-and-exchange-pleasantries kind of meeting. An interview is so much more. It's an exploration of what makes someone tick.

In the pages that follow I've tried to bring you into the room with me as we do our *One on One* interviews. In some cases you'll see the behind-the-scenes activity that takes place, and in others you'll get a sense of what was on my mind when I decided this was the person I wanted to talk to that week. Through these pages I hope you'll get to appreciate the men and women who have sat across from me these past ten years, just as I did.

CONRAD BLACK

I FIRST MET CONRAD BLACK at the wedding of a mutual friend in Toronto. In fact, Black, Mike Duffy and I were three people rolled into one to give a little spine to the man about to end his years of bachelorhood—quite a combination. And who, pray tell, was the lucky groom who had entrusted these three musketeers with such an important role on such a critical day? The internationally respected globe-trotting correspondent Brian Stewart, whom Black had gone to school with when the two were growing up in Toronto, and whom Duffy and I had worked with in the Ottawa bureau of the CBC during the 1970s and early 1980s.

Brian's two lives, personal and professional, came together on a beautiful summer day in September 1989, and the three of us were determined to do our part. Black had the chore of managing the ring; Duffy and I were to ensure that the guests were directed to the appropriate seats. And we would all, of course, be up front when the ceremony took place. Everything was going perfectly: arrivals were on time, Brian was in an acceptable state of nervousness, and the minister was ready, willing and clearly able. With everyone seated, we were standing at the front and could hear the arrival of the bridal party, with the beautiful, incredibly charming and seriously funny Tina Srebotnjak at centre stage.

The next moment was supposed to involve a musically accompanied procession down the stately centre aisle of St. Andrew's Presbyterian Church. But there was a problem, and for what seemed like an eternity we had no idea what it was. Feet shuffled. Throats cleared. The crowd began to murmur. And then word was relayed from aisle to aisle that no one had escorted Tina's mother to her seat. She was stranded at the King Street entrance.

At the very moment that I was realizing this had been my blunder, my eyes met Black's. He had a look on his face that I suspect he normally reserved for his butler. His head was slightly lowered, and then he sharply tilted it back with his nose pointed directly down the centre aisle to where Vida Srebotnjak was waiting. He didn't say anything. He didn't need to. It was clear what the message was: *Get her. Now.*

The rest of the wedding went off without a hitch, a wonderful start to what has been a wonderful marriage. And then it was back to our respective lives, Black to managing his millions and building his newspaper empire, and the rest of us to the more basic grunt work of journalism. Our paths crossed a few times over the years, but it wasn't until 1999 and the very first *One on One* that I actually had a chance to sit down and talk with the man, who at that time was a London-based major international tycoon. He was also involved in what had become a bitter fight with the then prime minister, Jean Chrétien, over his citizenship.

Black had been offered a British peerage—a seat in the House of Lords—but Chrétien countered that if Black took the offer he would have to renounce his Canadian citizenship. To back his position, the Prime Minister relied on an eighty-year-old parliamentary document, the Nickle Resolution, in which Ottawa called on London not to bestow any titles of honour on Canadians. Chrétien's critics argued that his position had nothing to do with Nickle and everything to do with one of Black's newspapers, the *National Post*, which had been attacking Chrétien on a variety of issues with a great deal of vigour. When we had our conversation, Black was still a Canadian, the peerage was on hold, and the fight with Chrétien was very much at play.

1999-09-12

Peter Mansbridge: I was thinking on the way into this interview, what would I have been calling you if the Prime Minister hadn't blocked this appointment?

Conrad Black: Same as you are now.

PM: Would it have been Lord Black?

CB: In the first place, that wouldn't apply to you. And in the second place, part of the understanding, and indeed what we were told by the Canadian government a week before the Canadian Prime Minister's intervention, was that as long as I didn't use the title in Canada there'd be no problem.

PM: Let's assume I was in Britain.

CB: But in any case, incidentally, I wouldn't expect anyone to call me that.

PM: Even in Britain?

CB: No. I mean, they can if they want. If I were the bearer of the title, they could if they wanted. But I'm not a very formal person.

PM: I was wondering about it though, because, as Max Aitken decided on Lord Beaverbrook, he came up with a name to go with the "Lord." Did this never cross your mind? As close as it got— It did get awfully close, and you may still get it?

CB: The British have signed off on it. I can pick it up as soon as the Canadian objection is removed.

PM: You must have thought of a name.

CB: No, I haven't. And in any case, this is a life peerage. Beaverbrook was a hereditary peer. I haven't really thought of it, no. Normally life peers take their surnames and just use that title, but it is premature to talk about these things. The British Prime Minister's note to me said that I could work that out with the King of Arms, and he will be calling eventually, he assures me.

PM: Before we get into actual details of this suit [Black would be facing Chrétien in court over his alleged abuse of power], I want to try to understand the relationship that you have with Jean Chrétien, because you've known each other for several years.

CB: Certainly he was very cordial for twenty years, up until a couple of months ago.

PM: But what was the extent of it? Were you friends, acquaintances? How would you—

CB: I would say friendly acquaintances. He used to come to our annual dinner sometimes, and he spoke at it once very amusingly, and I used to call upon him in Ottawa sometimes. I would see him when he came to London. So it was very cordial.

PM: You even had a lunch for him, did you not, when he was running for the leadership?

CB: That's right.

PM: How often was the contact while he was prime minister, before this event? Did you talk on the phone?

CB: Sometimes, yeah. Oh, things would come up where he would quite rightly—there's nothing wrong with this—want to mention something of national interest that he expressed a perfectly reasonable hope that we'd editorially be supportive of. It was usually not on partisan matters; there was never anything wrong with it.

Usually it was things to do with constitutional questions and that sort of thing. And he phoned me sometimes. I almost never phoned him, because I don't believe in bothering holders of great offices. Their lines are busy enough and I assume if they want to talk to me they'll call me, but that happened sometimes.

PM: In any of these conversations over the years, up until this happened earlier this year, did you ever raise this possibility with him, that you may be approached? Because, I assume, most people were expecting this. The owner of the *Daily Telegraph* has always been in the British House of Lords. So you must have been expecting this was going to happen at some point. Did you ever raise it with him?

CB: No, because I never thought that it really was any of his business. You see, years ago, when it first became a deemed possibility, I commissioned some legal research, and there was no legislation in this country and there was no policy, and I'm a British resident. And since it wasn't an area where there was any legal obligation for the Government of Canada to express an opinion, I didn't feel, in the first place, that he had any particular standing in it, and in the second place, it was hypothetical until it happened.

PM: We'll get to that in a moment, because I guess that one is the debatable point: whether the Nickel Resolution has some impact.

CB: Look, Peter, that really isn't the core of this whole matter. The core of the matter is that on the recommendation of the Government of Canada, as communicated to me by the British Prime Minister, I applied for and was granted British citizenship while retaining my Canadian citizenship. That was the Canadian government's recommendation. I followed the recommendation. Then the Prime Minister of Canada purported to intervene and claim that the Queen of the United Kingdom, on the recommendation of the Prime Minister of the United Kingdom, could not confer an honour on me as a citizen of the United Kingdom for services rendered in the United Kingdom. That is the core of this. The Prime Minister has no standing whatsoever. The Nickel Resolution is a sideshow, and no, it isn't binding, and that didn't pass the Senate. There is no policy in Canada, but I accept there is some prerogative for the Canadian government in matters of Canadian citizens. But there's no prerogative for them to try to create a category of citizen in a foreign country that is inferior in rights to other citizens of that country, particularly when they've recommended the individual in question become a citizen of that country.

PM: All right, I don't want to lose everybody on this, but the Nickel Resolution we both referred to is—what, eighty years old? It was 1919. It was a statement passed through the House of Commons asking Buckingham Palace not to appoint Canadians to titles.

CB: Not quite. What it actually did was ask the Canadian government not to request the British monarch to appoint Canadian citizens resident in Canada to titles. So even on that basis it has no application to me.

PM: All right, let me get to what is perhaps one of the other cores of the lawsuit, and certainly the one that has grabbed a lot of the attention. That's the suggestion in the document that the Prime Minister acted because of his unhappiness with the stories that have been written in one of your papers, the *National Post*.

CB: I don't think his objections are confined to it. I think he's a little grumpy about what the *Ottawa Citizen* has written too.

PM: Let's see what it actually says in the statement. "He, the prime minister, also stated he was not kindly treated by the *National Post*, a paper published by the plaintiff"—yourself. "This reference to newspaper articles about the Prime Minister was the third occasion within six months that Jean Chrétien mentioned to the plaintiff his dissatisfaction with published comments in the *National Post*." Now, how did those conversations, or that exchange of views, take place?

CB: I don't think we can try this case *ex parte* on this program. There is a judicial process and we have to respect that, so I'm not going to go too much beyond what's public knowledge now.

PM: Part of the public knowledge is your lawyer suggesting that the Prime Minister phoned you in Austria at three o'clock in the morning with an—

CB: No, he didn't suggest it; he stated it, and it's true. The Prime Minister hasn't denied that. In fact, I think his office confirmed that. And it was following that conversation and that lengthy letter that he wrote complaining about our coverage of the question of economic development grants—

PM: In his riding.

CB: —in his constituency was published. And I encouraged him to send this letter and promised of course we would publish it and we would flag it prominently and publish it without comment, which we did then.

PM: So how do you react? I suppose it's not unusual for a prime minister, and you've known many here and abroad, to suggest to you that your papers are being unfair to them. Or is it unusual?

CB: He's been a little more consistent and—to take a needful word—imaginative in his putting forth of that view than other prime ministers whom I have known here and elsewhere.

PM: What do you mean by that?

CB: He— Again, we're not adducing evidence here, but this is a theme that is going to emerge when we get to the pretrial phase. I haven't had a conversation with him in the last two years that he didn't mention some aspect of my status as a press owner— not always threateningly, but rarely particularly appreciatively. I must be clear here, I'm not suggesting there were direct threats of any kind. But it has been a theme, and this whole issue of freedom of expression is one that counsel was right to put in our statement and will be focused on when evidence is taken, including the Prime Minister's.

PM: Do you think there is linkage from one to the other?

CB: Yes, and I think that will emerge clearly in the evidence. There is no question there is linkage, and my counsel in fact confirmed that with all sorts of people from whom we shall also be taking evidence.

PM: But you mean linkage between the fact that he was unhappy with the *National Post* and the fact that he blocked your appointment?

CB: Yes. Yes.

PM: You're comfortable in saying that.

CB: I'm comfortable in the accuracy of that assertion, but I'm not—I regret that it's the case. Incidentally, I don't accept that our coverage of him has been unfair. After that call, particularly. I was in Salzburg at the time, in Austria.

PM: This is the three-o'clock-in-the-morning call.

CB: Yeah. But I go to bed late. I don't want to martyr myself; in fact I wasn't asleep, but it was under active consideration when he phoned. But I read the entire file after that to make sure I hadn't missed anything, and I don't think our coverage was unfair at all. But that's another issue. If we had defamed him, if we'd really done anything other than point out the facts, then I certainly would have asked the editor to be much more careful and publish corrective pieces if we had been unjust. And not because he was prime minister. We're not in the defamation business. All we did was point out that in fact the person to whom he supposedly sold his shares in this enterprise sent them back with liquidated damages to his trustee, and he knew perfectly well he was still the equitable owner of those shares. And for him to assert in the House of Commons and to the public that he wasn't is in fact not true, and that's all we wrote.

PM: We're moving into another story there, but suffice it to say that you are comfortable with the stories that were written in the *Post*. Were you comfortable the time you talked to him on the phone, or did you refresh yourself?

CB: Well, I was concerned because he clearly felt aggrieved. You know, I get letters from people all the time, much less prominent than he is, who have been referred to in newspapers of ours in this country and in other countries, and I always look into them because, you know, we've got to be careful about things like this. We run a quality operation and we're very concerned about matters like this. As is well-known, I've often been libelled myself, and I myself have often sued. I've certainly received a great many libel writs, and I'm very sensitive to the virtue of always having truth as a defence, or indeed as the basis of a complaint. So you always want to find out what the facts are. And I always look into it, and I did particularly for him, but I would for anyone.

PM: Why the British House of Lords? Why would you like to be sitting there?

CB: First of all, I want to address this myth that's been propagated that I've been slaveringly chasing after a peerage. I have not.

All I did was answer the phone. It's an honour, like the Order of Canada, and one accepts honours, and it's a nice honour. Secondly, it is contrary to the second myth that is now being propagated, that it's so absurdly anachronistic a place that it's almost shaming to be asked to join it.

PM: So it's not fox hunts and tea parties.

CB: It is now going to be an entirely meritocratic place, including the one hundred hereditaries who elect themselves out of a total of many hundreds that are there now, and you find there the leading figures from practically every field in British life. The retired field marshals, the Archbishop of Canterbury, the former prime ministers and senior members of the government, the previous governments.

PM: You can quite possibly be in the British Cabinet from the British House of Lords.

CB: Carrington was foreign secretary.

PM: Right.

CB: But—

PM: Some say you put out hope one day for that.

CB: Please.

PM: I'll take that as a no.

CB: Yehudi Menuhin was a peer, Bertrand Russell was a peer, Field Marshal Montgomery was a peer. It is a place where you do encounter a lot of interesting people, and particularly the foreign policy debates are very interesting. You get all the former foreign secretaries and great authorities in the field like the late Max

Beloff, for example. Great academics. It's really quite an interesting debating chamber, but—

PM: It's similar to the Canadian Senate.

CB: No. Good heavens, no. With all due respect, there are some
impressive senators, but the Senate is not taken all that seriously.
The House of Lords has in it practically all the outstandingly exceptional people in virtually every walk of British life, including all the
academic disciplines; as I said, the military; the established church,
at least, and some others—the former chief rabbis, for example.

PM: Why not a Canadian Senate seat for you?

CB: I haven't been asked.

PM: But if you were.

CB: I haven't been asked.

PM: If you were, would that in any way interest you?

CB: I don't know. I'd think about it, I'd think about it. But
(smiles) I see what you're *deviously* creating here, inciting in the
minds of your viewers this idea that I'd be interested in a British
honour but not a Canadian one.

PM: No, I'm just wondering whether you could do both.

CB: Now that you've— You know something, that's a very timely
comment, because in the last conversation I had with Jean
Chrétien, I mentioned that sort of jokingly, saying that I could
be a senator too. And I said, "As you know, generally I support
the Liberals," which happens also to be true, by the way. I haven't
always, but I generally am.

PM: That will frighten a few people.

CB: It may do, but it's the case. I supported Mulroney because he was a friend of mine, as Turner was, but I was in favour of free trade and that was a big issue at that time. But I was not a supporter of Mr. Stanfield or of Joe Clark. Not that I don't respect them as individuals, but I wasn't a supporter of them.

PM: So what did Mr. Chrétien say when you suggested . . . ?

CB: He didn't respond. Didn't respond. He found the whole idea so esoteric that he went on to other things.

PM: But you obviously don't.

CB: No, I think it is rather esoteric, and it was in that vein that I mentioned it. At that point I was emphasizing the fact that I was not prepared to renounce my Canadian citizenship as Thomson did, for example.

PM: Right.

CB: If I did, then I could collect the peerage tomorrow. But that's not the issue.

PM: Why wouldn't you?

CB: Because the real issue here is not the honour. The issue is the principle. If what the Canadian government was doing was trying to prevent my right to buy a new toothbrush, I would object just as strenuously. I hate to belabour this point because I accept that the honour is not terribly important. But whether I'm a member of the House of Lords is of no interest to anybody, not, frankly, of overwhelming interest to me. But what is of interest to me, and it should be an interest to some of your viewers, [is] this business of the Prime Minister of Canada committing illegalities to discriminate against an individual and to abridge and infringe upon his rights as a Canadian and as a Canadian and as a citizen of the U.K.

PM: "Illegalities."

CB: Illegalities, yeah.

PM: And some of the language here—"illegalities," "abuse of power," "malfeasance of power" . . .

CB: I didn't say "crime." "*Mis*feasance," yeah.

PM: It's almost sounding Nixonian here.

CB: He's not— We're not alleging crimes. These are not, these are not—

PM: Illegalities.

CB: —offences that carry custodial sentences.

PM: Illegalities?

CB: Illegalities, yeah.

PM: That's not a crime?

CB: Not necessarily. A parking ticket is an illegality.

PM: All right, so it's somewhere between a parking ticket and a crime.

CB: Yeah. The fact is, he gave wilfully erroneous advice to the chief of state for reasons that we are confident will be proved to be malicious. Now, if you brush up on your Bagehot* or the constitutional specialist of your choice, you'll find that that's not what prime ministers are supposed to be doing. But as I said, the core of the case of the other matters—the misfeasance—is the Canadian government gave us advice, we acted on the advice and they reneged a week later. But the real core of the case is the one I said earlier. They've no standing in my status as a U.K. citizen.

PM: Let me briefly go back to the devious point you were suggesting that I was coming up with—that actually you came up with—and that is that you'd go for a British appointment before a Canadian appointment.

CB: No, I wouldn't. The fact is, I think if I was offered [one] in Canada I would probably accept, but it was never offered. It was sort of hinted at by Trudeau once but it wasn't offered, and I didn't leap at it. But I had peerages hinted at quite a few times and I didn't leap at them either. In general I accept honours when they're offered. I have the Order of the Southern Cross of Brazil; when it was offered to me by the Brazilian ambassador in London, I accepted it.

PM: You didn't clear that one first of all with Ottawa?

CB: As a matter of fact I suspect that they did clear it, but not because I asked them to.

PM: Mulroney, your friend, never talked to you about the Senate?

CB: No, never did.

PM: Does that bother you?

* *Walter Bagehot (1826–77) was a British businessman, essayist and political and economic analyst. His book* The English Constitution *explored the nature of the constitution of the United Kingdom, specifically the functioning of Parliament and the British monarchy.*

CB: No, not a bit.

PM: How far is this going to go? Both sides seem to be really pawing the ground in their preparations for this.

CB: We'll try the issue. If we want judgment and we're convinced— When I say "we" I'm not engaging in some sort of baronial collective noun here. The counsel—and I've shown that to a number of distinguished barristers—are convinced that we're going to prevail.

PM: But they [Chrétien's legal team] sound equally convinced that they can prevail. And it just seems to be one of these things that could be in the courts for a long time.

CB: That's what we have courts for.

PM: How far are you prepared to go? If you lose one round, does this keep going? Can you see this in the Supreme Court one day?

CB: Not as a result of our taking it there. No, I don't think so; I have my doubts about that, I'm not sure. I certainly have no standing to speak for the other side. I'm not engaging in games-manship, and I don't really see where their case is. I think what we're going to get are a lot of dilatory procedures and spurious motions to change venue and change the court, and delays and motions to strike and requests for particulars. But when we start taking evidence on discovery, then I think things will move along.

PM: You like military analogies. Is there room for this battle that's shaping up?

CB: I wish to emphasize, Peter, whether I'm a peer or not really has no importance, but there is an issue of principle involved here. That's the only thing that lends this any significance. I mean, I agree that it's a news story because of the personalities involved, but—

PM: Do you think the public cares about this?

CB: No.

PM: Or does it have any impact on the way the public sees you?

CB: I can't judge that. I feel—pardon the ghastly expression—that my "image" is that of a Frankenstein monster that's been lurching about for twenty-five years, and I have absolutely no idea what animates it at times, but I must say, from the press reception, the letters and things that I've received, most of what I've heard is quite favourable. I think a good many people see this as a case of an individual abusing a political office for petty reasons and overreaching his jurisdiction. And as we take his evidence and that of all those around and beneath him, I think that impression is going to be reinforced. I don't know why they're persevering with it. If they want to, we'll stick with it until the judicial system renders judgment. That's all we want.

PM: That could be years?

CB: No, I don't think so. The dilatory procedures won't go for more than about six months. After that we start taking sworn evidence. Then that raises the game quite a bit.

PM: So within the next year.

CB: Yeah, I think we'll have—

PM: Will it resolve—

CB: —six months of posturing. After that I think you'll start to see things moving along.

—

IN THE END, Conrad Black gave up his Canadian passport. He became Lord Black of Crossharbour and along with his wife, Barbara Amiel, the two became fixtures on the London social scene—but not for long.

The lord now sits in a Florida jail. The early years of the new century proved his downfall, and after a lengthy trial in which he never confessed any guilt, he was sentenced to six and a half years behind bars for fraud and obstruction of justice in the operations of his own company, Hollinger International. There are occasional suggestions in London that he will lose his peerage over the conviction.

In a delicious irony, for Jean Chrétien at least, the former prime minister now enjoys membership in an even more exclusive London-based club than Black's House of Lords. In the summer of 2009, the Queen appointed Chrétien to the Order of Merit, only the third Canadian in history to be so honoured. No one dredged up the Nickle Resolution debate when it happened, even though Chrétien will now be one of only twenty-four members worldwide, including Prince Charles and Nelson Mandela, who can have the letters O.M. follow their name.

From the robes of wealth and power to a prison jumpsuit. Conrad Black is said to be writing the latest instalment of his memoirs while he is incarcerated. I know I'll be buying it.

DIANA KRALL

IN THE EARLY 1980s I rented the main floor of an old house in downtown Toronto, and I used to buy my groceries at a small, trendy market at the north end of Rosedale. It was a proven spot for a reporter on the lookout for a good story to bump into some of the city's political movers and shakers. Sometimes you get a lot more out of aisle talk than just wise advice on how to pick a ripe melon.

Apparently during those shopping moments someone had noticed me but I hadn't noticed her: a young, struggling jazz pianist and singer by the name of Diana Krall. At least that's the way she tells the story these days. She claims she knew of me from watching the news but was too nervous to walk up in the store and say hello.

Right. Years later, who's nervous now? Heading up to a suite in Toronto's posh Four Seasons Hotel, where our *One on One* interview was scheduled, I kept trying to forget that I'm a guy who can't carry a note, doesn't understand music and might have a hard time describing the difference between jazz and opera. Yet I was about to sit down by the piano with a musical icon and talk about her work. After we shook hands and she had told me the eighties grocery-store story, she had another surprise. "Oh,

Elvis wants to meet you. I've told him all about you." Sure enough, out from one of the adjoining rooms came the equally iconic and, as it turned out, very pleasant Elvis Costello. Together they were one very happy, and very excited, couple—twins were due within months.

So after all that, how did I get through the interview? Here's my confession. The night before, I had asked my wife, actor, dancer and *singer* Cynthia Dale, what questions she would ask Diana Krall. I suggested that she tell me the questions she wished reporters would ask of her. It took her only a few minutes to give me a list (see if you can guess which ones they were). We started our conversation by talking about the Nanaimo, British Columbia, restaurant where, at fifteen years of age, Diana Krall had her debut evening as a singer.

2006-09-16

Peter Mansbridge: Your first paying gig was at the NHL Restaurant in Nanaimo when you were fifteen years old. What were you thinking that night?

Diana Krall: That I was very fortunate to have my family around. My mom took me there for an audition. Fortunately Peter Ward, a bass player, already had a gig there. The deal was that I would play piano and he would play bass. I became a student again working with Peter, who showed me how to play with charts again.

The restaurant was owned by Lloyd Gilmour, a former NHL referee, and his wife, and it was right on the water in a beautiful spot. The carpet was covered with NHL logos and the waiters all wore referee shirts. It's very funny, when I go to America, if anybody asks me the story about my first gig, because it sounds like something that they would have expected. You grew up in Canada and you got your start playing in a hockey-themed restaurant.

PM: What kind of ambition did you have at fifteen? Could you see a way that you could go from the referee's bar to the big time of jazz?

DK: Quite a bit of ambition. I wanted to go and study in America. And my band teacher, Brian Stovell, was very, very wise in counselling me against that, because right in my hometown I had the best music program, the greatest band director (who was also a bass player). So I was playing in jazz trios. Going to a big American school that had these big stage-band festivals wouldn't have been the best thing for me. I was better staying in Nanaimo, where I was able to play jazz in a quartet with people who loved me and I was at home.

I just had ambition to learn and play with people who were jazz musicians. When I met Ray Brown—the great bass player who was my mentor and my friend until he died just four years ago—he was playing in a restaurant in Nanaimo! So you just don't know who you're going to meet in your own hometown. That time was a good time.

PM: The people who have been important in your life—like him, like your mother, like Rosemary Clooney—

DK: Yes.

PM: You lost so many of them all around the same time.

DK: Within a six-week period. First my mother, and then Rosemary, who was like a second sort of mother to me, and then Ray Brown, who was very much a father figure as well as the most important musical influence in my life. It was a lot. A lot.

PM: Why jazz? Why was it that Diana Krall at fifteen was focused on jazz?

DK: When I was about fifteen years old, I discovered records that were quite intense—people who sang on them had been through a lot. I hadn't been through a lot at fifteen, but maybe I knew I was going to. I was drawn to artists like Billie Holiday and Frank Sinatra early on. The music of Fats Waller and Nat King Cole appealed to me—its feeling of improvisation and swing. When I discovered Oscar Peterson, it was about the feel of the music, and the freedom to improvise within that context of standards, the music that I already knew, and how you could take something and stretch it and make it your own. That was very interesting to me, even at that age.

PM: Is there such a thing as a perfect song?

DK: I think there was a time when American popular songs were perfect to be interpreted by jazz musicians—songs from the 1930s to the 1950s. Ella Fitzgerald interpreted "A-Tisket, A-Tasket" and made it her own. But you could look at the sixties and into the seventies for songs written by Bob Dylan and Joni Mitchell. Maybe "Blue" was the perfect song. Or a lot of Joni's songs are the perfect song for different reasons.

PM: You wrote some of the songs on your album *The Girl in the Other Room*. When you sit down and you're in song-writing mode, what are you thinking? You say it was hard. Tell me about that.

DK: It was a very intense process, and I'm so thankful that I had Elvis to help me with that, because it was right after I had lost my mom. I just couldn't sing the songs that I'd normally feel good about singing, like "'Deed I Do." I just couldn't do it. I couldn't find a way of expressing how I felt through those songs. Honestly, I felt like I was telling a lie. And so I decided to write. It was very frightening, though it was more frightening after I'd seen what I'd written. Being in it was very cathartic and very helpful. It got me listening to a lot of different artists, like Joni, whom I just idolized for many reasons. And Bob Dylan. Not trying to be them, but trying to have their courage to say something. But then you realize that you can never do what they did, so you just be yourself and you do the best you can. But it was a very important time for me to start writing and expressing myself directly.

PM: What do you mean when you say "frightening"?

DK: It was frightening to me to expose myself in that way. It was more frightening to have to talk about the songs on the press tour, for instance. I felt really exposed, and like, "Okay, I've written all these personal things but I don't want to talk about them." But I have to talk about them, because it's a different record. It's something new, so it's exciting. You want things to be challenging, and difficult, and wonderful all at the same time. But it was hard afterwards because talking about it is always difficult for me, no matter if I'm doing standards or writing.

But I couldn't have done this record so joyfully without going there. And something like "Departure Bay" still stays with me always. You do what you do, you write about how you feel honestly. It's just a reflection of how you are at that time, and then it changes.

PM: How do you feel, honestly, now?

DK: Happy.

PM: Yeah?

DK: Yeah, very happy.

PM: It's the marriage. The twins on the way.

DK: Yeah. I think you finally let yourself feel. It's still hard, especially now. I miss my mother, but I can say I'm happier than I've ever been. I'm excited about having a family and being happily married and happy in my music. And I think I just know myself better, if that's possible. For now, for the time being, I think I feel more settled in myself. It's not an arrogance, it's just . . . maybe it's turning forty. I don't know. I'm just more accepting of myself and what I do. It doesn't mean I'm not still searching and frustrated—all those wonderful things that drive us as artists and people—but I don't know. Something lifted.

PM: If you could sit at that piano and sing or play with anyone, any other artist, dead or alive, who would that be?

DK: Frank Sinatra.

PM: And why is that?

DK: 'Cause he's *great*! I don't know, that's the first thing that comes to mind, probably because we were watching Frank Sinatra videos while I was getting ready today. You know, I've come pretty close to experiencing that. Recently, I played with Tony Bennett—"I Left My Heart in San Francisco." Now, I've practised that song since working at the NHL Restaurant. You know how many requests I had for that? And I practised it for . . . how many years? Every bar I played in. And then it came time to accompany Tony Bennett, and I was really scared. It was an incredible experience to hear him, to accompany him in that song. He just comes right in. So that's pretty big.

PM: Have you accompanied Sinatra through the magic of playing his CD and singing along with him?

DK: I learn songs by playing people's records. There are lots of people that I would love to play with. I wouldn't think that I'm worthy of playing with them, but—

PM: You know, hearing you say you're not worthy—that's the little girl from Nanaimo.

DK: It's a little *Wayne's World*, yeah.

PM: Isn't it? Here you are, one of the biggest-selling jazz artists of all time—

DK: I didn't live the way Billie Holiday did, I didn't go through what she had to go through. So I would never put myself in the same place. I would just be honoured—and I have been honoured—to play. My dream as a sixteen-year-old was to play with Ray Brown. I wanted to know what that felt like.

When Oscar Peterson turned eighty, he invited us to his home. There was one point in the evening where he said, "Do you want to go play?" And I went, "Please, this is not happening to me!" So now I'm remembering seeing him at the Orpheum in Vancouver with Ella Fitzgerald when I was a sixteen-year-old kid. First time I'd ever seen him. So he says, "Go play the box." The "box" is the ten-foot Bösendorfer, which is scary enough, you know? And I thought, "Just don't even let your ego or anything get in the way of the joy of this. Just play. Go and play."

And then we ended up singing a Nat Cole tune together. He'd say, "Di, do you know this?" I just couldn't believe it. The next day when Elvis and I woke up, we thought, "Did this really happen?" So you never know. You have to put aside all that kind of ego stuff that holds you back—"Oh no, I can't do it"—so that you can experience the joy of that. That was one of the best days I've ever had: playing with Oscar Peterson.

KARLHEINZ SCHREIBER

IF YOU'VE MET BRIAN MULRONEY, you'd be puzzled to understand how Karlheinz Schreiber could be his nemesis. Mulroney stands tall and confident, Schreiber not so much of either. Mulroney has walked the halls on equal footing with presidents, kings and queens; he's a man who achieved the very heights of political and business success. Schreiber has only ever dreamed of such glory. Yet Brian Mulroney's entire legacy, in fact, his standing in life, rests on the outcome of his battle with Schreiber.

Schreiber's background leads to the ever-present mystery around him. At different times he's been a West German spy, an international arms dealer, a lobbyist in both Europe and North America and a political party fundraiser on both continents as well. The image of Mulroney, the former Conservative prime minister of Canada, "cutting up the cash"—to use a term he himself used when attacking the Liberals—in an overseas hotel room with a shady German-Canadian businessman seemed ludicrous. But it happened. And Schreiber, when I first met him face to face in December 2007, was enjoying the notoriety he had gained by forcing Mulroney to admit it.

Schreiber had pursued me through one of his lawyers in Toronto. "Karlheinz is a great admirer of your program" was the approach, a not uncommon one when it is believed flattery will accomplish the goal. But these things work both ways, of course, and as we had been trying a different route to get Schreiber before our cameras, things moved along quickly. I wanted the interview to run just before Mulroney's much-anticipated testimony before a parliamentary committee investigating Schreiber's allegations. So we agreed to an interview session in a suite in Ottawa's Chateau Laurier hotel, two days before Mulroney was scheduled to appear.

Schreiber is short, somewhat stout, and very charming. Within moments you can see how he managed, both in Canada and abroad, to navigate rooms full of lobbyists and fixers to settle on his prey: people in power. When he shook my hand, I tried to imagine just how many other palms had clasped his before he settled in with his story, whatever the story happened to be that day. As his wife and his lawyer sat just out of camera range listening to every word, Schreiber tried to make his case about how and why money had changed hands between him and Brian Mulroney.

2007-12-15

Peter Mansbridge: I'm sure there aren't many Canadians who don't know who you are right now, but they may still be wondering what it is you're trying to tell them when you say this is "the greatest scandal in Canadian political history." What is the greatest scandal?

Karlheinz Schreiber: It is more or less the payback for helping [Mulroney] come to power, and then the interest to make big money. This is how it was, in short: Brian Mulroney became prime minister, and Frank Moores got the business for Altanova GCI.

PM: Frank Moores, the lobbyist. GCI, the company.

KS: Yes.

PM: Did he do something wrong?

KS: No.

PM: That was his job—he was a lobbyist. He made a lot of money.

KS: Yes.

PM: You paid him millions of dollars.

KS: Not me, the international companies.

PM: But through you.

KS: I controlled it, yeah.

PM: But it does open the door to me trying to understand what your relationship is, or was, with Brian Mulroney. I've seen his inscription on a picture: "To my friend Karlheinz." But you know and I know that political leaders and prime ministers and presidents write that on thousands of pictures. Was he really your friend? He says he only met you a couple times.

KS: We met quite often, and I have quite a few photos from him. This photo was special because it's a photo taken in the house. He sent his gratitude. So that was what related to the meeting at [the Prime Minister's retreat at] Harrington Lake. My friend? I have a different understanding what friendship is. In a friendship you can really trust somebody. No, we never became that close.

PM: You met at Harrington Lake.

KS: Yes.

PM: Nobody seems to deny that. You met in at least three hotel rooms.

KS: Yes.

PM: And nobody denies that. Today you told the parliamentary committee about having breakfast with him at 24 Sussex Drive . . .

KS: Yes.

PM: Were there other meetings?

KS: Many. Many.

PM: Where? Did you meet in the prime minister's office on Parliament Hill?

KS: Yes, quite often. In the lounge, his office. But we had a lot of meetings before that, Peter. In the early eighties, at the Ritz-Carlton in Montreal. His office was across the street.

PM: Was this before he was the leader?

KS: Yeah. This is when it was all discussed that he should become the prime minister. And there was Frank Moores, the president of the party. There was Walter Wolf, who brought me there. He was the fundraiser. And Gary Ouellet.*

PM: But why were you sitting there? You were representing a variety of arms firms. Were you looking at it as future potential business, or did you actually think, "Wow, this guy's great. He'd make a great prime minister." You'd just become a Canadian.

KS: First of all, I never represented arms firms. That's number one. Thyssen was the exception, on the request of the Canadian

* Walter Wolf, an Austrian-Canadian businessman, was a key fundraiser for Mulroney. Gary Ouellet was a lobbyist along with Frank Moores at GCI.

government. But I was asked by Mr. Strauss* to go to Canada and support the Conservatives, which I have done around the world quite often, by helping them win an election. It's called the Insider Foundation, and we had a substantial amount of money. I had the briefcase, and I brought it to Central America. I was involved in the whole Nicaragua crisis, and all these things.

PM: So you're used to travelling around the world with a suitcase full of cash?

KS: Yes. I brought it for political purposes.

PM: And did you see anything wrong with that? Was there anything illegal with that?

KS: No.

PM: Not at that time.

KS: No. It was support from one political party to another political party. I think even today they can do this.

PM: Did Mr. Mulroney know, as far as you're concerned, that that's why you were there? To bring cash from overseas?

KS: I don't know what Walter Wolf told him, but I am convinced they [Mulroney and Wolf] were aware through Michel Cogger† and Frank Moores that I was supporting them from the German side, and that the Strauss family was also behind this. We bought property from Moores. That enabled him to have his own cash ready to help Mulroney, with the aim that everybody

* *Bavarian Premier Franz Josef Strauss was an associate of Schreiber's and had Schreiber work on numerous family business deals. Strauss was chairman of Airbus when Air Canada awarded the company the $1.8 billion contract for new planes in 1988.*

† *Michel Cogger was a political advisor to Mulroney and a lawyer for Walter Wolf and the Strauss family. Mulroney appointed him to the Senate in 1986.*

gets something. I mean, Cogger went to the PMO [Prime Minister's Office]. Doucet went to the PMO. Others, like Bob Coates, became ministers. And Mr. Moores had decided he wants to have the lobbying business. He wants to make money, and that was clear. That is what he would get if Brian Mulroney would become prime minister.

PM: So when he did become prime minister, did you feel like you'd won the jackpot? That there were real possibilities here now for the firms you represented and the sales you wanted to make?

KS: Yeah. It was [a two-way street]. The government approached everybody in Europe; they wanted the jobs and they wanted success. And jobs come from industrial contracts. At the same time I'd look for potential business in Canada. So, yes, to do both.

PM: If you were travelling the world and now making stops in Canada with a suitcase full of cash, that word kind of gets around.

KS: But that was nothing new for me. This was—

PM: No, I'm not saying it was something new, but word gets around here. Did people come to you looking for cash?

KS: Sure.

PM: Who?

KS: The party. Frank Moores. Wolf. Everybody wanted support to get Mulroney elected. At least, that's what we financed.

PM: No, I'm talking about after he was elected.

KS: After he was elected?

PM: When the product of all the work done by people like you and Moores and others to get him elected—did people come to you thinking that somehow you were now going to be able to help them in some fashion or another? Whether it was contributions or—

KS: This happened once in a while. We all set our fundraising dinners and donations. I was asked by Frank Moores and by Mulroney to help him through. I asked him to send another bill to my company and gave him $25,000. Yes, favours like this happened.

PM: Let me get to this issue of the three meetings with Brian Mulroney and cash. Have you been following the Conrad Black story? Have you had an opportunity to follow it?

KS: Not so much.

PM: The one thing that everybody understood in the Conrad Black trial, or at least they thought they understood, were pictures of Conrad Black on a security camera taking files out of his office. Everybody understood that and they felt it was wrong. Right?

KS: (laughs) Yes.

PM: In your story of you and Brian Mulroney, the thing everybody understands—because neither of you disputes this—that you handed him an envelope three times with one hundred thousand-dollar bills.*

KS: Yes.

PM: How thick is that? Does it look like . . . that? (gestures with thumb and forefinger)

* Mulroney alleged on December 13, 2007 (two days after this interview was recorded), at a parliamentary ethics committee that he accepted $225,000 from Schreiber.

KS: Not so thick, sir. The problem is to get rid of [the thousand-dollar bills] in Canada. It's a huge problem.

PM: Okay, we'll get to that. But the public understands this image. They have this image of you giving a man who was a former prime minister, and in one case who was still a sitting MP, $100,000 cash.

KS: Yeah.

PM: And the public thinks that's wrong. Is there anything wrong with him taking that money?

KS: In my opinion, no. Not at all.

PM: Okay. How long was that first meeting at Harrington Lake?

KS: Perhaps two and a half hours.

PM: Two and a half hours.

KS: Yeah.

PM: What'd you talk about?

KS: About what he was doing, what the children do, what I would do, what the project is.

PM: And at no time did you discuss how much money you would pay him to help lobby.

KS: No. And he said, "When Kim Campbell becomes the next prime minister, I am in Montreal, in Quebec." And he's happy the job is much easier for me than him being in Nova Scotia. I can help a lot.

PM: Okay, stop there, because I don't get that. I don't understand why you would think he could help you on a project while he was no longer prime minister, when as prime minister he didn't help you on the project. Why did you think he could help you then if he didn't approve it when he was prime minister?

KS: Yeah, but the point I always learned from him is that it was all the Liberals, like Paul Tellier and [Robert] Fowler and these guys, who were against the project.* He would have loved to do it.

PM: Okay. But it didn't happen while he was prime minister.

KS: Didn't happen.

PM: Then Kim Campbell loses the prime ministership.

KS: Yup.

PM: The Liberals are in power. They're cancelling contracts that the Tories made.

KS: Yes.

PM: The helicopter contract right away, like Day One. Chrétien marches down and cancels it.

KS: Yeah.

PM: But you meet again with Mulroney and give him a $100,000 second instalment.

KS: Yes.

---

* *Paul Tellier and Robert Fowler were senior bureaucrats through the 1970s and '80s. Under Mulroney, Tellier was Clerk of the Privy Council; Fowler was Deputy Minister in the Department of National Defence.*

PM: One hundred thousand dollars cash.

KS: Yes, in December.

PM: Because he's going to help you.

KS: Yes.

PM: His party's not in power. He didn't deal with the project when he was in power. And now the Liberals, who are in power, don't want anything to do with Tory contracts. And you're still giving him money.

KS: Yeah.

PM: Why?

KS: Because I thought that there could be use for Brian Mulroney as he is doing today, lobbying all these big companies very successfully.

PM: Okay, I want to get back to this idea of giving out the cash, because it still is—the image is the thing that Canadians have; they can't shake it. Now you seem to not have a problem with this, giving out cash.

KS: No. Never had.

PM: Did you give cash in envelopes to other politicians or former politicians or senior bureaucrats or former senior bureaucrats in this country at any time before you started giving it to Brian Mulroney?

KS: No.

PM: Well then, why was it cash?

KS: Because the cash was there in that account.

PM: This is the account in Switzerland.

KS: In Switzerland.

PM: And so you give him an envelope—

KS: Yeah.

PM: —with the cash. And what does he do?

KS: "Thank you."

PM: Puts it in his pocket?

KS: Yeah.

PM: Or puts it in his briefcase?

KS: "Thank you." In his pocket or his— No, his briefcase. His briefcase.

PM: Did he have any idea what was in the envelope?

KS: Sure, I told him. The first $100,000.

PM: Did you tell him that it was cash?

KS: Sure. It was not sealed. You could see it. It was open.

PM: But did he look at it?

KS: Sure.

PM: He opened the envelope?

KS: But he didn't count it. I said, "It is what it is," and bingo (smiles). Mr. Mansbridge, I have to tell you something. At that time and even today we have a different relationship to cash in Europe than you have here. Credit cards are not that common. People don't like too much paper, and [with credit cards] people have to pay 8 percent or 5 percent. You get a much better bargain when you pay cash. And you don't want everybody to know what you're buying.

PM: What did you think Mulroney was going to do with thousand-dollar bills?

KS: That was his problem, not mine. Do you think I could bring $100,000 in twenty-dollar bills?

PM: But why didn't you just cut him a cheque?

KS: There is no cheque at that account.

PM: You paid a bank transfer?

KS: I could have put the money in my account—my personal account—and given him a cheque from there.

PM: But why wouldn't you have done that?

KS: No, because I took money from the account where the money was.

PM: The issue is, was this supposed to be money that nobody was ever going to know about? Did you think that when you gave it to him?

KS: No, and I will tell you why. I expected him to give me something—either send me a bill or receipt or tell me for what company it should be.

PM: Did you ask him for that?

KS: No.

PM: Why not?

KS: Because I met him then and I met him a time later and nothing happened. So I said, "Okay, he may organize it himself." I didn't know whether it was Mr. Mulroney, private citizen, or it was his company. If he would not have said that he received this money from me, I could not have proven that he received the money. But this is in that world—there's no proof of anything.

PM: But that's the world that I'm asking you about. It makes it sound like you were dealing in cash because you didn't want any record of it and he didn't want any record of it.

KS: I didn't care.

PM: Who's money was it at that moment?

KS: My money.

PM: It was your money that Thyssen had given you—

KS: Yeah.

PM: —to do what?

KS: To push the Bear Head project.

PM: Push?

KS: Yeah. The work for the Bear Head Project. [. . .] The only thing that you can say is, "Why was it cash?" Because it was cash.

PM: No, the thing that is wrong with it, for one, was that there were rules against former politicians lobbying for anything for two years after they left office—rules that the Mulroney government had put in themselves.

KS: Yeah. I didn't know that, by the way.

PM: Two, on the cash, it ends up looking like it was cash to get around that rule so there was no record. There was no invoice. There were no receipts. There was no nothing. It was, "Here's the money, you do what you have to do, and hopefully we can get that contract." Because, as you just told me, you never recall ever paying anybody cash in an envelope for anything else previous to that. So it was an unusual moment.

KS: You speak [about] here, in this country?

PM: That's right. Here, in Canada.

KS: There was no need for anything. Nobody asked me for—

PM: But there was a need that day—

KS: Yeah.

PM: —and you decided that all on your own, that it should be cash. Nobody suggested to you it should be cash.

KS: No, I took it from there and [withdrew] it, and that's it. Didn't even think about it.

PM: How can anybody get to the bottom of all this, if in fact there was something? As you say, you didn't know there was something wrong.

KS: Mr. Mansbridge, may I say something very funny?

PM: Yeah.

KS: Bill Clinton.

PM: Bill Clinton?

KS: And Monica Lewinsky. If they both would have kept their mouths shut, who would have known? This is what it is. Brian Mulroney, if he would have said, "Schreiber is nuts. He never gave me any money," how could I prove it? There was no receipt. There was no wire. There was no cheque.

PM: Were you surprised when he agreed?

KS: Not really, because as I said in my letter to him, "Why didn't you tell the truth from the beginning?" There was nothing to hide. He made it so complicated, so crazy and so nasty. At first saying nothing, then denying, coming out with false statements in his settlement thing, and then inventing all kinds of stories . . . I don't get it. Why? And this is exactly the point why I asked for an inquiry. I have certain ideas about what went on. Because when I see what's going on today, it is pretty clear what happened then. As I said to you earlier, I have no problem with taking a polygraph. Let's see whether the others are prepared to do the same.

PM: Do you think there will ever be a day when Canadians understand everything that happened here?

KS: A great part, yes. But Canadians must understand that there will always be a couple of places where they cannot find an answer, because there's no answer available.

—

IMMEDIATELY AFTER THE INTERVIEW aired I offered Brian Mulroney the same opportunity: a seat on *One on One*. The offer still stands. He's chosen, at least so far, not to accept it.

There's an irony about our Karlheinz Schreiber interview. After he and his entourage left the Chateau Laurier suite, our crew began the lengthy process of packing up: taking down the lights, rolling up the cable and putting the ornate pieces of furniture back where we'd first found them. By early evening we'd checked out and I was back in Toronto airing the interview. The Chateau cleaning staff went to work changing the linen, polishing the chairs and tables and preparing things for the suite's next guests, due to check in the following morning. They were from Montreal—the Mulroneys.

THE AGA KHAN

THERE ARE ABOUT EIGHTY THOUSAND Ismaili Canadians in our country, and when I decided to interview their spiritual leader, the Aga Khan, his Canadian representatives told me that every single one of them would be watching. They weren't kidding. Every time I meet an Ismaili Canadian, whether in Edmonton, Calgary, Toronto, Ottawa or any of the other urban areas they seem to favour, I'm stopped and told how great the interview was. *One on One* airs at least three times every weekend on the CBC, and one of those airings is in the middle of the night. The audiences at that time are understandably small—often no more than fifteen thousand. So I had to smile when I saw the overnight ratings the first time the Aga Khan's interview ran: eighty thousand.

Ismailis are a minority in the Muslim faith; in fact, some Muslims don't even recognize them as Muslims. Their history is deep, ancient and to a degree bitter. Ismailis broke away from the main Shiite Muslim faith about twelve hundred years ago over who best represented the true Imam, or leader of Islam. I've seen some Ismaili friends at work shunned by other Muslims, who refused to accept them as friends and barely acknowledged them as colleagues.

His Highness Prince Karim Aga Khan is the leader of the world's Ismaili community, and he has spent many of his fifty years as the Aga Khan trying to counter those differences. He's become a well-known and well respected international figure and his admirers exist far beyond his faith. He established the Aga Khan Foundation to improve living conditions and opportunities for the poor, whatever their faith, origin or gender. He was a great friend of Pierre Trudeau; his trips to this country during the Trudeau years were frequent and they continue that way now. While the Trudeau relationship became broader in scope, it was based on the former prime minister's decision in the early seventies to admit to Canada thousands of Asians who had been expelled from Uganda by the brutal dictator Idi Amin. Many of the new arrivals were Ismaili, and they, and the Aga Khan, have never forgotten Canada's open doors in their time of need.

All of those points had made me determined to invite the Aga Khan onto *One on One* during one of his frequent Canadian visits. The opportunity came in early 2007.

When I flew to Ottawa for the interview, I took with me a good friend and colleague. Sherali Najak is the executive producer of *Hockey Night in Canada*, and years ago he worked with us on *The National*. He'd begged me and my regular director, Fred Parker, to let him direct the Aga Khan shoot. Freddie, normally very protective of his turf, said, "Absolutely," and so did I. Sherali, you see, is Ismaili. His family story traces back to those Uganda days, and for him this opportunity to be in the same room as the Aga Khan was going to be a life-defining moment.

The interview was enjoyable and informative. The Aga Khan is a moderate Muslim leader at a time when many Muslims and Christians are wondering if they will ever get along. His thoughts on that topic were provocative, but we started by trying to understand his fondness for Canada.

2007-02-17

Peter Mansbridge: You must love Canada—you keep coming back here.

Aga Khan: I do.

PM: What is the quality that you most admire about this country?

AK: I think a number of qualities. First of all, it's a pluralist society that has invested in building pluralism, where communities from all different backgrounds and faiths are happy. It's a modern country that deals with modern issues, not running away from the tough ones. And a global commitment to values, to Canadian values, which I think are very important.

PM: Let's talk about that a little bit, because I wonder whether your confidence in Canada has in any way been shattered a little bit in these past few years, especially since 9/11. There have been tensions in this country, as there have been in many other Western countries, between Muslim and non-Muslim societies—on any number of levels, on both sides, about history, religion, tradition and integration within society. How much has that concerned you?

AK: It concerns me and at the same time it doesn't, in the sense that, to me, building and sustaining a pluralist society is always going to be a work in progress. It doesn't have a finite end. And so long as there is national intent, civic intent to make pluralism work, then one accepts that it's a work in progress.

PM: Let me go a little deeper on that, because it raises a question you have often raised, and that's the issue of ignorance. You reject the theory of a clash of civilizations, or even a clash of religions. You believe there's a clash of ignorance here, on both sides of that divide. And you've felt that way for a long time. I was looking through the transcripts of an interview you gave in the 1980s in Canada where you were warning the West that it had to do a better job in trying to understand Islam. That clearly hasn't happened.

AK: No, it hasn't happened. A number of friends and people in important places have tried to contribute to solving that problem, but it's a long-established problem. It's going to take, I think, several decades before we reach a situation where the definition of an educated person includes basic understanding of the Islamic world. That hasn't been the case. And the absence of that basic education has caused all sorts of misunderstandings.

PM: What's been the resistance?

AK: I think it's essentially historic. I think that Judeo-Christian societies have developed their own education, and basic knowledge of the Islamic world has simply been absent. Look at what was required for an education in the humanities; for example, I was a student in the U.S. and education on the Islamic world was absent.

PM: Is this a one-sided clash of ignorance?

AK: No, I think there is ignorance on both sides, and I think very often there's confusion. I think more and more there has been confusion between, for example, religion and civilization. And that's introducing instability in the discussion, frankly. I would prefer to talk about ignorance of the civilizations of the Islamic world rather than ignorance just on the faith of Islam.

PM: What we've witnessed in the last couple of years, not just in this country but in other Western countries as well, is what we call "homegrown terror," where you see young Muslim men—born in the West, educated in the West—moving towards a fundamentalist view, a militant view of Islam. Why is that happening?

AK: There is without any doubt a growing sense amongst Muslim communities around the world that there are forces at play that it doesn't control, that views the Muslim world with, let's say, unhappiness or more. I would simply say, however, that if you analyze the situation I don't think you can conclude that all Muslims from all backgrounds are part of that phenomenon. Secondly, if you go back and look at the communities where this is common, you will find that there's a long-standing unresolved political crisis in the community. It's very, very risky, I think, to interpret these situations as being specific to the faith of Islam. It is specific to peoples, sometimes ethnic groups, but it's not specific to the face of Islam.

PM: That must really concern you. Your followers see you as a direct descendant of the Prophet Muhammad, the same prophet that some of these minority fundamentalist militant groups hold up and claim as the reason they're doing the acts they're doing.

AK: Again, I think one has to go back and say, "What is the cause of this situation?" With all due respect, if you look at the crisis in the Middle East, that crisis was born at the end of the First World War. The crisis in Kashmir was born through the liberation of the Indian continent. These are political issues originally; they're not religious issues. You can't attribute the faith of Islam to them. I think the second point I would make is this tendency to generalize Islam. There are many different interpretations of Islam. As a Muslim, if I said to you that I didn't recognize the difference between a Greek Orthodox or a Russian Orthodox or a Protestant or a Catholic, I think you'd say to me, "But you don't understand the Christian world." Let me reverse that question.

PM: Canada's role in Afghanistan is well-known, has been since 9/11. So is the Aga Khan Foundation, which is in there in a big way in development matters. The question is simple, really: with all the help that's been given to Afghanistan, why is the Taliban resurging? Not only in numbers, but in popularity as well. Why is that happening?

AK: I think there are a number of reasons, but the one that I would put forward as the most immediate is the slow process of recon-struction. There was a lot of hope that once there was a regime change and a new government and the political process had been completed, the quality of life would change. It hasn't changed quickly enough. It's taken much more time than I think many of us had hoped to get to isolated communities in Afghanistan and improve their quality of life. It's an organizational problem. Even amongst the donor countries there have been differences of opinion. The management of the drug problem has not been a united effort by any means. So there are a number of things that have slowed up the process. And there are still acute pockets of poverty in Afghanistan: people who don't have enough food, people who don't have access to any education, any health care. It is clear this sort of frustration causes bitterness and the search for other solutions.

PM: Is there time to turn it around? Because you get a sense that the pendulum has swung back considerably in the last year or so. There's this growing sense of frustration among the Canadian people and a belief that it's a war that cannot be won.

AK: I would beg to differ on that. I think what we're seeing in Afghanistan, at least from my own network of activities, is an increasingly visible two-speed process, where in the north and the west you're beginning to see quantifiable change. In the east and the south you're not seeing that. Two-speed change is going to have to be managed with great care, but it's not a good reason to give up by any means.

PM: Can you do both at the same time? That's the debate in Canada: to run a military operation—talking specifically about the south—while trying to introduce aid and development in an area that is not secure.

AK: It's very difficult to do, but necessary. Every step counts. Certainly in areas where there's insecurity, I think the availability for populations to participate in these development activities does go down when quality of life changes. And I believe the same thing with regard to the drug problem.

PM: How much of the problem in Afghanistan is a result of the decision on the part of the Americans and the British to move into Iraq?

AK: Very substantial indeed. The invasion of Iraq was something which has mobilized what we call the Imamat—the community of Muslims around the world. Every Muslim that I have ever talked to has felt engaged by this.

PM: On what level?

AK: Baghdad is one of the great historic cities of the Islamic world. Iraq is not a new country; it's part of the history of our civilization. It's been a pluralist country and has produced great philosophers, great historians, great scientists. Reverse the question again. What would the Christian world think if a Muslim army attacked Rome? I think there would be a general reaction in the Christian world, not just an Italian reaction.

PM: But it seems that even in the Muslim world, that invasion has caused major divisions—the clash inside Islam itself, between Shia and Sunni.

AK: That was entirely predictable. Entirely predictable. What you are effectively doing is replacing a Sunni minority government in a country that has a Shia demographic majority. And again, what would happen—I'm sorry to come back to this, but it's important—if a Muslim army went in to Northern Ireland and replaced one Christian interpretation by another? Imagine the fallout that that would cause in the Christian world itself.

PM: So what happens now? Can Iraq be put back together? And who would be doing the putting back together?

AK: I think that's a very, very difficult question, and I would not want to predict the answer. Because I think that the whole process of change in Iraq has regional dimensions which have got to be managed. They're not national dimensions in Iraq. Those regional dimensions also were predictable, let's be quite frank about it. I think they're going to need to be managed with very, very great care.

PM: Is the answer, as some suggest, the splitting of it into three regions with the main two combatants, the Shia and the Sunnis, actually separated by borders?

AK: That's really, I think, an issue where the leaders of the three communities have got to agree or not. In my life, in the past fifty years, I have been uncomfortable with the creation of unviable states. So I would ask this question: if you did do that, what components of Iraq would be stable, viable states in the future?

PM: Who's showing leadership in this world right now in terms of the major global issues? Who do you look to as a leader, whether it's a political leader or not?

AK: I think there are a number of people in the U.N. system who've shown leadership, who have shown balanced judgment on these issues. Because when all is said and done, it's the balance of the judgment that counts. And it's understanding the issues. I think, amongst others, Kofi Annan has been remarkable in his understanding of the issues. He's also had a team of people around him who are very good.

PM: It's quite a condemnation though of the political leaders of our generation that you don't point to one of them, no matter which side of the divide we talked about earlier. You don't see one there?

AK: I'm looking at the regions of Africa, Central Asia, and I'm asking myself within this context who's having the greatest influence. I think that certainly the U.N. Development Program . . . I think the World Bank and Jim Wolfensohn changed direction very significantly and dealt with real human issues and has done a wonderful job.

PM: Some people suggest that there's been a movement in terms of real leadership away from governments to private foundations, philanthropic organizations—yours being one, the Gates Foundation, and you can name a number of them. Do you see that happening? Is that a good thing?

AK: I see it happening, and I welcome it wholeheartedly. Because what we're talking about, I think, is accelerating the construction of a civil society. I personally think that civil society is one of the most urgent things to build around the world. Because one of the phenomena you see today is the number of countries where governments have been unstable. Progress is made where there's been a strong civil society, and that's a lesson that I think all of us have to learn. My own network is immensely committed to that. And so what the Gateses and others are doing is providing new resources, new thoughts to create civil society. Whether it's in health care or education, it's the combined input which is so exciting and so important.

PM: We touched briefly earlier on the new Global Centre for Pluralism, which will be established here in Canada through the Aga Khan Foundation and the people of Canada through the Government of Canada. What is your hope for that? What do you see that doing, accomplishing?

AK: I hope that the centre will learn from the Canadian history of pluralism, the bumpy road that all societies have in dealing with pluralist problems, the outcomes, and offer the world new thoughts, new ways of dealing with issues, anticipating the problems that can occur. Because in recent years I think we're seeing more and more that no matter what the nature of the conflict, ultimately there is a rejection of pluralism as one of the components. Whether it's tribalism, whether it's conflict amongst ethnic groups, whether it's conflict amongst religions, the failure to see value in pluralism is a terrible liability.

PM: Why Canada?

AK: Because I think Canada is a country that has invested in making this potential liability become an asset. I think that Canada has been perhaps too humble in its own appreciation of this global asset. It's a global asset. Few countries, if any, have been as successful as Canada has, bumpy though the road is. As I said earlier, it's always going to be an unfinished task.

PM: Next year is your golden jubilee: fifty years. What's your— I was going to say what's your dream for the world in that year, but I guess dreams are dreams. What's your realistic hope?

AK: In areas of the world which are living in horrible poverty, I'd like to see that replaced by an environment where people can live in more hope than they've had. I'd like to see governments that produce enabling environments where society can function and grow rather than live in the dogmatisms that we've all lived through, and which I think have been very constraining. And I'd like to see solid institutional building, because, when all is said and done, societies need institutional capacity.

PM: Those are grand hopes. I'm sure they're shared by many. How realistic do you think it is that we can achieve anything like that?

AK: I think we can achieve a lot of that. I think the time frame is what we don't control. I remember in the mid-fifties reading about countries in the developing world being referred to as basket cases. Fifty years later those are some of the most powerful countries in the world—enormous populations. They're exporting food when fifty years ago we were told they'd never be able to feed themselves. They had an incredible technology deficit fifty years ago. Today they're exporting technology, homegrown technology. So I think there are a number of cases out there where we can say what we don't control is the time factor. But society does have the capability to make those changes.

PM: So there is reason for hope.

AK: I believe so, God willing.

—

AS INSPIRING AS HIS MESSAGE WAS, the lasting memory I take from that day was more personal. It was the beaming face of Sherali Najak standing next to the Aga Khan for that special photograph he had so wanted to get. The man who regularly bosses Don Cherry around looked pretty tame all of a sudden.

RANDY BACHMAN

THE FIRST THING YOU WANT to get right with Randy Bachman is his name. If you are a BTO fan, you would say "*bawk-man*"—and you would be wrong. "Bawkman" is the way the name was pronounced by a record executive who decided it would sell much better than the way the Winnipeg-born rocker was christened, which is "*back*-man." So that was issue number one when this front-row-centre icon of the Canadian music scene came by for our *One on One.* The former Guess Who, former Bachman-Turner Overdrive, former Brave Belt, former Ironhorse guitarist and singer has been a major force for the past forty years. When he's not been in front of a microphone, he's been behind the glass producing others.

With the name pronunciation bit out of the way, he softened me up with that line I never quite know how to respond to: "My mother is a big fan of yours. She's very excited that I'm going to be on your show." I hear that a lot. It leaves me wondering where the division between the merits of flattery and demographics lies. I find it especially challenging when I'm asked to speak to university students and afterwards there's a lineup for pictures or autographs. That's encouraging—until they start saying things like "My mother loves you" or "Can I have your autograph, but please sign it for my mom. She *always* watches you." Or the always popular "Mom goes to bed with you every night." But enough on that. Suffice it to say, in this case I was very flattered that Mrs. Bachman was a viewer, and now it was on to trying to impress her by interviewing her son.

I feel that if an interview can leave viewers with one good story to repeat to friends, then it's been a success. Bachman gave me that and more, especially on the issue of how signature tunes come about. "Taking Care of Business" is probably his most famous signature song; it's certainly the most repeated from classic rock radio to the most up to date of commercials. Bachman's story of how a pizza delivery man helped make "Taking Care of Business" the hit it became is certainly one I'll never forget.

2002-03-10

Peter Mansbridge: There are so many things we could talk about, but I want you to tell one anecdote because it's great. It's about the song "Taking Care of Business." It's the story of recording that song and the pizza man.

Randy Bachman: The song was written by accident. It was a song that the Guess Who had passed on earlier, and I desperately put it together one night on stage when Fred Turner, who was the main lead singer in Bachman-Turner Overdrive, had lost his voice and I had to finish the last set. We were going to record it a few weeks later. After we were recording it with just guitar and bass and drums, there was a knock on the recording studio door.

This is in Seattle. Steve Miller was down the hall recording the *Fly Like an Eagle* album, and War was down the hall doing their album, and there is a great big guy there. I'm big, so when I say a big guy, I mean a *really* big guy—about six foot six, three hundred something pounds, and hair like Fidel Castro, big beard. And he was wearing the full army fatigues and the hat just like Castro, standing there with about five pizzas. He said, "Did you guys order pizza?" I said, "No, it must be down the hall." And he's standing there listening to the song, and it was "Taking Care of Business."

So he went down the hall and dumped the pizza with whoever—Steve Miller or War—and then he came back and knocked again. And he said, "You know, that song sounds like it could really use a piano." It was two o'clock in the morning, and I said, "Look, we're going home." I'm closing my briefcase and everything and he says, "Please, please, I'm a piano player. Can I have a shot?" And I said, "Oh, who am I not to give a guy a shot, right? Okay, you have one pass."

He took a napkin and he wrote down the key and he said, "What should I play like?" I said, "Well, Little Richard, Elton John, Dr. John"—all this kind of stuff. Normally you would try a whole pass like Little Richard, then a whole pass like Dr. John, then a whole pass like Elton John. He went and did it all at once. When it was all done, I said, "Great, that's it. Thank you very much."

I was going to wipe this track the next day, just erase it. The head of our label, Charlie Fasch, flew in because he wanted to hear this album and hear some songs to get us on Top 40 radio. We played him the song, and he says, "This is really good." Suddenly the engineer brought up the fader that had the piano on and he went, "Wow, BTO with a piano? This gives you a whole different sound on radio—let's leave it in! Who played piano?"

I said, "I don't know, a pizza guy."

"What do you mean 'a pizza guy'? What musician did you pay?"

"It was a pizza guy."

"Well, we have to get him and put his name on the album and pay him!"

So I went down the hall and said to Steve Miller, "Where did you order the pizza from?" He said, "Are you kidding? We've all been here two months, and every day about two in the afternoon it's Chinese or Mexican, and every night it's pizza. Here's the

Yellow Pages." I went to the front of the studio and I said to the girl, "Would you please start phoning in the As and I'll go half through the alphabet—I'll phone from the Ms to the Zs."

PM: Come on, you're kidding.

RB: And we asked them if they delivered pizza to this studio on this date. Now two days have gone by, and we had to find him.

PM: And you found him?

RB: I got it, but they wouldn't tell me his name or anything because they didn't know why I was calling. Finally I got a really good Italian guy and he said, "Oh yes, there's this musician that only works for us the last day of the month. When he can't pay his rent, he delivers pizza."
    And I said, "Can you give me his name and number?"
    "No. But if you order a pizza we'll send him out."
    So we ordered a pizza and the guy came out. His name was Norman Durkee, and this was his entrance into show business. He went on to become Bette Midler's musical director on her first national tour. About six years ago I was playing with the Ringo Starr All-Star Band and we played at the Greek Theatre in Los Angeles, and before us the L.A. Symphony was rehearsing—and he's the rehearsal pianist. So that's the story of the pizza man.

PM: Songs like "Taking Care of Business"—and you've had so many of them—have become anthems for a number of different generations. Do you know at the time you're writing them or recording them that they're going to be?

RB: No, because a lot of them are accidents and happenstance, things that just kind of happen. And when they're happening you're kind of bewildered, like, "Why is this happening?" I've learned to go with the flow, that somebody somewhere is making these things happen, that there are angels guiding people and it comes together.

And then, very soon, you realize that moment is a real moment in your life—that you will never forget that moment and that song.

When it first comes out and gets on the radio, you're so thrilled and so happy to be driving along, especially to land in Toronto or go to L.A., rent a car, put on the radio and hear your song, it's just—there's nothing like that. To go back ten or twenty years later and still hear that song is really unbelievable. This is a dream we never had, you know—of a resurgence, like getting back together with the Guess Who. This is not a dream we had when we were twenty: "When we're in our mid-fifties, let's all get back together and go coast to coast and have a sell-out tour!" No one would dream of this.

PM: You talk about how your mid-life crisis was different than for so many of your colleagues and people your age. But also your whole career has been different than so many who are in your business: no drinking, no smoking, no drugs.

RB: Well, that allowed me to buy the guitars.

PM: Ha! Yeah, right.

RB: Literally, I'd save my per diem on the road—$20 or $30 or $50, depending on which band you're with—just save all that up.

PM: But how did you do that when you were eighteen, nineteen, twenty years old, when the temptation on the road must have been incredible?

RB: I was allergic to smoke. I tried smoking once. I'm from a non-smoking family, so that kind of sets a standard. When I was going to college, I wanted to be cool, and guys had a pipe. So I went and bought a pipe and tobacco, and I'm stuffing it and I'm trying to light my first pipe—and my mother is running around saying, "Something's on fire! The house is on fire!" because nobody smoked in our house. I said, "It's me, I'm being cool, I'm going to smoke a pipe." I was eighteen or nineteen, and the phone rang and she called me to the phone. I was sitting in my dad's chair, the Archie Bunker chair in front of the TV, with this pipe. I got up to walk into the kitchen and I fell down, and my throat had swollen up and I was dizzy, just from a few puffs on this pipe. That's when I realized I was allergic to smoke. So I threw away the pipe.

And then there's another instance when Chad Allan had left the Guess Who and Burton Cummings was joining the Guess Who. We had a big blast of a party on the edge of town with Jim Kale, the bass player, whom I used to live with, on the edge of St. Vital. I made a fool of myself at this party. I got so drunk I backed a car up over my own foot, and my dad had to put the car in drive and drove it off. Luckily it was all snowy and I didn't break my foot or anything. He said he was ashamed of me and that I was a drunk. I stopped drinking that night. Then I joined the Mormon church, which preaches abstinence from tobacco and alcohol, and I was so glad to have a support group, like I had joined Alcoholics Anonymous or something. The Mormon church said, "Don't do this. This will kill you."

PM: Winnipeg is a part of your roots. You're still very connected to that city and it's still a lot of the reason for your success.

RB: I believe so. There's something about the isolation of Winnipeg, that you had to drive many, many hundreds of miles either to Minneapolis or Regina, or further to Toronto. There wasn't that great a deal to drive to. *You* know—you've spent your time there. You're indoors a good six or seven months. And when I grew up—same with you—there are no indoor hockey rinks. As a kid you're playing hockey and the coach would say, "It snowed last night. Come an hour early before the game," and you'd have these big shovels push the snow aside and play hockey. When you get to be twelve or thirteen, you figure you don't want to play hockey any more. That's what a lot of guys did—me, Neil Young, Fred Turner—you start a band and you copy the Beatles or you copy Jimi Hendrix or you copy Bob Dylan. And you go to the garage, which is now all insulated in Winnipeg, with a little pot-belly stove, or down in your basement, and you try to be someone.

But meanwhile, as you were growing up, all that music that you heard at the weddings and bar mitzvahs and parties—that influences you in a way. So I find that whichever part of Winnipeg you were from, whether you were Crash Test Dummies or BTO or the Guess Who or Loreena McKennitt, your music was totally different from everyone else's. It wasn't like the cloning of music that's coming out now. Neil Young and all the hit musicians that came out of Winnipeg—that music is just totally different. It's from their ethnic celebrations that were going on. You saw people dancing and reacting to the music. There was just something about being able to hibernate in a cocoon there. Winnipeg, being very ethnic—there was a Ukrainian part of town and the Jewish part and the British and Irish part—they all had their own wonderful things that they don't have any more: community centres that the people played bingo in and you had dances in, and that's where you changed into your skates to go skate outside on the outdoor rink, and you changed your baseball uniform when you were playing Little League baseball.

Suddenly the dances evolved to Neil Young and the Squires playing at the River Heights Community Centre and the Guess Who playing at the West Kildonan Community Centre. Then you'd go to play on the other side of town, and suddenly Winnipeg in the mid-sixties was like Liverpool. There were eighty or a hundred community centres, and all these discotheques that started, and no worry about drinking or drinking ages. It was a teenage phenomenon. There must have been 150 bands that were all cross-pollinating and lending each other guitars and drums, helping each other and going to watch each other. I remember going to see Neil Young and the Squires and cheering him on, and they'd come and watch us and cheer us on. It was just the most wonderful high school or college for us all to get into the music business.

—

WHILE WE AT *One on One* take no credit for it (although secretly we try!), it was shortly after his visit to our studio that Randy Bachman took over the chair in his own studio with CBC Radio. He's the host of what has become the very popular Saturday evening program *Vinyl Tap*, and his storytelling and music selection have become a weekend highlight.

SIR MARTIN GILBERT

WING COMMANDER STANLEY MANSBRIDGE of the Royal Air Force had completed two tours as a navigator/bomb aimer with 5 Group, 49 Squadron, when King George VI pinned the Distinguished Flying Cross on his chest during a wartime ceremony in Buckingham Palace. My father had been on many famous Bomber Command missions in the Second World War, including an August 1943 attack on the Nazis' Peenemunde rocket site that seriously delayed Adolf Hitler's V-1 and V-2 rocket production at a critical time during the war.

Like so many veterans of the greatest generation, my father rarely talked about the war. He'd "lost far too many friends," my mother used to say. One Remembrance Day I remember catching him gently crying as he watched the 11:00 a.m. ceremonies from Ottawa. I was twelve or thirteen, and it was the only time I would ever see him tear up. After that I decided that if I was ever going to get him to open up about his experiences, I'd have to start by learning the history myself. I became an avid student of the Second World War as a result. One of the first times I brought the war up with my father, I asked him if he'd ever met Sir Winston Churchill. He looked me in the eye and said, "I never met him, but one night I talked to him."

In the last year of the war, his missions behind him, Wing Commander Mansbridge had been assigned to Bomber Command headquarters, where major operations were mapped out, assigned and coordinated. One night at about four in the morning, with the latest mission over, he was filling in as duty officer when a certain phone rang—only one person called on that line. "Yes, Prime Minister?" my father answered, as firmly as he could. "How many aircraft have not returned?" was the only question asked. That it was that question, as opposed to all the others he could have asked, has always struck me as characteristic of Churchill's leadership style.

Much of what we know about the most famous British prime minister of the past century we have learned from British writer Sir Martin Gilbert. With access to literally tons of Churchill's private papers, he has given us a close-up view of Churchill during his most challenging years. I've been buying Gilbert's books— there have been dozens—for years, and whenever my father unwrapped one as a present, he'd retreat immediately to his favourite reading chair to begin devouring its every word. When Sir Martin agreed to come by our studios for a conversation, I'll concede that I was a bit nervous, fearful that this icon of Churchill lore would be a bit stiff, overly fact-laden and dismissive of anyone not up to snuff on his many writings. I couldn't have been more wrong. We began our conversation on the topic of leadership, and what Churchill taught us about it.

2006-10-21

Peter Mansbridge: As somebody who's studied one of the greats, do you have a definition of what great leadership is?

Martin Gilbert: I think a great leader has to have a sense of moral purpose. He has to know exactly where he stands on the crucial issues of the day. And if he's going to be a leader of Western democracies, he's got to have a real sense that democracy matters—that it has to be defended. He must have real conviction in his beliefs, and of course an ability to transmit his convictions. There are many people who have intense and good convictions but don't, for one reason or another, have the means to transmit them, to get them across to you and me.

PM: So it's a combination of knowing where you want to go, being convinced that you are right and having the ability to attract others not only to follow you but to help you get there.

MG: Absolutely. And to understand that, on the one hand, you have to reflect public opinion, but on the other you have to be able to lead the public opinion in directions it's a little reluctant to go. It is a very complicated balancing act.

PM: How do you judge leadership? Some people suggest that you can't really judge a leader at the time that he or she is leading, that you have to wait for some time and allow the historians to make that judgment. Often the leaders are the ones who say that, especially those who are leaving at a time when perhaps they are not particularly liked. But how does one judge? Can you judge at the time?

MG: I think it's difficult. And I think Churchill's case is interesting in that he judged himself to have been a failure. During the great appeasement debate of the thirties, when he was in opposition and no one was listening to him, he felt he had failed to produce acceptance for his views that war could be averted by armament, by alliances, by faith in one's own ideological democratic position. So he judged his leadership to have been a failure. And being called in to, as it were, pick up the mess—he didn't see as a great achievement.

Of course, for us it was a great achievement and one has to always think what would have happened if he hadn't had full confidence in his convictions. What would have happened in December 1941, when the Blitz was at its height, if he had said to himself, "I don't think I can go ahead with this"? And he came near to that. He came very near—not to losing his nerve but to feeling, "The task is too big for me."

PM: I don't want to pick on Bush or Blair, but they're convenient targets, especially over these past couple of years. I recall a speech you made near the end of 2004, where you suggested that it was far too early to judge either man. The criticism was beginning to build in the post–Iraq invasion time, and their approval ratings were dropping. Do you still feel that way, that it will take time to judge the leadership of George W. Bush and Tony Blair?

MG: I think it will take time. Of course, there may be some intractables which will never be resolved in their favour. It may be that weapons of mass destruction will never be found in Iraq and therefore some element of Bush's leadership will be perceived to be flawed. Similarly with Blair. My impression of Blair is that he has adopted a very strong Christian moral tone with regard to world affairs, in both Africa and also, of course, Iraq and Afghanistan. And I'd like to feel that this is the case. I think it is. But it will only be in thirty years' time when the historian opens the archives, and I shan't be around because I'd have to be a hundred—well, perhaps I will be around! (laughs)—but, you know, it will be sad to find, say, that he is revealed to be cynical or not quite believing in what he did. I think you have to judge on trust, and you have to have an instinct that a man is genuine and hope that you're right.

PM: Going back to that definition of leadership: is it different in wartime? We tend to judge certain politicians as great wartime leaders. And so you're making the judgment more instantly than you do with leaders who are in peacetime the majority of time. Is it different?

MG: I think it is different. It's also much harder to really get to the bottom of what wartime leadership is. Because even for

Churchill's conduct in the war, so much of wartime leadership is working with a large group of people and letting the fighting men and women get on with the job and not being a micromanager. Even Churchill was not a micromanager. There were all sorts of people on his staff of whom he approved, and they got on with the job. So there, leadership came from being an inspiring presence but not a finger in the pie. Now, it may be in times of peace that the leader has to be more proactive.

PM: You know, there are those who say it's hard to be a great leader now, not necessarily because of the people who come forward, but because television has changed the dynamic.

MG: I think it probably has. People often say to me, "Would Churchill have been any good on television?" Essentially we don't know.

PM: But you must have a guess.

MG: Probably in his prime he would have been magical on television, but—

PM: When was his prime? When you consider that he was in his, what, mid-sixties when he became prime minister in the 1940s, was that his prime?

MG: I think his greatest days were in the five or six years before the First World War, when he spearheaded the great social revolution and created the social system in Britain under which we still live. His other prime was in those first months of the Second World War, when everything seemed hopeless and he too believed that it might all be over. He confided to a friend six months later, "I awoke every morning in May 1940 with dread in my heart," yet he was able to go out and about and people said, "He doesn't think we're beaten." Even the V-for-victory sign was a little cocking a snook at what seemed to be a disaster.

I have one extraordinary story I was told by his principal private secretary. Churchill was going into 10 Downing Street, fumbling with his key in the little back entrance. And there was a group of men on a statue of Kitchener putting up scaffolding so it wouldn't be hit by shrapnel—which indeed it was in the end—and they started cheering, "Good old Winnie, good old Winnie!" The private secretary was puzzled that he kept pushing to try and open the door. Normally he'd go over and he'd chat with them or he'd wave to them. So the private secretary tugged at him and said, "Prime Minister—the men on the scaffolding." And suddenly he saw tears streaming down from the old boy's eyes, and Churchill said, "There's nothing I can do for them." And at that moment he probably thought it was hopeless. But he never appeared with his tears. He appeared always with his grin and the defiance and the cigar.

PM: Wow. I interrupted you as you were answering the question about whether or not he would have been able to perform on television in a way that could ensure that his leadership would continue. Do you think he would have?

MG: I hope so. He was a very adaptable person. He was in parliament for sixty-four years, and he had to adapt to all sorts of different aspects of politics. I think where he was very good—and that was unexpected for his contemporaries—was on the radio in its early days. In fact, I was astonished to discover that in 1926, when the BBC wanted to have someone make the Christmas appeal for the blind, they chose him. And it's a wonderful appeal that he made, because he spoke with wit as well as with oratory, and with light touches as well as with heavy touches. So he adapted to the radio, as we now know, of course, because of the famous Second War speeches. But in 1924–25, it wasn't certain he would.

PM: Did he write his own speeches?

MG: He did. In the first, oh, thirty years of his political life he wrote them all by hand, and wrote and rewrote. He was a tremendous rewriter. Then he dictated. His secretaries typed them out in sound form, rather like poems, phrase by phrase. Then he went over them and over them and over them again. And he knew them by heart when he gave them, but he always had the little sheets of paper in front of him just in case. He worked harder on the speeches than any other public man about whom I've studied.

PM: We see a kind of leadership now in countries around the world, formed by the hangers-on who work in the office of the prime minister or the president, the image-makers, the speechwriters, the what-have-you. Did he have that kind of a group around him?

MG: He had a very good team; it was called the private office. There were five members. They rotated so two of them were with him every day, and they knew his thoughts. He also had two secretaries. He would speak; he wouldn't dictate. Whenever he said something, they would immediately put it down on their silent typewriters, never making a mistake. And so whenever he spoke, what he said was down on paper. And any idea he had, the private office followed through with it.

He didn't use image-makers, but I came across a fascinating example. When General de Gaulle arrived in London—the one hope, really, of maintaining France in exile—Churchill saw him and was impressed that this man wanted to go on fighting the Germans. I found a wonderful note which he wrote to the Cabinet Office, saying: "General de Gaulle is our man, but he has such a poor personality and presentation I propose we use government money to get the leading PR firm to boost up his image." De Gaulle was trained for a month before he made his great speech to the French people.

PM: What about Churchill? Did he need a PR agency, even in those days?

MG: Not really. He was his own PR machine. He wrote a lot and published many magazine articles, and he was very good at promoting his articles. For that he had an amazing literary agent, as we now call him, who got his articles in fifty newspapers every week around Europe and in Canada and the States.

PM: During the war years, once he was well established as the leader, was he seen by the British people as a great leader at that time?

MG: He was always a slightly divisive figure. It took four months into his premiership before the Conservatives cheered him in the House of Commons.

PM: And he was their leader!

MG: He was their leader. They sat glum and silent. And there were always people who didn't like him because of the pre-war political quarrels. But he established the basis of his war government, let pre-war hatreds die, and he brought around his strongest opponents. On one occasion his son, Randolph, said, "How can you make Margison Secretary of State for War? He was the Conservative Party chief whip who even tried to remove you from your constituency in 1938." Churchill wrote to Randolph and said, "Look, he's the best man for the job, and if he shows one-half of the energy against Hitler that he's shown against me, we're on the winning ticket!"

PM: Of course, he did lose in 1945 as the war ended. Churchill, the country's greatest leader through its most difficult period, was turfed out.

MG: As he said, "It's the will of the people." The wartime coalition had dissolved. The Labour leaders had wanted to remain for a year and bring in an all-party social reform, but the Labour rank and file said, "Forget it. We've been fifteen years out of power, we want an election and we want it to be Labour versus Conservative."

So the wartime coalition dissolved, Churchill became prime minister of an interim Conservative administration, and the public voted against it—and he had been one of the people who had most discredited the Conservatives for their neglect of Britain's defences before the war.

PM: Were people as surprised at the time that he lost, as we are now when we look back, and say, "How could that have possibly happened?"

MG: They were surprised. I met a lot of people who voted against him—basically Labour voters, of course—who said, "But I'd assumed that Churchill would remain prime minister. He's going to have a Labour government, but he would still be there, particularly, of course, as the war against Japan was still going on." No one knew at that point that it was going to end so quickly.

PM: Six years later—he's well into his seventies now—they come back to him and elect him again, even though he's a man in poor health and beginning to fade. But they come back to him. Why?

MG: I think he saw that the Conservative Party had to be revitalized. It couldn't be that terrible pre-war Conservative Party based on privilege, so he brought in lots of young men like R.A. Butler, Harold McMillan, and said to them, "I want a modern conservatism. I want education for all. I want housing for all people. I want a proper national program for the needs of the country."

PM: And these were his ideas?

MG: They were his ideas, and they performed well. And the public said, "We'll give it a try." Unfortunately Attlee's socialist government had made a mess of things. They'd perhaps gone far too quickly with the nationalizations, so the public expected panaceas and miracles, which you never get with any government. So Churchill was brought back.

Once Stalin died, which he did shortly into the second premiership, Churchill's own interest was to try to bring about détente with the Soviet Union. He was really devoted to this, but of course his powers were failing. He had a massive stroke in 1953, but he dragged himself across the Atlantic to say to Eisenhower, "Come with me to Moscow. Let's try and end this nuclear confrontation by discussions." But Foster Dulles said no, and Eisenhower made an incredible remark. He said, "What makes you think that underneath the new Soviet leaders it isn't the same old harlot?" Churchill was disappointed.

PM: Over the years, in writing those twenty-nine books on Churchill, you have been through fifteen tons of material looking at his life and writings. If he were alive today, what would be the one question that you still have unanswered in your mind about him and the way he led and the way he lived?

MG: It would be a question he asked, and I'd like to know what his answer is. As the Second World War was coming to an end, he asked one of his closest intimates, "Do you think I've spent so long focusing on the German danger that I've neglected to see the emergence of the Soviet danger?" In other words, although he never fell for Stalin, had he in those last three years of the war allowed Stalin to take too many advantages, among other things the destruction of Polish independence? It worried him, and I'd really like to ask him today does he still feel that. Was there really anything he could have done while Stalin was our ally to halt that westward spread of Communism?

PM: What do you think his answer would have been?

MG: I'd like to feel it would be no, that he did his best. But he was a very self-critical person and he probably feels that he did fail in that regard.

PM: What's his greatest contribution in helping us define leadership?

MG: I think it was a combination of drawing on experience and perseverance. So often knocked down, so often marginalized. So often out of power, out of office, and never giving up. On one occasion, when he came to Canada in 1929, he thought, "Perhaps I should give up politics all together, buy a ranch in Alberta and become a Canadian rancher."

PM: Really?

MG: Somehow or other, yeah. He wrote to his wife, "If Neville Chamberlain becomes leader of the Conservative Party, that's it." But luckily, by the time he sort of completed his holiday . . .

PM: Might have been unlucky for you. My gosh, who knows what would have happened to us if he'd been here!

MG: Perhaps he would have become a great oil baron!

MARC GARNEAU

I AM ONE OF THOSE CHILDREN of the sixties who spent hours and hours, sometimes days, in front of an old Sylvania black-and-white television watching Walter Cronkite vamp through the endless delays of the early U.S. space program. It always seemed to be early in the morning as we waited to see NASA astronaut Alan Shepard or John Glenn or Gus Grissom or any of the "right stuff" boys launch into space. It was a time for patience; rarely did takeoff occur as scheduled. But it was an incredibly exciting period as great new frontiers were being explored, and for a youngster it was a chance to place astronauts up there with hockey players as heroes.

So the aura of Cape Canaveral was ingrained in my being, and I couldn't wait for my first trip to the famed Florida launch pad. It was October 1984, and the first Canadian astronaut, Marc Garneau, was about to head into space aboard NASA's shuttle. We were to cover the event live, so I arrived a few days early to get all the appropriate briefings.

The drive between the launch site and the strip of hotels in nearby Cocoa Beach is only about twenty minutes, and we made it a few times a day. Often there would be hitchhikers trying to grab a ride, and as this stretch was used almost exclusively by those with a direct interest in what was going on at the Cape, success was almost guaranteed. On one of our trips we picked up a fellow, and as he climbed into the car he asked where we were from and what we did.

"From Canada, to cover Marc Garneau's mission."

"Nice man, that Marc," was the response, leaving us to wonder who this guy was and how he knew Garneau. So we asked.

"Oh, I'm an astronaut too."

An astronaut? Hitchhiking? That broke every image I had of the "right stuff" gang. I was still caught in that sixties mode where it seemed that astronauts were kept locked in special air-tight, germ-free vehicles that chauffeured them around. Not so, apparently—our passenger's explanation involved something about lousy per diems. What a downer.

Meanwhile, Marc Garneau, small per diem or not, was on the shuttle about to head into space and a place in the hearts of Canadians everywhere. Even though this was a generation after the first manned space flights, it was still exciting, and as a Canadian first it was doubly so. In the media zone a few kilometres from the actual shuttle pad—the same spot where the great CBS newsman Walter Cronkite had called those earliest shots into space—I'll admit I was caught up in the thrill and the history of it all. A new Canadian hero was born that day. Many honours would follow. Garneau would even have a high school named after him in the years following his first flight. For our *One on One*, on the eve of his third and final ride into space in 2000, I went to the NASA facility in Houston where he was training.

2000-10-08

Peter Mansbridge: The moment of takeoff—the fifteen seconds before or the fifteen seconds after—what goes through your mind?

Marc Garneau: In the two hours before you lift off, when you're sitting there with nothing to do, you think about a lot of things.

You realize that you're going to do something that could kill you, so it's a point of reckoning in your life. You hope that you've squared everything away and that you're at peace with yourself and you're not leaving anything undone. The trick then, when you're actually in that last little countdown, is to focus. You have got to put all of that out of your mind and realize that you are now focusing 100 percent on making your contribution to that flight.

On this particular flight coming up, I've got to be focused to support the commander and the pilot and back them up on everything. I can't think about anything else. This is no longer the time to think about my family or about what I'm going to do after my next flight. I've got to be focused on supporting them, so it's an exercise in concentration.

PM: What surprised you most about being in space, which I assume would also surprise us?

MG: I think what surprised me was just how fast we go around the Earth. We go around the Earth sixteen times in a day. It's something that you can never think about when you're back down on Earth, when you live on the planet. It puts it into perspective, the fact that you're going eight kilometres per second, that you're going around your planet in an hour and a half.

PM: What would be the biggest misconception that we have about space that you don't have as a result of having been in space?

MG: I think a lot of people imagine that, when you're in the space shuttle, you're way, way above it, that you can see the whole planet. Well, no, you can't. When you're in the shuttle—and, indeed, in the space station—and you imagine the Earth as a basketball, then you're really only about half a centimetre above its surface. The views you get at that height are amazing, but you're really still very close to your planet.

PM: What's the most important thing that you've learned from being in space and from being an astronaut?

MG: I think, on a personal level, what's left after this whole experience is over is a different consciousness about the planet. The fact that we have the potential to destroy it, certainly damage it. When I am up in space, I am able to see the evidence of man's effect on our planet in terms of pollution, in terms of the deforestation.

PM: Give me an example of that.

MG: For example, if you look at a very striking country, Madagascar. It has been 90 percent deforested, and the result of that is that all the sediment is being washed off. The earth that's being washed off in the previously forested mountains is just washing down into the rivers. It's a red kind of soil—it looks like blood leaching out into the Indian Ocean. That's very dramatic. You go over South America—and I'm thinking back to when I flew in '96—you see large wafts of smoke covering hundreds of thousands of square kilometres. And you go over Canada and you see the stripping of the forests in British Columbia. You're aware of these things, so they strike you.

And because you go around the Earth and you see all of it, you realize that it's not as big as we think. That very, very thin little layer called our atmosphere, which is like, as many astronauts have said, the first layer of an onion—that thin layer is what allows us to live. That thin, thin atmosphere, which most of us don't see when we're here on Earth—we look up into the sky and say, "Oh, we've got lots of atmosphere." No, we don't have a lot of atmosphere. And when we deplete its ozone, and when we fill it with carbon dioxide and other gases, then we risk destroying it and destroying our life on Earth. So you become very, very conscious of that, and that stays with you.

PM: What about space in general, for those of us who still dream one day of its being more accessible? Clearly it's not going to be accessible to the general public in our lifetime, but will it ever be?

MG: It will be accessible for people initially, if they've got a lot of money. For example, if you were prepared right now to spend $20 million, you could go into space with the Russians. There is a company called Mir Corporation which will fly you up to their *Mir* space station for about ten days, if you've got the money to do it.

PM: One of the reality TV shows actually wants to do that. You know, run a contest for somebody to go up to the *Mir*.

MG: That's right.

PM: And after looking at the *Mir* the last few trips, I'm not sure . . . Would you really want to do that?

MG: It has been around for a while, but it's still a serviceable space station and the Russians clearly believe that it has many years to go and want to be able to get some commercial profit out of it. So there's the situation where you can go up to that particular space station if you wanted. But the general sense of people having the opportunity to go into space—yes, it's going to happen.

PM: Would the reason be for general access to witness the kinds of things you talked about just a little while ago? Is there any reason to be there other than to experience?

MG: In terms of the general public going into space, it's to experience it. And I think that by the end of this century, I can very easily see people going to the moon for their summer holidays or for a honeymoon. I think there will be a settlement on the moon where you will be able to fly, go to the moon, spend a few days there and return, strictly for the experience of it. For much the same reason why people are attracted to going to different parts of our planet: because there's something exotic and special about it.

PM: You really believe that? You're not just saying that.

MG: No, I believe that by the end of this century—look, it's still a hundred years away—that kind of thing is going to happen. But it's going to be expensive.

PM: That's a long way to go for a holiday.

MG: Yes, it is a long way to go for a holiday.

PM: It's not going to go any faster, is it?

MG: Not appreciably. Not in the next hundred years. I think we're still going to be stuck with chemical propulsion for a while.

PM: When you're off duty up there, is it a private time or are you constantly being monitored? Is "Big Brother" always watching you or hooked up to your pulse, your breathing patterns, everything?

MG: No, they're not. You know, there's a part of you that is glad that there is a whole bunch of people on the ground, on duty, making sure that everything is going well. But they haven't got a camera in your face and they're not monitoring your vital signs, unless you're doing a scientific experiment that specifically calls for those things to be monitored. In my particular case I think that despite the fact that the shuttle is very small and that we all live together—in fact, we'll be a crew of five on my next mission—there is a sense of privacy when you put on your Walkman or your music and you go and stick yourself in a corner and lose yourself there. Because it would be a tragedy for any person who goes up in space to come back and say, "I did a great job but I didn't have a chance to savour the experience." And so everybody is going to take that time, and I certainly did do that.

PM: What do you listen to on your Walkman when you're looking out that window?

MG: On my first flight I went all classical. I love baroque music. And I would sit there, and that is to me probably the most beautiful experience in the world—to be looking out the window at the curve of the Earth, and you see a country or continent beginning to come over the horizon and you are listening to maybe the "Jupiter" suite from Holst's *The Planets* or something that moves you—and to listen to that, to me is just an exquisite experience.

The other experience that's great is to have music in your ears and to suspend yourself in the middle of the middeck. It's a kind of sensory deprivation, except that the music is flooding your head; nothing else is distracting you. There are no hot points on your body, there's no other sound bothering you, you're not touching anything, your eyes are closed—that's just wonderful. I wish everyone could feel it.

PM: (laughs) What kind of music this time?

MG: I've gone very seriously into jazz. I will definitely be taking up some Oscar Peterson, some Diana Krall, some Miles Davis. I still love classical music, but I want to take some jazz with me along with some classical music.

PM: This is your third mission; it might be your last. When you leave, what do you tell your kids? They must be fascinated by what you do and what they could do in the future.

MG: I've got a three-year-old son who thinks I go into space every day, and he loves the whole idea. He's one of the few children who learned to count from ten down to one before he learned to count it the other way. So he thinks it's wonderful and he thinks it's mundane. He thinks it's all possible—lots of people go up into space. He hasn't quite realized that it's still a fairly new occupation.

—

GARNEAU STOPPED FLYING after that mission and became president of Canada's space agency. Ever since that first 1984 flight he has been wooed by the siren song of politics, but there was always the hope of one more mission. Retirement from space travel obviously changed that. The Liberals are his party of choice, and these days he can be found sitting on their benches in the House of Commons.

DEVRA DAVIS

MY MOTHER DIED OF CANCER. She'd been diagnosed in early 2006, and for two years she fought the disease, at first nervously, somewhat in denial and a bit afraid, and then courageously and with incredible class. Near the end, when she finally decided that she could no longer live alone, she made what for any of us would be a very difficult move, in her case from her beautiful downtown London, Ontario, condominium to the palliative care wing at London's Parkwood Hospital.

On the day she left home, we all knew that she was almost certain never to come back. Nobody mentioned it, though it was a reality tearing at us all from the inside. But she was determined not to show any sense of that. Instead, when my sister came to pick her up, my mother had laid out on her bed the clothes she wanted to wear for her arrival at the hospital. She loved grand entrances, and this was going to be the grandest. There on her bed, which she had just made up—perfectly—for the last time, Mother had placed her finest clothes. If she was on the final journey, it was one she wanted to take in style.

Cancer can be beaten and is, regularly, by millions of people. Sadly, as we all know, like my mother, millions of others lose that fight. Through all the battles, though, the same question keeps coming up: "Why me?" or, even simpler, "Why?" After all, we have spent billions trying to determine how to fight cancer. Why are we still dying? Why are we still asking why we get it? Why do we still sell cigarettes? Are cellphones really a hazard? Why do men get cancer at a rate far greater than women? Do we spend too much on looking for a cure and not enough on prevention?

Dr. Devra Davis asks those questions and many more all the time. Too often, for some people. She's an epidemiologist and director of the Centre for Environmental Oncology at the University of Pittsburgh Cancer Institute. She's also a writer. When I read her 2007 book, *The Secret History of the War on Cancer*, I knew I had to talk with her. She may not have the answers to that string of questions, but after reading her book and hearing of her struggle to seek the truth, I knew she wouldn't sugar-coat her answers. She didn't.

2007-08-12

Peter Mansbridge: When I started reading your book, I assumed that I was going to be scared. But very quickly I realized, I'm not scared. That's not the right word. For me, page after page, especially in the first half of it, it's about being angry, being sad, being depressed, because in so many ways it's a story of lost opportunities, our past in the war on cancer. Is that the kind of reaction you expected?

Devra Davis: I think it's important for people to understand the past, because only if you understand it will the future be different. And it is true that we missed a lot of opportunities in the past, but it's also true that I am able to tell about those things today.

PM: Let's talk about some of the statistics that most people know. One of two men will get cancer, one out of three women—which is interesting, in the sense that there's a difference.

DD: Yes.

PM: But they're kind of accepted—you know, that's life, that's gonna happen.

DD: Well, I don't accept it. I don't think cancer needs to be thought of as the price of modern society. We know we can do a better job and we look at that when we see cancer patterns throughout the world. Why is it that people in Asia have a fifth less chance of breast cancer, prostate cancer and brain cancer than we do? And why do those people, when they move to Canada or the United States, develop the risk of breast cancer and prostate cancer that we have here? There's a lot of evidence that the environment is playing a role in cancer. And even though in the United States cancer deaths are dropping, they're dropping mostly because fewer men are smoking and we're getting better at finding breast and colorectal cancer. But we still have more cases of cancer in children. And we still cannot explain why most people get cancer that isn't related to smoking or aging.

PM: Men versus women. Why is there that difference?

DD: We're not really sure, but I think one of the factors has to be that men on average work in dirtier jobs, have more access to the blue-collar world and tend to have more exposure to things that may have caused them to have cancer in the past. Cancer takes a long time to occur. It arises from many different exposures that we have throughout our lifetime, and historically men have had more exposures to things than women may have had.

PM: Not hereditary, then?

DD: In fact, all cancer comes about when your genes stop doing their job of suppressing growths that are out of control. But only one in ten cases of breast cancer arises because a woman was born with defects in her genes. That means that nine out of ten women who get breast cancer and most other cancers are born with healthy genes and something happens to them in the course of their lifetime.

PM: You talk about the situation with identical twins.

DD: Identical twins come from one egg that splits at conception to develop two embryos. At age three their chromosomes look pretty close to identical. But I have studies and I have data that I can show you that show that by age fifty, they don't even look related to one another. So if identical twins can look totally different by the time they get to age fifty, that's telling us that the environment is playing an incredible role in shaping how our genes develop and how they're affected. We can say that genes give you the gun and the environment pulls the trigger.

PM: As you say, you obviously learn from history. What stunned me is that you go back hundreds of years to reports and studies on cancer— We're not going to go into them all here, obviously, but I want to talk about one, because there was a conference in 1936.

DD: Amazing.

PM: An amazing conference, a lot of people there, small circulation of the results afterwards.

DD: Of course.

PM: Of which you managed to find one copy. In 1936, some of the things they were saying then—we haven't advanced that much since then.

DD: It was astonishing to me to find that in 1936, the world's leading cancer scientists understood that sunlight caused cancer, diagnostic radiation caused cancer, synthetic hormones that had already been created then were understood to cause cancer. Tars were

understood to cause cancer, whether from fuels or tobacco. Cobalt
and uranium mining were understood to cause cancer. In 1936.

It was amazing. They even showed that if you took sunlight and also added hydrocarbons like you could find in fuel,
like benzene, you could increase the amount of skin cancer that
you could produce in animals. And that animals exposed to
these elements very young would have more of a response than
those who were exposed when they were older. It's an amazing
work. I was astonished to find that the world scientists understood this in 1936 because they took all of the evidence, the
totality of the evidence: they looked at experimental studies in
animals, they looked at clinical reports of individuals and they
looked at preliminary crude public health statistics, which are
the forerunner of what we call epidemiology today.

PM: So what happened? It was all looking at them in the face.
One assumes they presented them to governments. What was it?
Did World War II get in the way, or what happened?

DD: Absolutely. The world went to war and then in some sense
it never got off the war-like footing. As John Maynard Keynes
famously quipped, "In the long run, we're all dead." And cancer
is generally a long-run disease. When you're fighting for your
life, as the world was at the outbreak of World War II, people
aren't thinking about the long run. One of the things I document
in my book is that some American companies well understood
the dangers, the long-term dangers of some of the chemicals that
the Germans and some others were using. They got that information and kept it in their own files and did not share it broadly.
You have to realize that the world was very different back then.
There was no Internet. There was no way to share information,
so I was astonished to find this report from 1936 on the dusty
shelves in a library in Brussels. It's a pretty amazing document.

PM: This raises this issue of where and how to focus properly on
the war. Should it be on the search for a cure or should it be on

the desire for better treatment or should it be on attacking the root causes—you know, the preventive measures.

DD: With all due respect, it's not an either/or situation. Of course, as someone who was a cancer orphan, who faced the sad situation of having both parents diagnosed with the disease, you want treatment. But the truth is, we've been fighting the wrong war, with the wrong weapons, against the wrong enemies, because the war started out ignoring tobacco, even though we knew long ago about the dangers of tobacco.

PM: The war started out by looking for a safe cigarette?

DD: The safe cigarette. We spent $35 million on a campaign led by the chain-smoking, four-pack-a-day leader of America's National Cancer Institute to develop a safe cigarette. But we also ignored benzene as a cause of cancer. We ignored what we knew about pesticides, which after all were made out of poison gas. We ignored a lot of good clues that we had about environmental causes of cancer.

PM: Were we ignoring them or were we being led down a path to ensure that we ignored them?

DD: Let me put it this way: The leaders of the American Cancer Society went to work for the tobacco industry in the early days. The chairman of the board and many leaders of the National Cancer Advisory Board of the 1980s were leaders of the chemical industry. So it's not an accident that they focused more on finding and treating the disease instead of dealing with some of the chemical and radiation factors that can increase the cause of cancer.

PM: One of the first things you said when we started talking on this program was that the past is sad. It does make one angry. We both lost our parents. But here you are, still optimistic.

DD: Absolutely.

PM: Why?

DD: Because I'm here. I'm talking to Peter Mansbridge, after all. And that's a sign of how much things have changed during this issue. I think the world is listening. I think the Canadian Cancer Society is waking up. I think that we are ready as a society to acknowledge that we've made mistakes and we've got to move forward. And the problem is not one of us; it's all of us together. I think the world is different and that's why I'm optimistic. That's why I'm here. But I also think it's important to recognize that we can't do it all as individuals. There's an African proverb: "If you want to go far, you must go together, but if you want to go fast, go alone." And so we have to go together to go far. I think that that's what's happening now.

PERDITA FELICIEN

THE LOONS ON THE LAKE in Quebec's Gatineau Hills were so startled they began their haunting calls almost immediately. This just seconds after I'd broken the late summer night's silence as I shouted in glee. I was at my log cabin watching the legendary sportscaster Don Wittman in Seoul, South Korea, do the play-by-play as Ben Johnson raced towards the 1988 Olympics hundred-metre finish line in 9.79 seconds. It meant a gold medal and a world record, and pretty close to dancing in the streets across Canada. It was a moment well worth all the fuss.

But, as we all know, it didn't last. Three days later came the shocker: Johnson had been on steroids for the race, he was stripped of his medal, his record no longer stood and Johnson himself was on his way out of Seoul, both he and his country in disgrace. That took a lot out of Olympic boosters; people just weren't sure anymore whether to invest themselves in athletes they suddenly realized they knew little about. I know that, as a fan, it certainly took me aback. But one gets over these things, and by 1996 and the Atlanta Olympics there I was again—now in my Toronto living room (no loons this time)—standing up and screaming as Donovan Bailey made it all look so terribly simple as he blew the competition away in the hundred-metre race.

In their Olympic years, Johnson and Bailey had both been considered contenders for gold but not "locks." Pickering, Ontario, hurdler Perdita Felicien was considered a lock when she ran for gold in Athens in 2004; in fact, more than a few analysts were already guaranteeing her gold in the medal counts they were predicting. It didn't happen, and in one of those "agony of defeat" moments in sports, we all felt her pain. She clipped her first hurdle, something that no one had foreseen, and there she was, left in a heap on the track as everyone else crossed the finish line. That heartbreaking image was front-page news across the land the next day. It spoke to the loneliness of an athlete whose four-year struggle had suddenly gone horribly wrong because of the misjudgment of a fraction of a second.

It was months before she wanted to talk about it in front of the cameras, but when she did, it was on *One on One*.

2005-06-05

Peter Mansbridge: Let's talk about the Athens Olympics. What do you remember about that day, about the minutes beforehand? Because, watching you, you didn't look nervous. You didn't look uptight. You really did look like this was your moment.

Perdita Felicien: If I look at the aftermath, then I'm being unfair to myself. And if I tell myself that I'm not good, I'm not talented, then I'm lying to myself. Because I'm so proud of how I handled myself up until that point. And even after, how composed I was.

We went to the track. You know, me and my coach and my team. We got ready. We warmed up. Everything was on point. And that's why I wish there had been some type of indication that I wasn't on that night. Because, looking back at my warm-up, it was just the best I've ever felt in my career. We're taught to be in tune with our bodies and how things feel. And I just knew I was on fire—like, nothing could have told me otherwise.

I'm just proud of how I handled myself up until that race. I never said this was my gold medal to win. I've never said that, but I believe that I could win it. I definitely believe that, and that hasn't changed.

PM: When you say you were on fire, some have suggested that maybe you were almost too on fire. That when you sprang out of those blocks, it was like you were too ready.

PF: Right.

PM: Is that possible?

PF: I don't think so. I don't think in track and field that really exists. Because that "being on fire," that being "too ready" has won me races. It helped me win in Paris. It helped me win in Budapest.* So for me, that's my style. That's how I do it. And maybe I was too good that night, but you know what? I'm going to learn from that. I'm going to harness the power that was evident that night and learn how to make it work for me, learn how to time it properly. And you know, that's going to win me another race.

PM: You don't watch the tape, do you?

PF: No, no.

PM: Why is that? I don't think I'd want to watch it either if I was in that position. But I guess some would say you've got to watch to understand what went wrong.

PF: Right. It's still very painful. I mean it's still very painful for me to watch, so when I see it, it's kind of like reliving your worst nightmare. I don't think many of us want to do that. You know,

* In 2003 Felicien took the gold in the hundred-metre hurdles at the world championships in Paris. In March 2004 she set a new record in the sixty-metre hurdles final at the 2004 World Indoor Championships in Budapest.

our failures don't always happen on a global stage. And how many of us go home at night and relive and rehash things that happen, in private? For me, I have to face it. If by chance I'm surfing the television and it's on, I choose not to look at it, not to watch it. And my coach hasn't either. I think there's going to be a point where we're going to sit down and maybe have a seminar. We can talk about biomechanics and what happened. But for right now, I'm not at that place. And I just, you know, I know how it felt. I know, believe me, I know what it is, and I just don't feel like seeing it.

PM: The fact that you were on the global stage, and not just this country but everyone was watching you and talking about you— was that hard to deal with? Was that extra pressure?

PF: Not at all. I think for most of the time I kept myself in a cocoon, in this little bubble where I was just preparing for the Olympic Games. And it's fun. You get fan mail and you go to different countries and you get a glimpse of that. People are looking at you and people are expecting some things from you. But the people that are around me have kept me grounded. And with or without that Olympic gold medal, I'm still me. I'm still Perdita. I'm still successful. And I'm still in pursuit of the ultimate challenge, because I'm a competitor. I actually relish and like that kind of attention, because it's like they're telling me, "There's a level of excellence that we expect from you. We're looking at you because you're going to set the bar high." And that's what I want to live up to.

PM: The public moments afterwards were amazing on your part. You were very composed. Privately, though, I guess it must have been tough.

PF: Oh yeah. And I just kept telling myself, "I have to be strong. One, for my mom, who's probably watching and probably just so devastated. And also because there's just a certain type of person that I want to be, and a certain type of athlete that I want to be."

The way I dealt with Athens was privately, and with my close friends and family. But at the same time, I'm not going to let my competitors see me cry and whine and complain and mull and sulk. There are no pity parties. I don't believe in those. Those aren't the theme in my life.

It was hard, it was devastating. I had moments where I'd be at home alone and cry about it or think about it. Or pick up an article and oh, there's the one shot of me on the ground. But that's life, and that's sport, and that's why I love it and that's why I do it. Because, you know, there's agony in defeat, definitely, but it's just so amazing when you win. And all the hard work that you've done just pays off in those moments.

PM: I remember one of the things you said the day after. You said that there was a message in what happened to you, but you weren't quite sure at the time what that message was.

PF: Yeah.

PM: Do you know what it is now?

PF: I think slowly I'm finding out what it could mean. I don't think I'll know until that great big feat is accomplished. I don't know at all. But I think there's a sign, because honestly, I felt that I could have been severely injured, you know? So for me, I've never come to a point where I've been unthankful for where I am. I've really been thankful. But I started getting a lot of success really early—still in college, winning a major title like that, a lot of acclaim—and I started getting a little subtle. I don't want to be like that again.

PM: What do you mean, "subtle"?

PF: Just a little, you know, comfortable. Maybe a little too comfortable. I wasn't necessarily comfortable going to Athens, but I thought if I did win that title, which is— Come on, you know, that's like the granddaddy! There's nothing better than that. What does that mean for my career, you know, after my rookie year? Year one—what does that mean?

PM: So you think things happen for a reason then? Do you think fate played a role in this?

PF: I don't know. I don't know if the stars were aligned properly, improperly. But I definitely feel that this has propelled me, motivated me beyond belief, and has told me, "There's something better out there for you." And I'm chasing, chasing, chasing that gold medal.

PM: Maybe that was the lesson then, that in the remarkable year that you'd had there had to be some kind of setback to—

PF: —to propel me.

PM: Yeah.

PF: Yeah. I don't know what it is, but I'm holding on to something—that something better and bigger is going to happen to me. And it's going to make me understand Athens. I don't know when it's going to be, you know, but it's going to make me understand Athens and be like, "Okay. It's okay. The moment is gone; I'll never get it back. And I can cry over my spilt milk for the rest of my life, but I won't do that." I don't know what the lesson is, but I believe that I'll find it out one day.

—

IT HAS BEEN A STRUGGLE for Perdita Felicien, both physically and competitively. Her comeback was progressing nicely, then injuries got in the way, costing her an appearance at the 2008 Beijing Olympics and hopes of redeeming her Athens performance four years earlier.

THE GOLFERS:
MIKE WEIR AND LORIE KANE

STANDING ON THE FIFTEENTH TEE of the Weston Golf
and Country Club on May 5, 1996, I was enjoying a gorgeous
spring day of golf. My playing partner, Bob Lewis, the then-editor
of *Maclean's* magazine, gave his usual "swing through the ball"
advice as I stood over my shot. With a slight wind in my face, I
steadied my stance and swung through the ball with my three iron.

"That was a strange sound," I said to Bob as we watched the
ball soar towards the green, and we both laughed about the odd
noise the club and the ball had made at impact. While everything
had looked fine from the tee, when we got to the green we couldn't
find the ball. Bob walked over to the hole almost as a joke, and
to our combined astonishment there it was, at the bottom of the
cup. "Well, now we know what that sound was," he said in that
tone where you know something profound is still to come. "It was
the sound of a perfect shot." (It should be noted that neither Bob
nor I have heard that sound again from any of our swings.)

Mike Weir hears the sound of great golf shots all the time, and
many of them are his own. He's become one of the world's elite
golfers, the first and at this writing the only Canadian to win one

of four annual tournaments that golfers call the "majors"—the Masters in 2003. I remember that Sunday afternoon getting my three-year-old son, Willie, to come and sit with me on the couch for the final holes—playoff holes, as it turned out. "This is history, Will. You'll be telling your grandkids about this day." Will watched and Mike delivered, as he does quite often these days.

But all golfers, even Tiger Woods, have their off moments, some so serious that they actually change the swing they've used for a lifetime. That's what Weir had done in the months before we last sat down together one on one.

Mike Weir

2007-07-25

Peter Mansbridge: I spent a lot of time on the weekend watching the British Open. One of the nice things to hear was the commentators talking about you and saying, "It's so great to see Mike Weir's back, that he's got his game back." Are you back?

Mike Weir: Yeah, I feel like I'm back. I didn't feel like I was that far away, you know. Even last year was a pretty darn good year, but I guess sometimes others' expectations get high, as mine do too. Injuries have kind of held me back, really, more than anything. I think with the changes I've made in my game, it's been a lot easier on my back, a lot easier on my neck, and I've been able to practise harder. So, yeah, I'm starting to see some good results now.

PM: I want to talk about that swing change, the change in your swing as you approach the ball. Is it because of your back and your neck?

MW: Yeah. That's why I went with Andy [Plummer] and Mike [Bennett], my two teachers. Their concept is that you're not going to be moving off the ball. There's not as much lateral movement.

I had been tilting back behind the ball. When I was swinging with a lot of speed and a lot of tilt, I was putting a lot of stress on my spine. I went to work with Andy and Mike to biomechanically make my swing more efficient so that it would last longer without injuries, and it's done that. I've practised harder than I've ever practised, probably, hit as many balls as I ever have in my career, and I haven't had any problems this year. So it's been great.

PM: Psychologically there must be something there in making that decision to change it, because it's not like the old swing was bad for you. For a significant period of time you were consistently one of the ten best golfers in the world—through 2003, '04, a bit of '05. To decide that that swing was no longer going to work for you, that must have been a tough mental adjustment.

MW: Yeah, I think it kind of came over a gradual amount of time. I saw the writing on the wall in 2004, which I wasn't happy with. In 2005 I started getting a little bit more injured; I wasn't able to practise as hard. I think it was just time for a change. But, you know, I think it became an easy decision at that point. It's like, "Yeah, I'm not happy with where things are going. I'm injured, and, you know, I need to do something different."

PM: Clearly something's been working well for you, especially in the last few tournaments: a couple of top tens in a row, which puts you back in a very elite club. But is it good enough for the President's Cup, which I know you want to be in because it's being hosted in Canada this year? To automatically qualify you've got to be one of the top ten of the non-Americans, non-Europeans. You're not quite there yet, but you could be picked by the captain.

MW: I could be.

PM: Do you feel you're playing well enough that you should be considered on that front?

MW: No question. I've earned my way on the last three teams. You know, with my experience and winning a major championship and the tournaments that I've won—if I were the captain, I'd be taking a good look at myself. Not to be boastful, but I think I'm playing well enough now. I know Gary's always said he wants someone playing well into the President's Cup.

PM: Gary, of course, is Gary Player.

MW: Yes. But I can't argue if he picks somebody else, because other guys are good players as well. But I have three weeks here to play my way right onto the team, and I have some good momentum going. I want to win. That's what I want to do. Winning will take care of that.

PM: You've talked about the game and how, when it comes right down to it, it's between the ears. What do you mean?

MW: It is a lot of power-game playing. You see a lot of the power players really doing well. You look at the British Open at Carnoustie last week; I'll use that as an example. Padraig [Harrington], to have the mental fortitude to gear up after he's hit two balls in the water and be able to get that ball up and down—that's between the ears. If you're not with it mentally and knowing what the situation is—that's a seven or eight. Depending where he took the drop, how he got the angle, and all those little subtle details are the mental part of the game that you really have to pay attention to.

You know, there are plenty of guys that can stand here all day long and it's the most beautiful thing in the world; they're just pounding the ball out there. But when they get out there, how do they handle adversity? How do they handle when they make a double bogey? When things are going along smoothly, you are under par, you make a double bogey. Can you handle that mentally? Those are the little subtleties of the game that challenge competitive professional players compared to just regular golf.

PM: What's the secret to doing that? As you say, on the eighteenth hole in regulation play, he hits two in the water, in the berm. How do you put that behind you? How do you forget that?

MW: It's very hard. It's a challenge, every shot, every day. Some days you can handle it better than others. I guess that's one of the real challenges of golf. It's to be able to—it's kind of a cliché—take the shot you have right there and do your best job of focusing on that particular shot, no matter if it's for six or seven or if it's for an eagle or whatever it is—to take the value out of the shot and just play it.

I remember playing with Bernhard Langer in Valderrama in my first year there, the year before I won at Valderrama; I guess it was in '99. We were both playing okay on Sunday. We got to the sixteenth hole, I believe. He hit it in the trees and kind of fumbled around in there. By the time he got it out, he was hitting his sixth shot into this par four. The way he went through his routine, getting the yardage—I was just amazed at the discipline, and that's why the guy's won fifty or sixty tournaments around the world. Because he's not thinking, "I've got to get this up and down for a triple bogey." He's looking at it as just a shot. He has to do the same preparation for that shot, and the most successful players treat it that way. Some players do it better than others, but they try not to get wrapped up in what the actual score is.

PM: Let me talk for a moment about the Canadian Open. Every year we go through this debate in Canada about where this tournament is actually played in the calendar within the PGA. And it's a debate once again this year, because it's positioned right after the British Open. In spite of the fact that many of the world's top players are here, not all the top players are here. What's wrong with the Canadian Open in terms of the way the players look at it and the way the tour looks at it? Does the Canadian Open have an image problem?

MW: I think it has. I think the last couple of years they've done a better job. I think the golf courses we've played the last few years are getting a lot better, and that's a big motivation for the players, when they know they're playing a good championship golf course. I don't think you can underestimate that, how important that is to the players when they're looking at their schedule. If they really like a golf course, they're going to come play.

But the scheduling has been a little bit tough, after the British Open. After any major I think the top players sometimes really want to take a break because it's so mentally fatiguing. I know the media sometimes talks about the lack of players, but we still have a good field here. I wish they'd sometimes focus a little bit more on that. One other thing is that it was considered the "fifth major" for such a long time. I think we lost focus of that and how well it was run. Also, the rest of the tournaments have really stepped up their game. Probably the Canadian Open didn't keep pace, and that's where it kind of lost ground. I think they're getting back to that now. The Royal Canadian Golf Association has done a great job within the last couple of years with all the little details that go into it. So I see it getting a lot better.

Lorie Kane

ONE OF THE MOST PLEASANT PEOPLE you will ever meet in golf is Lorie Kane. This native of Charlottetown, Prince Edward Island, is one of Canada's leading female golfers, and her legion of fans on both sides of the border is proof of her popularity. So is the fact that after years of no better than second-place finishes, when she finally won her first LPGA tournament, in 2000, her opponents lined up to applaud her last putt for the victory.

2001-03-04

Peter Mansbridge: Let me remind you of an event from a year ago. It was one of those heartbreakers where it looked like you

were going to get your first win. It turned out you didn't; Karrie
Webb won. Here's what was said that weekend, not by you but
by Karrie Webb, right after the tournament: "When I hugged
her I apologized to her. I feel bad that she hasn't won. But she's
going to win one day, and when she does she'll win a lot." That's
a remarkable thing for your opponent to say. But it says what a
lot of people felt then, including your opponents: that you were
going to win, and you were going to win a lot. Did you always
have that same kind of confidence in yourself that they had?

Lorie Kane: Yes and no. Now, looking back, I think I wasn't supposed to win. I think I was supposed to learn through those nine
second-place finishes that I was going to win, and win a lot. And
having people, like Karrie and Annika Sorenstam, who have said
great things after having beaten me—I don't like when they
apologize for winning, because that's not what they're there to
do. They're not there to help me win. They're there to be the
best that they can be. In Australia—that's Karrie's hometown,
her country—I'd worked really hard, and in that case it was my
tournament to lose. And Karrie did the things that she needed
to do to win, and it worked out. I couldn't get it done. But I
learned from that. And I think now I have a solid foundation
under me that just brings more confidence to the fact that, yes,
I am a winner, I can win, and I can handle anything that comes
on the golf course.

PM: I want to talk about how all this started and talk about your
family and the importance of PEI. I guess you must have learned
to play on the course that your dad was a pro on. Talk about PEI,
its importance to you, and your family background in golf.

LK: It's where I was born, basically raised. My family is the
reason I'm having the success I'm having, because they've been
my number-one supporters from the get-go. My older sister,
Mary-Lynn, and I were introduced to golf about the same time
as kids, when my dad was taking his summers off from coaching

hockey and was the first golf professional at Brudenell. And that's where we were introduced to the game.

PM: How old were you when you first played?

LK: I think Mom and Dad say we were like five or six when we shared a set of clubs. I can remember the day the clubs came to our house, because the inventory was coming for the shop. They were PowerBilt junior clubs, and I still have them. They've been passed down to many a kid who's wanted to try golf. We were told that golf would always be there, but we were also introduced to all kinds of other sports. And I definitely think that my athletic background has helped my golf game. But Dad said to me, "You know, you have a gift." And I argued with him and said, "Dad, I don't want to practise every day." When I was younger, I wanted to go to the beach and hang out at my grandparents' cottage and do all that kind of stuff. And then one summer that I didn't really play very much, I realized how much I did miss being at the golf course. I guess I realized that the junior boys were at the golf course—they weren't at the beach—so that's where I went.

PM: Did your dad always know you could do this at this level?

LK: He told me. He said, "You have a God's talent and you need to pursue it, and you need to be the best that you can be and test yourself." I guess with their support, both Mom and Dad's, I found the courage to keep working and to keep trying to get better. I remember a comment, Peter, that my mom made to me when I went to Acadia University. I was very much a homebody, and still am. On the way to Acadia, when they were dropping me off, she said, "Lorie, you can always come home." And knowing that, even now being out on tour, knowing that I can always come home is a real nice feeling. Regardless of how things end up, win or lose, home is home, and I'm welcome there. I think I carry that with me. People ask me if I miss home and

I miss PEI, and I do, dearly. But knowing that I can go there whenever I like is a very comforting feeling.

—

GOLFERS ARE CONSTANTLY LOOKING for the perfect swing, and in spite of Mike Weir's confidence during our conversation that he'd found it, he's since changed his swing yet again. But his results prove that however he handles his clubs, he continues to be one of golf's elite players. He remains comfortably among the top golfers in the world and consistently ranks in the top finishers each week on the PGA Tour.

As for Lorie Kane, things have been a bit of a struggle in recent years. After her flurry of victories in 2000 and 2001 (four in total), she's cooled off to where 2008 was her lowest-earning year since she joined the LPGA Tour in 1996.

COLM FEORE

COLM FEORE IS ONE OF THE FINEST theatre actors in the world today. Most everyone agrees on that—his friends, his fellow actors, the critics and, yes, even Colm himself. And they're all right. Simply put, he is amazing on stage.

But if you think he's good on the boards, you should see him at dinner. In Rome. On your honeymoon, no less. That's what Cynthia Dale and I discovered in 1998 when we spent a week in Italy. We remembered that our fellow Stratford citizens Colm and Donna Feore were living in Rome while Colm was filming *Titus* with Sir Anthony Hopkins. After all, we'd already had an audience with the Pope (as had many others, I should add), so why not one with Colm? Donna picked the restaurant and it was what every Italian restaurant seems to be—so good it hurts. But it isn't the food I remember from that evening; it was Colm's brilliant offstage performance. As he does in the theatre or on film, he carries the moment. That night Colm spent much of the evening mimicking fellow actor Hopkins, for whom he obviously has enormous affection.

Cynthia, whose stage and film career is pretty stellar too, had known Colm for years, but I hadn't, so for me that night was an introduction. I was blown away, and I knew right then that someday I'd like to try to capture that energy in an interview. My moment came a couple of years later when Colm was filming in Hollywood, where he gets a lot of work, often as the villain in countless big-budget action flicks. In fact, he was juggling three different movies at the same time. I'd been in Phoenix giving a speech and used the proximity to fly over to Los Angeles and talk to Colm on one of his days off. He had just been picked to play Pierre Trudeau in what would become the hugely successful CBC made-for-television movie *Trudeau*, but it hadn't been announced yet, so we could talk about that only over coffee. But that was okay, because what I really wanted to get at was the difference between stage and film, and how he weighed the balance between the two. Once again, he didn't disappoint.

2001-05-01

Peter Mansbridge: Wow, you've got three movies going right now. How can you be doing three movies at the same time?

Colm Feore: Appear briefly in all of them and try and not get them confused (smiles). I'm a repertoire kind of guy; I like this. If the hair doesn't change and the clothes are the same, no problem. What's peculiar about them is that they're all spread out over the course of three months. I kept saying to my people, "Look, I've got two days off. Why? I've got other movies I could be in here." I don't like sitting around here not doing anything, but at the moment it's strictly a question of scheduling. If I do a day here for them, two days there for these guys, and go to the rifle range to shoot with these guys, then that's another day here. So, you know, I don't find it all that taxing. It's certainly not as hard as many other things I've done. It's really rather a lot of fun, and you keep meeting different people and, depending on which face you see, you go, "Oh, that movie. I remember what I'm supposed to do here now."

PM: A lot of people are going to be getting used to your face in the weeks and months ahead, when *Pearl Harbor* opens. You have a role in that, and just from the advance publicity, it sounds like it's going to be huge. What was that experience like?

CF: It was pretty terrific actually. I mean, it was very straightforward. It sounds peculiar to say it was easy, but for me, and many other guys in the same boat as me—no joke intended—we weren't there to establish the plot lines. Peter Firth, a wonderful actor, showed up and I said, "Peter, nice to meet you. What are you doing here?" And he said, "I'm here for the disembowelling." And I said, "Oh, I beg your pardon?" And he said, "Yes, I come and I get disembowelled as the captain of the ship and then Cuba Gooding Jr. holds me together for a few minutes, grabs a gun, shoots something down and then I go home." I go, "This is fantastic; this is really cool!" And that's what we were doing.

PM: You're the commander?

CF: I play Admiral Kimmel, the commander of the fleet in the Pacific, who may or may not be guilty of not quite paying enough attention. I happen to think not, obviously. But it was a very easy thing to shoot. I mean—hello!—you get a week in Hawaii in February. And in Stratford February is really ugly. So I had to pretend to my wife that the lapping surf was in fact rain and the lovely warm breezes were storms, because it was really hard to say, "I'm here standing in the ocean with a couple of friends from the Honolulu shoot and it's really hard, dear."

PM: When people see this, they're going to see a sky full of aircraft.

CF: It's actually going to be an astonishing movie to watch.

PM: More so than it actually was to do? Because I assume a lot of the effects will have been put in during what they call post-production.

CF: Well, yeah. Michael Bay was very excited about showing us the stick-person animation that they had sketched out for the bombing of Battleship Row.

PM: Michael Bay's the director.

CF: He's the director, and the director of *Bad Boys*, *Armageddon*, *The Rock*—big things, he does beautifully. Fourteen cameras, everything blows up, seven ships here, just get your line right. And that's why I think a lot of us were there, because the casting director, Bonnie Timmerman, who'd had some experience with us, had said, "You need guys that, whenever something is blowing up, they're likely to get it once right before the sun goes down and you won't have to hit them really hard with a stick to do it." That's kind of how I advertise myself, you know. "Hire an actor— think of the savings."

PM: One of the other ways you advertise is how you really research the roles you do.

CF: Yeah, sometimes.

PM: You put a lot of work into that. Did you have to research Pearl Harbor beyond the obvious?

CF: No, we didn't. We—and I say "we" because my wife, Donna, is very often extraordinarily helpful at saying, "Oh, I happened to be on the Net and the Pentagon says . . ." and she will send me packages of information on what I need to know— so we collaborate to prepare, but some things don't need a lot of preparation at all. And in fact, I don't want to make light of it, but essentially it's about standing on this mark and wearing these clothes at this moment and looking that way when all hell breaks loose. Knowing that the guy had oatmeal with cranberries for breakfast is immaterial at this point; nobody really gives a damn about it. So at some point it's just like John Hirsch* used to say: "Just learn the lines and show up and then don't bump into the furniture and go 'oh.'" It's really quite simple. You know, if the cheque doesn't bounce, to me it's been a huge success. And the level of commitment that you have to it is the moment between "Action" and "Cut." Do I feel more secure with a lot of research? Yeah, but very often then you're struggling trying to get it in and there isn't the opportunity. Greater minds than mine are always at work organizing the details for these movies.

Last night I was covered with flame retardant—"Oh no, it's very safe"—and a guy is putting jelly behind my ears and stuff. It's for this wonderful shot where I'm reading a book by an arson investigator, and these horrifying details are really happening in real life. He's written a book he's trying to sell. I am an ATF [Alcohol, Tobacco and Firearms] agent, and I found this book and I'm staggered. How do you communicate that in a film? You have an actor like myself sitting there and pretend to be reading while behind him, the wall blows up. And if he's got enough jelly on the back of his head, he won't burn before the shot's over. And he won't squeal like a pig as you pan off him down to the money shot, where there's a half-naked girl about to be engulfed in flames over here in the bathroom. How much research is necessary for this? Very little. I showed up, said hello, collected my per diem cheque, was charming and gracious with everybody, sat there, held the book, pretended to read and tried not to burn.

PM: It's not quite Stratford, is it?

CF: No, but I will say one thing. Without that as a foundation, it would probably be immeasurably harder. Because I say, "This needs *just* this layer, because that's all they're going to see and that's all they're going to use and that's really what they need. They don't need you to complicate it. They don't need to know what your motivation was. They don't need to know that you are deeply engaged

* *Canadian director, 1930–89. Hirsch founded the Manitoba Theatre Centre in Winnipeg and was artistic director of Canada's Stratford Festival from 1981 to 1985.*

in it. Just don't burn." Because I've had all that experience, because I've had that extraordinary opportunity to build a foundation, I'm free to have fun with some of this stuff, and that's what I'm doing.

PM: You know, you're known as one of the country's greatest Shakespearean actors.

CF: Really?

PM: (smiles) I read that somewhere.

CF: I must have written that. I think I did.

PM: But is it difficult sometimes, given what you have to put into that—establishing that reputation—to be doing the fire-retardant scenes?

CF: No, it's delightful; it's absolutely magnificent. It really is and, you know—I'll be honest with you—it pays a hell of a lot better. You let them slap you with that goo and light a fire, they're handing you money. Shakespeare isn't like that at all. I think that one of the basic, fundamental things actors need is a chance to explore. A lot of people get frustrated and never get a chance to play this or "I'm yearning to play this." I am spoiled rotten. I got to play Hamlet, Iago, Petruchio, Giacomo, Richard III, Cyrano, Romeo, Mercutio. I have had an extraordinary career, and it's hard for me say, "Now what would I like to do next? Do I want to go back to Stratford and work for them?" I'm a huge fan of Richard's and—

PM: Richard Monette?*

CF: Yes, and we talk all the time about the possibility. What I learned from Shakespeare and the power that he gives you can

* Artistic director of the Stratford Festival, 1994–2007.

go to another level, because of simplicity. Now I've had the pleasure of working with some rather extraordinary directors and some terrific actors. Guys like Anthony Hopkins—you watch the meticulous way he prepares something and you know this comes from the theatre; you know he was Olivier's darling and you know that he knows what he's doing. And when you see him on the set and how he spots the camera—(eyes camera, nods, imitating Hopkins) "How're you doing, Charlie?"—he knows everybody, has his Stephen King book, everything's fine. The work is already done: he knows what he's going to do and he's going to be fine; just leave him alone and let him do it, let him go home and give him his book. He will go from "Action" to "Cut" and be transported, but once "Cut" comes, it's all over. He goes back and lands firmly in the support structure of his work, which is all, I think, from the theatre, from Shakespeare. And so, watching him, I thought, "All right, I know how this goes. In order to get really good at doing this movie thing, I have no choice but to use this as a foundation." And interestingly enough, I found that there were many parallels between him and myself insofar as the theatre.

PM: And he also sometimes goes back to the theatre. As you said, you went back and did Hamlet in New York.

CF: Yes, I played Claudius to Liev Schreiber's Hamlet—Liev Schreiber, who incidentally has just killed me yet again in *The Sum of All Fears*. He slit my throat twelve or thirteen times and finally got it right.

PM: But there is something about going back to the stage? A lot of actors who do well in film, who don't need to go back, do go back for a summer. Why do they do that?

CF: Some of them go back for vindication: "See? I am a serious actor. See? I really, really am an actor." Because there are "real actors" and then there are the others. And those of us who want to be in the "real actor" column think we can survive privation and poverty and all of that as long as we can call it art. The moment you start not being able to call it art, you get into trouble and you start looking for some way to establish yourself, your prestige or name, in a legitimate venue. So you'll get a lot of people who really have no business being in the theatre getting into the theatre. Because, of course, it's what's done, and it gives you the patina of the right stuff. I don't buy it. Acting is acting is acting. You do television, you do radio, you do theatre—it's all the same stuff. The differences are really technical. I feel very fortunate that my foundation was something as strong as Shakespeare, and there's so much further I have to go in order to get good at acting. I'm very fortunate that this is the base, and now, on top of this, what I strive for is simplicity. But I'm having a very hard time getting to that.

PM: What do you mean by that?

CF: It's about being simple in the face of extraordinary whirlwinds of activity. And I like to be accommodating. I like to think that the essence of a film set is like a helicopter taking off: it needs to get up to 3,500 rpm or the damn thing falls apart. Usually when it gets to 3,500 rpm, you've got the crew and everybody working wonderfully, and then you bring in the actors and the whole thing breaks down. It's my feeling that we should be able to seamlessly come in and just let the clutch out, change the pitch of the thing—*vroosh*, and away we go—and the crew can sit back and say, "Oh yeah, that's why we do it."

PM: Let me ask you one other question about the differences between theatre and film, because you said acting is acting is acting and really there's not a lot of difference. One of the differences that I've always sensed when I've been to the theatre is that the actor, he or she, can get instant reaction to their performance.

CF: Sure.

PM: Whether the audience is into this and is appreciating your work—that you never see on a film set.

CF: I tend to disagree with that, because on a film set you've got a lot of people paid to be very interested in what you're doing and making very sure you do exactly what they need, and or more. So there is a focus and attention on it. You know the old cliché: that the crew guys are off having hoagies and cigarettes and beers and then (feigns yawning), "Here it goes, acting again." That's not really true. The crews that I've had the pleasure of working with pay attention to the shot as needed and then get on with the next one. And you can sense when people are paying attention.

In the theatre you can sense when they're not, and in certain theatres you can see them asleep. It's enormously difficult to manage an audience, to take this huge creature that they've become three or four minutes into it and manoeuvre them around at your will. It's enormously fun to do, but it's really hard work and you have to be sensitive—not to the people who are enjoying it, but to the people who aren't and to the people to whom you want to say, "You got dragged here, didn't you? She told you that if you came to this, you get to go to the hockey game. Fine." And you say to him, "It's going to be better than you think. Don't worry, you're with me. We're going to kill all the boring people and we'll have some fun"—and that I enjoy immensely. Maybe that's a power trip. It's not about the applause; it's not about any of that. It is about the liveness of it. It is about, "This could all go horribly wrong in a moment, but I don't think it will. I'm prepared, but— Oh no! It went horribly wrong there for a second. Whoops, it's live." So, you know, they all cross-pollinate, they all feed each other.

PM: What's the goal now for Colm Feore? Where do you want to take this to?

CF: My career mantra for the moment is just to keep showing up. I know that may sound simplistic, but it is really the foundation from which I build the next ten years. You keep showing up, you get a little bit better, you meet interesting, fascinating people, and you go up one step at a time. There is no ultimate goal except perhaps to be in that list. You know, *Vanity Fair* magazine every year has a "new Hollywood" list. And one of the pictures I like is a nice black-and-white of five or six guys in New York. It's Dylan Baker, Chris Cooper, David Morse, and they call them "The Co-stars"—the guys you can always count on to show up and do the job right. I'd like to be one of those guys.

—

COLM FEORE KEEPS RACKING UP the film credits, but since that interview he has also spent more time on stage, both on Broadway and in Stratford. In 2002 Cynthia and Colm starred in *My Fair Lady*, Donna staged the choreography and, while I am biased, the critics agreed with me that all three were brilliant. Colm can be a challenge to work with because he is as demanding of others as he is of himself, but as Cynthia often said that year, "He makes all of us better."

BRIAN CLARK

I WAS IN MY DOCTOR'S OFFICE having my annual physical when the first plane hit the World Trade Center on September 11, 2001. My cellphone buzzed moments later and one of the editors on the assignment desk let me know that there had been an "incident" at one of the WTC's two giant towers. At that point most news agencies were assuming it had been a small plane in a fluke accident—interesting, but unlikely to affect my day. Less than twenty minutes later my cellphone buzzed again. This time the caller was Mark Bulgutch, the executive producer of CBC news specials. His message was short and clear: "You better get in here right away. Two planes have hit the World Trade Center in New York in the last twenty minutes. It looks like a terrorist act."

I drove as fast as the law would let me along Toronto's University Avenue towards the CBC, but the closer I got, the more dense the traffic became. In every car I could see people anxiously listening to the news coming over the radio. You could tell they were listening by the frozen looks on their faces. In those few minutes of relative traffic-jam calm I gathered my thoughts, knowing this was going to be a very long day (as it turned out, I anchored forty-four hours of coverage over the next few days).

Having been thrust on the air to cover breaking news over the previous two decades, I knew the perils. Information would come in at warp speed, and much of it would turn out to be wrong. Like all my anchor colleagues, I would have to remain calm and patient and use my best journalistic skills, along with those of people like Mark in the control room, to decide what to share immediately and what needed more confirmation. There would almost certainly be mistakes, but viewers can handle mistakes if you are honest and upfront about the information you have, where you got it and how reliable you consider it to be.

I thought back to the lessons I learned the first time I was suddenly in the hot seat of a breaking international story. It was the shooting of Ronald Reagan in Washington on March 30, 1981. Within the first hour we had been told, in some cases by official sources, that Reagan had not been hit, then that he had been hit but it was just a glancing shot, then that he had been hit but it wasn't overly serious, up to the actual scenario that if he'd gotten to the hospital much later than he did, he might not have survived. It had been a chaotic afternoon, and not a shining one for many news organizations that went to air with "facts" that proved not to be facts at all.

Those few minutes of remembering the past helped prepare me for the challenge ahead. Brian Clark did not have that luxury on any level. First, he wasn't in the relative calm of a traffic jam. He was in the midst of the horror of a hundred-storey building on fire and about to collapse, where hundreds were already dead and hundreds were only minutes away from death. And second, he had no time to reflect on the decisions he had to make. Quite simply he had to decide, immediately and on instinct, whether to head up or down from where he stood on the eighty-fourth floor. Everyone else, it seemed, was heading up, convinced that a rooftop helicopter rescue would happen. Something inside him said, "No, safety lies in going down."

Brian Clark is a Canadian, and on that day he was working as the executive vice-president of the international brokerage firm Euro Brokers, in the south tower of the WTC. His story and

the way he tells it still leave me in a cold sweat. He joined us
on *One on One* for the fifth anniversary of 9/11.

2006-09-09

Peter Mansbridge: Your story is as compelling today as it was five
years ago. Do you ever get tired of telling it?

Brian Clark: I have been asked many times to tell the story, and
a little bit of tiredness does come into it, but I do feel an obligation to continue to tell the story.

PM: Is it cathartic in some ways for you to tell it?

BC: It's less difficult than it was. It's been a healing process. It
has helped me by downloading it so many times over the years.
And I'm left with a tremendous amount of sadness.

PM: What does it do to you when you see those pictures of 9/11?

BC: That day I felt like I was in control of things, except for the
ten seconds after the plane hit our building and the building
moved so much. In those ten seconds I was terrified. Other than
that I felt comfortable with myself, that I knew what I was doing.
I knew I was fine, so that stayed with me. The whole time I knew
that I had escaped and that I was fine. And I've been comfortable with that fact. I haven't been haunted.

PM: Your story is so amazing to hear. We won't go into every
detail here, but let me isolate a couple of points. The first one is
when the first plane hit, not the south tower where you were, but
the north tower.

BC: Right.

PM: Tell me about that moment.

BC: I was sitting at my keyboard at 8:45, 8:46 when that plane hit. All I sensed was this boom, an audible noise. The lights in my office buzzed and my attention was drawn upward. My peripheral vision caught something behind me, and I whirled around and, eighty-four floors in the air—that's where our office was, eighty-four floors in the air—there were swirling flames. It was such an unprecedented thing. You just don't expect to see that. And I incorrectly thought at that moment that there had been an explosion upstairs, and perhaps that was why my head jerked up with the lights. That was the sense that I had. I grabbed a flashlight and I put a whistle around my neck—I had volunteered to be one of the fire wardens on our floor. And went out to start evacuating our people, thinking that something had happened a couple of floors up.

PM: When you turned around and saw that image—it almost sounds like you're caught in a movie.

BC: Yeah. It dissipated after two or three seconds. And in the air, floating, like flaming confetti if you like, was newsprint—you know, paper from photocopy machines or computer paper—just floating in the air. Nonetheless I still thought it was something upstairs. Had I gone right up to the glass and looked to the north, looked to my right, I would have seen the north tower and seen the damage up on the ninety-second and ninety-third floors. I didn't do that then.

PM: In the minutes that followed, the discussion began about whether or not you should follow through with various announcements calling for an evacuation on the intercom. But then, about twenty minutes later, another shake. Tell me about that moment.

BC: Yes. I had made a couple of phone calls to home to say, "We're okay." I came out of my office and I was standing with a fellow who had gone down ten floors. He was just telling me he'd heard the announcement and come back up. He and I were closer than you are to me right now. He and I were that close, when—*boom!* Our room just fell apart in an instant. It's a very hard thing to describe what happened in that one second, but everything came out of the ceiling. Our raised floor—you know, computer floor— went all cobblestone-like, out of alignment. A door frame fell out of the wall; it tore jaggedly. And everywhere was just dust and soot. And then for ten seconds the building tilted to one side. It stopped—and came back. And then I was fine.

I reached in my pocket, got that flashlight, shone it around the room and gathered up a group of people, six of us altogether, who went into the centre core. We'd gone down only three floors when we met somebody coming up, and they said, "Stop, stop." A woman would not let us pass. She said, "There are flames down below. We've got to go higher." I was distracted by a banging noise on the eighty-first floor and went to grab the fellow beside me. "Ron," I said, "come on. Let's get this fellow," and we started in on the eighty-first floor. As we did, everybody else on the landing with me started up. And they all died that day.

PM: So many details you've just told me. Let's take them step by step.

BC: Sure.

PM: You were convinced you had to go down, not up—even in spite of what this woman who was coming up said: "Don't go down"?

BC: Yeah.

PM: Now what was it in you that told you, "I've got to go down"?

BC: Partly, I suppose, was the training from the Port Authority and the fire drills they had sent us through. And yet, at the same time, I didn't absolutely insist to those other people who were going up, "Where are you going? Stop!" Because I was now focused on this person inside on the eighty-first floor. Halfway to meeting that person, Ron, my co-worker who was with me, turned around and went back to the stairs. He was overcome by smoke, but around me was this bubble of fresh air. I found the stranger, we came back to the stairs, and that's when I made the decision. I pointed the light down and said to myself, without much thought at all, "I've got to go down and test it. I've got to see if what that lady reported is accurate." It was a kind of sensation that I just needed to go further.

PM: And the person you met that day, whom you didn't know at that moment . . .

BC: Stanley Praimnath is his name.

PM: Stanley. As he says, you saved his life, and I guess in some ways he saved yours, because he took you out of that argument. His dilemma took you out of the debate about whether to go up or down.

BC: That's exactly true. When we in fact got outside the building— I guess we were outside the building four minutes before it collapsed—we actually stopped about a block away. Stanley broke down a little bit. And in front of a couple of ministers who were at the backside of Trinity Church—he literally said it at the time, while the building was still standing—he said, "This man saved my life." And I said to him at the time, almost like a premonition, I said, "It may have been your voice in the darkness that saved my life, Stanley." And we had this back-and-forth mutual appreciation, if you like, at that moment. That's the first time we said it. And then, two minutes after that, we turned around and the building collapsed.

PM: You eventually made your way home.

BC: Yes.

PM: Stanley made his way home.

BC: Correct.

PM: You divided paths at that point. But you still know Stanley, you still talk with him.

BC: As the white wave of guck, dust and everything was catching up to us, Stanley and I dove into a building on Broadway: 42 Broadway, a building neither of us had ever been in before. And we shared stories for forty-five minutes. One thing he did in that forty-five minutes was give me his home personal business card, which I tucked in my shirt pocket. I still keep that card in my wallet to this moment, and I was able to get in touch with him as a result of that. He and I still talk to each other at least once a month.

PM: Really?

BC: And we see each other once a quarter.

PM: What does that relationship mean to you now?

BC: We're very different people. Very different backgrounds. Ethnically Stanley's an Indian, from Guyana. He's an immigrant to the United States as I'm a Canadian immigrant to the United States. He worked for a bank; I worked for a broker. So we come from different backgrounds. But I don't have any brothers or sisters; I'm an only child. And Stanley, through this if you like, has become my brother. We have this shared experience. When you think of who are your friends in life, they're the people you've gone through events with and shared events with. Well, he and I certainly shared an event, so we will be lifelong friends.

PM: As it turned out, only sixteen people from the impact zone and above in the south tower got out that day, you and Stanley being two of them. Do you believe in luck?

BC: That's a definition some people can use, and it's probably acceptable in some circles. Maybe it's luck. I felt like there were other things at work that day. Stanley is a deeply religious person. When the plane was approaching him, he said at the last second he just dove under his desk saying, "Lord, I'm in your hands." His Bible was on his desk when the plane hit.

PM: He saw it coming in?

BC: He saw the plane coming. It was coming right at him. He saw it. He picked it up when it was across New York Harbor above the Statue of Liberty. He was standing on the phone, standing along the south wall, looking south, talking to an associate in Chicago. And she was saying, "Get out of the building. Don't you know what's happened?" He said, "Not really." And then he saw the plane coming. At the last second it dipped down below him about three floors. A wing tip certainly went through his floor—the right wing was up as it entered the building. His room was destroyed, everywhere other than where his desk was. He had said, "Save me," and his Bible was on the desk. So he knows that's why he is alive. I had a choice in my exit to go right, straight ahead or left to a stairway. Without any thinking I just felt this push to the left. What was that push? Who gave me that push? You know, people could say, "Oh, it was lucky you found that stairway." I beg to differ. There was something else at work.

PM: You're a religious person; you have faith.

BC: Yes, I do. And there's another story. Halfway to Stanley, my associate Ron was overcome with smoke. Stanley, who was a stranger to me at the time, was screaming, "Help, help, I'm buried. I can't breathe." But around me—I noted it at the time—was this bubble of fresh air. There's no other explanation to me than it was a miracle. It allowed me to get to Stanley and get him out of there. So some people can call it luck, but I think I was being looked after. That raises an issue: Why me? Why not somebody else? I had been blessed and given a gift. I don't wrestle with what I consider to be unanswerable questions. I don't have nightmares about the event. I fall asleep very quickly at night. And I take no credit for any of that. It's just been a gift. It's the way it is.

PM: So you have no survivor guilt.

BC: I really don't. I've accepted it, I'm not embarrassed by it, but it's nothing to brag about. As I say, I take no credit for it. It's just the way it happened to me.

PM: What has it done to your faith in the five years since? When you look back at it, the bubble moment is obviously something, but what about on a broader level?

BC: I had a particular dream one week after the event. And the result of the dream was that any doubts I had about my faith just evaporated in a moment. Since that moment—I know this may sound strange, but I feel comfortable about what happened that day.

PM: That'll sound like a strange word to people.

BC: It does.

PM: Why do you choose it?

BC: Because for me, I'm not haunted by that day. I am left with this tremendous sadness and the futility of that day. It was a senseless event. It accomplished nothing but to stir up the hornet's nest. So many innocent people were just slaughtered that day, and for no reason. It just made no sense to me. But it happened. I have been able to rationally say it happened and you can't change it. It's in the past. So I don't dwell on it on a day-to-day basis. When people ask me to tell the story, I'll tell the story. So it comes back and rolls like a movie, very clearly for me, each time I tell the story. But I don't dwell on it when I'm not asked.

PM: And you don't get angry about it.

BC: I was angry at one funeral when I saw three young children— aged, I'm guessing, seven, five, three—following their mother down the aisle. I had this moment of anger, but it was just at one funeral. Our company lost sixty-one people that day, so the group of us two hundred survivors in our company went to many, many funerals for the following months. I had one flash of anger in all of that. I just knew the rest of it couldn't be changed. It happened; I accepted it. I didn't like it at all, but whatever is God's plan is unfolding as it should be. And I cannot change that. I can play my part in it—we have free will; that's a gift we've been given as well. But I can't argue with the events that have happened in the past.

PM: I guess it's *the* question: how has your life changed?

BC: I did learn from 9/11 that you can't predict the future with any certainty, so I do not worry about the future. If I don't dwell on the past and I don't worry about the future, it leaves me at the present. So I take every day as a special day. It's a gift. I live it as best I can and enjoy every moment. Conversations like this, a walk down the street—it's all wonderful, and it's all to be treasured. Enjoy every moment: that's how I'm getting through it.

—

BRIAN CLARK RETIRED FROM Euro Brokers in 2006, but not before he had helped raise $5.2 million for the families of co-workers who were lost on 9/11. He spends his time now doing the odd day trade, golfing and volunteering at a food bank. As for Stanley, they still connect at least a couple of times a year.

HAMID KARZAI

CANADA'S COMMITMENT TO AFGHANISTAN can hardly be questioned. We've lost good people, both men and women. We've spent billions of dollars defending the country and ourselves. We've trained the Afghan military and its police force. And we've been doing it for far longer than we fought in either the First or Second World Wars, Korea, the Gulf or Bosnia. And while there may be an end in sight for the current Canadian Afghan mission, there doesn't appear to be one for the overall challenge in that country. Stephen Harper has suggested that the insurgency may not be beatable, and Barack Obama has raised doubts about whether the war is winnable.

The NATO goal in Afghanistan is all about security: making it secure against the possibility of a return of al Qaeda and the Taliban; making it secure against the corruption caused by the drug trade; making it secure for women to live lives of equality to men; making it secure for Afghan children to go to school. And the list goes on, ending almost inevitably at making it secure, in the most basic sense, for the president of the country, Hamid Karzai.

Like most journalists who have covered major world events over the past few decades, I've seen a lot of security. The United

Nations, the White House, G-7 and G-8 summits, royal tours, papal tours, the Olympics—checkpoints and layers of security are all part of the norm. But I'd never seen anything like the security involved as I made my way to the presidential offices of Hamid Karzai in Kabul in 2003. He'd been president for less than a year and already there had been at least one serious attempt on his life. Afghanistan may have been liberated, but it was far from free. A huge sector of the city surrounding the presidential palace had been cordoned off to ensure that no unwanted visitors got near the man who NATO, Canada included, was hoping would bring calm and order to the country in which the 9/11 terrorists had been trained. As we entered the sector, a lengthy series of checkpoints lay ahead. At each one, guards searched first our car, then us in a process that got more intense the closer we got to our destination.

After what seemed like at least an hour, we arrived at the front door of the building where Karzai spent most of his time. It was surrounded by armed guards, some Afghan but most, it seemed, American, and they weren't saying whether they were U.S. Special Forces or private "rentals" who were just starting to make their mark in and around Kabul. Another hour of waiting and checking our papers and finally we were ushered into a large, sofa-filled waiting room just outside the president's office. We set up our equipment under the watchful eye of his most senior guards.

All of that was expected, but what followed wasn't. As the Afghan leader came into the room he reached out his hand and we shook, sat down in our chairs and exchanged the basic pleasantries that pass for small talk in the moments before an interview begins. Then the surprise. Sitting right behind Karzai and just out of camera range, but very much in my eye range, was a very large man with an equally large gun lying across his knees. Then I heard a noise behind me that I knew wasn't my cameraman, so I turned around and saw the same scene behind me.

Now, don't confuse this with media intimidation. Far from it. In fact this was a pretty honest reflection of how the security forces in Afghanistan measured the continuing threat almost fifteen months after the Taliban had been thrown out of the country. They were still so concerned that half a dozen checkpoints weren't enough to stop them from worrying about safety right inside the President's own offices. I wanted to know how all that security, in effect closing him off from the outside world, had affected the President's relationship with his people. What follows is part of that interview and part of another sit-down with Hamid Karzai a few years later, in 2006, during a visit he made to Ottawa—there were no big guns across any laps in that room.

2004-02-21

Peter Mansbridge: I wonder how close you feel to the people of Afghanistan, how close you *can* feel to the people, given the level of security that surrounds you in what are still difficult days for your country. How close is your relationship with the people?

Hamid Karzai: Almost daily I have meetings here in my office over lunch, and in the afternoon at times, with groups of people from various provinces or interest groups. We also have occasional visits by tribal chiefs and the clergy. I think my involvement with people on a daily basis takes up almost 50 percent of my daily routine. I took lots of provincial trips in the summer and in the autumn, and I'm going to begin the trips in the coming days again.

PM: I guess that's what I was wondering. How difficult is it for you to make those kinds of trips, in terms of the security concerns? Even here in the city, would it be out of the question for you to walk in the streets, to walk into, for example, the market area?

HK: I did that last year. My security is very tough in that they don't allow me to walk in the manner I did before. But if I want to, they prepare and I do go out for lunches or dinners sometimes. It's more difficult than I would want it to be. I would like it to be easier, but security is not something that I interfere with. But provincial trips are much easier. We ask in advance, the security guys prepare for it and then we go and make the trip and meet people en masse.

PM: How hard is it for you to see a time when you're not going to face those kinds of security constraints?

HK: The kind of world we have today, I think it's going to be difficult for any president of any country to roam around like they did ten years ago or before that. Afghanistan is no exception.

PM: But it is. You concede it's certainly different in Afghanistan right now than the rest of the world. There are a lot of people with guns around you, all the time.

HK: Oh yes, absolutely different, yes.

PM: What is your current understanding and your feeling about security in your country? There's a sense on the part of some that the Taliban, that al Qaeda are re-emerging in this country.

HK: There was a sense of that last summer. I think that sense has gone away.

PM: Why is that?

HK: Because they'd failed. People really don't see the Taliban as a challenge and they don't want them to come back. The towns-people have complained about security, but about a different aspect. They complain about the inability of the government to provide simple protection. They complain about the lawlessness of the government itself, including all police and the military. So for us, terrorism is not a threat in the sense that it was two years ago. I think there's a sharp decline, especially with the recon-struction picking up. And we're seeing changes in Pakistan. We've had some good announcements from the Government of Pakistan.

If that also is implemented, as promised, Afghanistan will be a much safer place. So I'm not worried about either a resurgent Taliban or terrorism or extremist activity, no.

PM: There's a feeling that the hunt for bin Laden and Mullah Omar is more concentrated now in an area between your country and Pakistan, that the Pakistan government is more involved now in that search. What do you believe to be the case on that?

HK: I hope they're captured soon. I will not be going into operational details on that; I just hope that they will be captured soon.

PM: Do you have reason to believe that there really is significant progress in that search?

HK: No fugitive can run away from the law forever.

PM: I'd like to talk a little bit about what you dream about for the future, and whether you feel you can realize it in your lifetime.

HK: I would like this country, first of all, to be even more stable, to be a partner with the rest of the world in the fight against terrorism, to find a way to end terrorism. I would like this country to be prosperous, to get off the world's back. I want this country to produce its own income and to produce its own security arrangements. And more specifically, I want this country to be able to have an income per capita of hopefully $1,000 in ten years from today. I want an Afghanistan that would be a productive member of the international community, paying for its own bread and butter and also helping alongside the rest of the world.

PM: Do you really think that's possible within that short a period of time? To some people ten years sounds like a long time, but for the challenge ahead for your country, ten years may seem a short time.

HK: We have made a lot of progress in the past two years, keeping in mind the Afghan potential: the potential of national resources, the hardworking nature of the people, and keeping in mind the strategic position of Afghanistan. In five years' time Afghanistan should be able to take a significant part of the burden of the security of its borders and country onto its own shoulders. In another five years we should be able to provide for ourselves in terms of economic prosperity. Why not? It takes hard work and we will do it.

PM: You referred to the stakes in terms of success in Afghanistan. What happens if it doesn't succeed?

HK: I would not say that it won't succeed. It will succeed. But the stakes of failure are going to be not only for Afghanistan but also for the rest of the world, and everybody recognizes that. And that's why neither us in Afghanistan nor our friends in the international community are allowing that to happen.

PM: But why is it that this country is so important?

HK: Because this country had been taken over by terrorism, because the failure of the Afghan state caused that kind of danger to the rest of the world. Do we allow it to go back to that way and affect the rest of the world the way it did? Just think of the Twin Towers. Could you ever have imagined that a threat like that could emanate from a country so far away? No. But that was the reality. It happened. So are we going to allow that to happen again? Never.

2006-09-23

PM: President Karzai, welcome to Canada. Of late there have been some pretty bleak assessments of conditions in your country. In the last few days you've been pretty blunt about the situation as

well, saying that terrorism is rebounding—those were your words
to the United Nations the other day. How tenuous is the situation in Afghanistan?

HK: It will not derail the peace process. It will not stop us from
what we are achieving. It will slow us down. For the Afghan people
four and a half years on, they see no reason why we should be losing
lives of those of the international community and of the Afghan
community. For Afghans the war against terror was over when,
together with your help, we drove terrorists out of our country
four and a half years ago over two months. And then life began.
Children went back to school by the millions, we created a constitution, we held presidential elections where eight and a half
million people participated. We elected a parliament with women
representatives, the economy bounced back, people found jobs,
trade with the neighbours increased. So now, for the Afghan
people, it's a question of "How can these terrorists be back?"

PM: What is the answer to that? The last time we talked was in
your office in Kabul less than two years ago. You were convinced
then that terrorism was on the decline in your country, that significant steps were being made. And now here we are with this
situation where many of the things we talked about in terms of
progress seem to have reversed themselves. What's happening?

HK: The economy slowed down for two reasons. One, we were
concentrating on the building of the army, on building the institutions and on building the political and economic process to
take the country forward, and perhaps did not focus as much as
we should have on creating a strong, effective police force for
Afghanistan.

PM: Who's the "we" when you say that?

HK: The international community and Afghans together, that's
"we." We should have focused more strongly on the police force.

About two years ago the people of the southwestern provinces, where we now have much of the trouble, came to me and said, "Mr. President, we don't have a strong police force in the southwestern countryside. The districts are not protected properly." For example, the district that shares a 250-kilometre border with Pakistan, with a population of 65,000, at that time had only 45 policemen. That means 1 policeman per 1,500 inhabitants of the district and for 250 kilometres of border with Pakistan. I began to work with the international community but unfortunately we did not implement the increased police force in time. Now we are all focused on it. On the other hand, when we drove the terrorists out of Afghanistan, we did not focus on the sanctuaries to be found outside of Afghanistan.

PM: Pakistan.

HK: They were regrouped, reorganized, trained, financed, equipped. And then, drop by drop, they were sent back into Afghanistan to hurt us the way they hurt us today.

PM: Are we in agreement that you're talking about Pakistan?

HK: (nods) We have to focus on the sources of terror, especially on madrassas in Pakistan. There are places that are called madrassas—schools for teaching—but actually they are places that teach hatred towards the rest of us in Afghanistan and the international community, where they take young, poor, desperate children and brainwash them into terrorists. That has to stop.

PM: Why hasn't it stopped? It's not like we just discovered that this year. We've known that in the West since 9/11, and I'm sure you did well before that. I thought there was now co-operation between you and Pakistan.

HK: There was co-operation on one aspect of the international terror organizations, on al Qaeda. But there was no focus on the regional elements of terror and extremism, especially on madrassas that are training young children how to make bombs and how to shoot people. That we should have done a long time ago. My plea today, through you, both to Afghanistan and to the international community and to our brothers in Pakistan, is, for the good of all of us, to get to that root—the sooner, the better.

PM: When you say you want more decisive action to try and curb what's happening in your country, what are you talking about? Are you talking about decisive military action?

HK: I'm talking about decisive action in any form—military, political or military and political. To go and hunt down the terrorists who are hurting all of us. And to go and drive out their sources, whether those sources are in Afghanistan or in Pakistan or elsewhere. We have to make sure that we get at where they get financed and trained and motivated, and stop it there. If we don't do that we'll be fighting the symptoms in Afghanistan or somewhere else in the world.

PM: The elephant in the room, as they say on this side of the world, would be drugs. A report by the U.N. body looking at the drug situation in Afghanistan would say that 90 percent of the world's opium comes from your country and that you are approaching becoming a "narco-state"—where the economy is dependent on drugs, where power is dependent on drugs, where terrorism is funded by drugs. What are you doing about that?

HK: It's a shame for us. We are embarrassed. Our country, or part of our country, became dependent on poppies because of years of desperation, from the Soviet invasion onward. People did not know if they were going to be in their homes the next day, or if they would have their families the next day, or if their children would be alive the next day. That's sort of been the past thirty years. Add to that eight or nine years of extreme drought due to lack of rain, which pushed people to destroy the pomegranate orchards, vineyards and other very productive food production to replace them with an easy-grow, easy-cash crop. The easy-grow, easy-cash crop was the poppy, because it also had the Mafia backing it from outside Afghanistan.

So we have a problem, and unfortunately, as much as it is bad, as much as it embarrasses us, it also is a reality. We began to tackle this five years ago, but I was naive about it; I thought we were going to destroy poppies in a year or two. And then the U.N. poppy chief came to me and said, "Sir, that's not going to be the case. You need much more time, perhaps ten years."

PM: Have you really got that kind of time, though?

HK: We have to. There is no option.

PM: How much time have you got to resolve this broader situation in Afghanistan? I was in Kandahar a couple of months ago and I talked to somebody in Kandahar City, a respected local person, who is in favour of the foreign troops on his soil but recognizing the fact, as in any country, that nobody likes foreign troops. He said to me that there's not much time left there for patience, that people have to see the value of this and they have to see it soon. I asked him how long, and he said a couple of years at most. People have to see the kind of progress we talked about, whether it's schools, water, electricity. They've got to see that soon.

HK: Yes, but they have seen some part of it. They have seen some good roads, they have seen some good schools, they've seen the economic benefit, they've seen a raised income for all of us. What they have not seen in some parts of the country, especially in Kandahar and the surrounding provinces, is security. They are attacked, killed, in mosques, in schools, in shopping places. So the man was right; we have to hurry. And that has caused some confusion in the Afghan population. They say, "With the presence of the entire world watching us, how come we are still vulnerable to attack by terrorism and how come they dare to kill international-community soldiers?"

That is why I am becoming more and more blunt, more and more clear in my demand that we need to get going to the sources on terrorism, going to where they train. Unless we do that, we will keep suffering. And unless we do we will keep losing the confidence of the Afghan people—which we must not, because it is vital for us to have this war won for all of us in the world and for the safety and security of the citizens of Afghanistan and in Canada.

PM: Let me ask you this last question. So much of the focus is always placed on you as the person to whom so much hope has been attached, when you first became president of Afghanistan and in the years since then. I read a quote about you the other day that said, "He's the wrong man for the job, but he's the only person who can do it," which in some ways sums up the difficulty of the situation in your country. How are you bearing up to all this?

HK: Afghanistan and the peace process are like a very beautiful, very delicate jar—a vase made of the finest crystal that I had to carry in my hands through storms and evils, in which I had to carry with me all Afghans of all faiths, of all considerations, and take it forward. I did that. Am I satisfied? I am. Am I not satisfied? Yes, I am also not satisfied. I think we would have been happier if there'd not been the loss of four Canadian soldiers last Monday, had there not been the loss of seventeen poor workers yesterday near the borders of Pakistan. So I have the feeling of happiness and sadness at the same time.

—

HAMID KARZAI'S FIRST SEVEN-YEAR TERM in office officially came to an end in the spring of 2009, a time when his popularity had dropped as Afghanistan faced a mounting and violent Taliban-led insurgency. The elections were postponed until August of 2009 and Karzai chose to run again.

ROYA RAHMANI

MOST OF OUR *One on One*s have been taped in our studio at the CBC Broadcasting Centre in Toronto. It's certainly the most convenient place, because everything is there: the cameras, the crews, makeup people and a dedicated set. But there's no doubt that being on location can capture a whole different mood and bring the viewer closer to the action.

I think back on interviews I've done in the Arctic, breaking through ice in the Northwest Passage, in Vancouver's Stanley Park shortly after a vicious windstorm wiped out hundreds of the city's oldest trees, or alongside the speed-skating track at the 2006 Torino Winter Olympics in Italy. But perhaps my favourite on-location *One on One* took place just outside the main terminal building at the Kabul Airport in Afghanistan.

We had just landed after a flight from Dubai, and a Canadian Armed Forces Hercules aircraft was parked on the tarmac waiting to transport us on the one-hour flight south to Kandahar. They told us we had forty-five minutes to make the transfer and they wouldn't wait a minute longer, for security reasons. That was just enough time for what we wanted to do.

The three-person crew rushed out of the terminal building and set up cameras on a small patch of long grass (in 2006 not much was groomed around the building; in fact it was mostly a mess of twisted metal and unkempt gardens). I went to meet our guest, who'd kindly agreed to come to the airport. Roya Rahmani was born in Afghanistan in 1978, but as civil war tore her country apart she and her family moved first to Pakistan and then to Canada, where she finished her education, graduated from McGill University in 2003 and became a Canadian citizen. Her degree was in computer science and software engineering, a background that could easily have landed her in a comfortable, high-paying private-sector job. But no, Roya Rahmani chose instead to go back to Afghanistan, as a project coordinator for the Rights and Democracy project, funded by the Canadian International Development Agency (CIDA).

The project is all about helping Afghan women understand their rights in a country hoping to find real democracy but still suffering from intense internal strife. I wanted to hear about that challenge, so we headed straight to where the crews had hastily established a makeshift *One on One* set. With military aircraft taking off and landing just metres away and our Canadian Forces escorts gently pacing as they counted down the minutes, we started to talk.

2006-03-11

Peter Mansbridge: I want to start by talking about the general situation that women face in Afghanistan. We all remember the difficulties faced during the Taliban years. In the almost five years since, how would you describe the improvement in the situation?

Roya Rahmani: It's a very difficult question but at the same time obvious. What has happened in the past five years specifically in terms of expansion of democracy and women's rights? I would say the fundamentals are in place. We have a structure for women's participation in the parliament and there is an elected government. But in terms of the reality for women and how they live within their household, the community, there is not a lot of change yet.

PM: That must be frustrating for someone like you.

RR: It certainly is.

PM: It must make it frustrating when you hear somebody like the President of the United States, who often cites, as an example of how things have changed in Afghanistan since late 2001, the new rights for women and how change has been significant. Now, he's not the only one; other Western leaders say the same thing. Are they overstating the case or is it fair for them to make that argument?

RR: It goes both ways, because they could make this statement. Obviously you do not see all women covered in burkas anymore. They're employed in all different sectors and they're out in the public. Still, women are facing the challenges that they were facing five years ago. In terms of domestic violence, there's not been much decrease, and actually some figures show that it has even increased.

PM: I want to talk about burkas, because a lot of North Americans can identify to some degree the plight of women in Afghanistan when they see images of women fully covered in burkas. That still exists certainly in more remote parts of Afghanistan, but also you just have to walk through the streets of Kabul and you still see that. You don't use that as the firm line as to whether or not women are progressing, because, as you've said in the past, some women want to wear burkas.

RR: That's right. I would never use that as some measure of expansion of democracy or not. In a lot of remote provinces, as you just mentioned, they still tend to wear them.

I do not think we're in post-conflict Afghanistan yet. Look at the amount of military we have here, and why we need so much

of it. Are we peacekeeping or peace-building? This is why I do
not see that Afghanistan is post-conflict yet, and therefore it's not
yet a secure place for women, who are not able to move freely.
And in the areas where they are not educated, where they didn't
have much access to different resources, some of them still want
to be seen as part of the private sphere of the household.

So they feel more comfortable wearing their burkas outside
because they still claim that the security is not in place, number
one. Number two, yes, the situation did improve for those who did
not want to wear a burka, to take them off where they couldn't do
it previously, and we cannot ignore that change. Obviously it is a
matter of giving the choice. Democracy is about giving the options
and choice, not forcing it either way. So if you have the choice to
wear it or not, I think that's more democratic than saying, "Okay,
so now all burkas are off—here is a democratic nation."

PM: Let's talk a little bit about your background. You're an
Afghan Canadian.

RR: That's right.

PM: You were here in Afghanistan but moved to Canada during
the difficult years in the civil war in the early 1990s. Canada,
though, gave you ideas about wanting to come back, through
your education and training at McGill. Tell us about that.

RR: Yes, I am an Afghan Canadian, and I relate to both countries
very much the same way. It depends on the mood, the momentum of the day—sometimes it's one side or the other. However, if
you're asking why I decided to return, it's that I was never separated from this country, specifically in terms of human rights issues
and women's rights issues. So once I graduated from McGill, I was
still very much involved with volunteer work, and thankfully I
found a fabulous group of Canadian women who are working to
help Afghan women in a very unique way. I became a member of
one of the chapters they run throughout Canada.

PM: Right across the country?

RR: We have thirteen chapters right across the country. I was a member of the Montreal chapter. And this is where I got more and more involved with Rights and Democracy. When there was the opportunity for me to return and take this position, I made the decision over three days. I had a job, I had an apartment, and I had to make the decision of returning back to this country and shifting pretty much everything. I thought, "It's now or never."

So this was why I decided to return to Afghanistan. I returned for a week in September 2004 just to see if I could do it. When I think about it now, I surprised myself how I made the decision, because I remember how everything looked to me and how strange and hard to handle it was. Yet whatever it was, there was this gravity that totally caught me. I went back to Montreal, sorted out my personal business and returned, and I have been here since.

PM: You talked earlier about the frustrations involved because of the slowness of the pace of change. But give us a sense what a normal day is like. Is there such a thing as a normal day trying to make the kind of change you want to make?

RR: I think pretty much everywhere in Afghanistan everyone's day is very busy. There is frustration, yet it's fulfilling. Though I only get to enjoy that fulfilment if I don't pass out on my bed, because the days are really never eight hours; the work never stops. It's very enjoyable work because I feel that every single woman I talk to might be able to learn something and we can have an exchange either way. I learn from them; they learn— probably and hopefully—from us, and we can plan something for a better tomorrow for women and children of this country.

Yes, the pace of change is very slow, but at the same time, probably, sometimes our expectations are too high. Ever since I can remember there has been war. And my parents say it was that way even before I came into this world. So we cannot make everything happen in a couple of years. But what still keeps us hopeful is the rate of growth of the civil society. The women of Afghanistan are really passionate, they are really working hard and they do need support to move on. Hopefully when they do, we'll have a better Afghanistan.

—

I FOUND ROYA RAHMANI to be a remarkable young woman, a Canadian making—as we often say when we meet special Canadians like her on our foreign travels—a "world of difference." She is still in Afghanistan, still trying to make a difference even as the country struggles desperately to stay on a road towards democracy as we know it.

TARIQ AZIZ

THERE WAS SOMETHING VERY SURREAL about driving around Baghdad in January 2003. Everyone knew war was coming, probably within weeks, and everyone had a pretty good idea that it would bring about the end of Saddam Hussein. Yet no matter where you went in the Iraqi capital you saw him—huge billboards and giant statues on almost every corner. It was very strange to pass them by, convinced that within weeks someone would be pulling them down to celebrate the end of a dictator's rule.

In the darkness of a Baghdad evening, my crew and I were taken to the old Iraqi Foreign Ministry building, a five- or six-storey structure in the middle of the city. I'd been granted an interview with Tariq Aziz, Iraq's deputy prime minister and a close associate of Saddam Hussein for fifty years, who was seen by many to be the country's Number Two. The cigar-smoking Aziz spoke fluent English, and as a result he'd become a much desired guest of the Western media, who were constantly trying to gauge what Number One was going to do next. The night I went to meet him was the same night the international community was waiting to hear Iraq's reaction to the final United Nations report on its inspection of the country's weapons sites. So whatever Aziz said was going to be a world exclusive.

We were ushered into a waiting room outside Aziz's top-floor office and offered Iraqi tea while the crew began setting up. I could hear a television blaring on the other side of his office door, clearly tuned to CNN's broadcast of the U.N. report—which was interesting, because CNN was banned in that country for ordinary Iraqis. Tariq Aziz was depending on it to get the information he needed before considering his country's next move. Within seconds of the broadcast's end, the door opened and there he was, alone and ready to talk. I was stunned. I had expected that officials offering him options would be surrounding him as he came out of the office. I had also assumed that he would spend at least some time on the phone getting directions from Number One. But no, neither of those things had happened. Iraq's reaction to the world as it was perched on the edge of imminent war was to come from one man, after no consultation with anyone else. And he was going to give it to me.

2003-03-03

Peter Mansbridge: If it does come to war, how do you see that war unfolding?

Tariq Aziz: Well, I'm sure that we will survive.

PM: How?

TA: We will. We survived in 1991, and we'll survive [now]. We are a very brave nation. Our people have ingenuity. We are a very active government and we can recover from the losses of war. In 1991 they inflicted great losses on us, but we recovered, we rebuilt, including this building which we are sitting in now. It was destroyed in 1991; now it's a fine building—we are working in it.

PM: I assume it would be a target again, would it not?

TA: It could be, yes.

PM: Can you win though?

TA: Win? Now you see, the concept of winning the war is different from the war that happened in 1991 and the First World War, Second World War. We are not fighting the Americans on their own homeland. We are not fighting them in Europe or in Asia or in the Sahara. We are being attacked by the Americans. If the Americans fail to achieve their objectives, then we'll be winning the war and they will be losing the war.

PM: There has been much talk that a conflict would be street-to-street, house-to-house in the cities of this country, especially here in Baghdad. Do you see that happening?

TA: While they are speaking about regime change, they cannot change the regime by remote control. And they cannot change the regime by using long-range missiles and long-range airplanes; that's clear. If they want to change the regime in Iraq, they have to fight the Iraqi people and the Iraqi army and the Arab Socialist Party on the ground. "Ground" means cities. They have to come to the cities to remove us from our places in government. So that means that they have to fight us here, in the streets of Baghdad, in the streets of Basra, in the streets of Mosul, and in the streets of each and every city and town.

PM: What do you think the people will do if it comes to that?

TA: They will fight the Americans. They will fight the Americans. The Americans are fancying—they are deluding themselves—that they will be received with flowers. They will be received with bullets, not flowers. We have distributed hundreds of thousands of arms, and we are confident of the reaction of our people. No government which is afraid its people might make an uprising against it will distribute so many arms, you see, to ordinary citizens.

PM: Are you actually giving guns to ordinary citizens, every citizen?

TA: Yes.

PM: There are some in the United States and in Britain who feel that if this does in fact come to a conflict, it would be over in a week or two weeks.

TA: Let them try. Let them try. They are deluding themselves in that. This nation, the people of Iraq are going to fight courageously and effectively for as long as it takes them to fight to defend their sovereignty.

PM: It makes it sound like it will be a massive killing ground, if that in fact happens.

TA: We are not killing anybody. They will be killing us, you see, and we will retaliate, and that's legitimate. We are not going to the streets of New York and Washington to fight the Americans. When they come to our towns and cities, we'll fight them.

PM: But how long could you hold out against—

TA: As long as it takes us to defend our country.

PM: But you can see this is the greatest military force that's ever been formed.

TA: It is, but we are not at war with America. We are not fighting the Americans in America. We are fighting the Americans in Iraq, and that's the difference. That gives you an advantage when you are fighting in your own homeland. You know every street, you know every corner, and you have the willingness, the determination to protect your sovereignty, to protect your national interests. This gives you an advantage which the Americans don't have.

PM: You were quoted in an essay by British academic Tony Dodge. I think you made these remarks last September: "People say to me, you, the Iraqis, are not the Vietnamese. You have no jungles and swamps to hide in. I reply: let our cities be our swamps and our buildings our jungles."

TA: That's correct.

PM: So you see yourselves as the new Vietnam?

TA: Well, I don't want to compare my country with another country, because differences are clear, but we do have the potential to defend our cities from the American invaders.

PM: Are you optimistic or pessimistic?

TA: I am optimistic about the future of my nation. I think this nation, which has survived for millenniums, will survive. The Americans are not going to break the will of the people of Iraq. Iraq will survive and Iraq will continue its path of progress and development.

—

AFTER THE INTERVIEW TARIQ AZIZ showed me around his cavernous office, bragging about how it had been rebuilt after being bombed in the 1991 war. He quietly acknowledged that the bombing was almost certain to happen again very soon. It did, but I suspect he knew that this time there'd be no rebuilding, at least not for him. In the chaotic days following Baghdad's fall, Aziz quickly cut a deal and surrendered to U.S. troops, becoming one of the first of the so-called "deck of fifty-five" to end up in American custody. It's said that Aziz was treated like every other prisoner. He was forced to dig his own latrine and allowed few amenities other than to shuffle around a prison yard with his hair uncut.

A few weeks after his surrender, I read in a Jordanian newspaper that his wife, who had been whisked to Amman as part of the original deal with the Americans, was upset that she hadn't been allowed to talk with her husband. She insisted he had been forced, under threat of death, to do Saddam's dirty work, even though he had always looked so comfortable defending the regime. He certainly did the night I met him.

After six years in captivity Aziz finally heard the results of some of the charges against him. Not guilty of crimes against humanity, but guilty of his role in the execution of forty-two merchants who in 1992 had been found guilty of profiteering. His sentence: fifteen years in jail. If he serves all of it, he'll be eighty-seven when released.

BRIAN WILSON

EVEN IN MY SIXTIES, I rarely do up the shoelaces on my runners. I blame the Beach Boys for that. After I first heard their *Surfin' Safari* album in 1963, I became addicted to everything Beach Boys—from the sun-bleached blond hair to the button-down shirts to the belief that a Beach Boy didn't do up his running shoes. Even though we were all sporting the British-invasion look within a year, something about the surfing sound of the California boys has always stayed with me. I can't sit still when I'm driving in the summer and "Good Vibrations" comes on the radio, even though everyone else in the car thinks my pathetic lip-synching and steering-wheel slapping is hilarious.

All this was the fault of one man. Brian Wilson was the artistic genius behind the Beach Boys and he played all the roles: singer, musician, composer, arranger, producer. While his life has been a troubled one of battling drugs, weight, depression and even the rights to the Beach Boys name (he lost), he is by all analyses one of the truly great rock icons of our time. So when producer and amateur musicologist Jasmin Tuffaha came to me and said, "Brian Wilson is coming to town to promote his latest album and his people say he'd love to do an interview with you," both of us were more than eager. I even suggested the untied-runners look. She said "Uh . . . no."

We set up in the balcony of Toronto's historic Massey Hall, where Wilson was due to perform that night. Jasmin had warned me that the sixty-something Wilson was a bit odd and that I should be patient. Right. "Odd" is an understatement. He arrived through a balcony entrance taking baby steps—literally, little tippy-toes across the carpet as if fearful of falling through the floor. After I said hello and shook his hand, I motioned him towards his seat, and he looked at me as if to say, "Why should I sit down?" That was my first hint that he thought the interview was going to be very short, like a few minutes, while my goal was half an hour. This was going to be a challenge. In fact it was more than a challenge, and as a result it ranks in the top ten of all the interviews I've ever done—not only because I'm convinced he almost got up and left within moments of things starting, but also because fighting to keep him in the chair helped me weave a conversation I'll never forget.

2004-10-09

Peter Mansbridge: *One on One* today in historic Massey Hall here in Toronto with the great—and it's the only way to describe him—the great Brian Wilson. Do you ever get tired of hearing yourself described that way?

Brian Wilson: No, I never do. I always get a thrill out of that. And I always will too.

PM: You know they mean it when they say it.

BW: Yeah, I know that.

PM: Your new album, *SMiLE*, is getting amazing reviews

almost wherever you look.

BW: I've been reading them. They're really good.

PM: What do you make of that?

BW: I think people like *SMiLE* because there's not much happening in the industry now, right? So I think people like *SMiLE*
because it's new, innovative music.

PM: It's new and innovative, but in a way it's old, isn't it?

BW: It's old in that it's drawing back to 1966. But it's new
because we finished it in 2004.

PM: But when you first started it, you felt that it was too
advanced.

BW: Well, Peter, we thought we were too far ahead of our time,
so we shelved it for thirty-eight years.

PM: Now why was it too advanced?

BW: We could tell that it was too advanced because we have good
heads. We could see what's going on.

PM: What was it about it?

BW: It was scary. It was very deep music. I can't explain it any more.

PM: But something obviously was affecting you to write it back
then. It was such a far different time than we live in now. As your
album says on the cover, Bobby Kennedy was still alive, Martin
Luther King was still alive, LBJ was the president. It's a much
different world we live in now, and yet it still connects now.

BW: The world is so crazy, you know. And I know *SMiLE* brings people back down to the Earth. It makes them feel at home because we're all—well, at least I spaced to the moon there for I don't know how many years.

PM: Yeah, we'll talk about that in a few minutes, but I want to try and understand a little more about what your message was then that people are responding to so well now.

BW: I can't answer that question. I will not be able to answer that question.

PM: Okay. There were some who felt that one of the reasons you didn't release it back then is the competitive nature between—

BW: The Beatles and us? No, it had nothing to do with the Beatles. We were working on *SMiLE* way before *Sgt. Pepper* came out. We were inspired by the Beatles, but not in competition.

PM: Tell me about that time and how that happened. How were you inspired?

BW: Paul McCartney and I met each other and he said, "I'm going to kick your butt"—in music.

PM: Really?

BW: "Just you watch." Yeah, he did say that.

PM: He really said that? When was this?

BW: In 1967. He says, "I'm going to kick your butt." I said, "Well, go ahead." Anyway, that's the most he said to me up until this year.

PM: And what did you make of it when he said that?

BW: I said he was a supreme egotist to say that to me.

PM: Was he kidding or was he serious?

BW: I don't know. I never found out.

PM: But did it scare you?

BW: Yeah, it scared me. Of course.

PM: This was right around the time of *SMiLE*, wasn't it?

BW: Right. Right around that time.

PM: And that inspired you to write *SMiLE*?

BW: It inspired me to write *SMiLE*. We were on drugs; our heads were all messed up. Let's go on to some new questions. Let's be done! Ha ha! Let's have some new questions happening here.

PM: Okay. One last question on McCartney, because, you know, that was a long time ago. Now you have a much different relationship. In fact, you produced a single of his on an earlier album of yours this year.

BW: Yeah, I produced him on a song called "A Friend Like You."

PM: And what was that experience like?

BW: Oh, it was a thrill, a big thrill for me to work with Paul McCartney. It was quite a thrill.

PM: He wasn't the supreme egotist?

BW: No, no, he'd mellowed out by then. He's real nice to me now.

PM: Tell me about your beginnings in music.

BW: My musical thing started when I was about ten years old. My dad taught me the boogie-woogie and from then on I was self-taught. No one ever taught me how to play the piano. I learned from Chuck Berry, Phil Spector, Little Richard, Fats Domino—you know, I learned from all the greats. I learned how to play rock 'n' roll piano.

PM: When you say you learned from them, you learned by watching them?

BW: No, I literally learned by listening to their records. Put on "Be My Baby" and I'd listen to the rhythm and it inspired me to want to write music.

PM: And you never took a formal piano lesson?

BW: Never took a formal lesson, no.

PM: And you also have a hearing issue.

BW: My right ear is shot to death. I can't hear out of it.

PM: Since birth?

BW: Yeah. It's shot. There's nothing to hear, so I have my left ear.

PM: So that's your musical ear then?

BW: Yeah. I overcompensate with my left ear. It works way better than most people's left ears. That's what they tell me anyway. That's what my mom told me.

PM: But what does that mean? Are you hearing in mono?

BW: I hear mono. I don't get to hear the spatialness of a room with people talking, or going to Disneyland and hearing all these sounds. I get to hear them mono.

PM: So you pick up the art, you learn, you become creative yourself.

BW: Yeah.

PM: With your brothers, a cousin and a friend, you write your first song.

BW: When I was nineteen—"Surfer Girl."

PM: Tell me about that.

BW: I was in my car and I was going, "Ba, ba, ba, ba, ba, ba," out of nowhere. I was just humming a melody. I drove right to my house and finished it. In about an hour, finished the whole song.

PM: And then you got the boys together and—

BW: Got them together and kicked butt. We kicked butt with that one.

PM: Now you've got "Surfer Girl," "Surfer," "Surf City," "Surfing USA"—you've got all these surfing songs, but you don't surf.

BW: I never learned. I was always afraid to learn.

PM: So what was it about surfing that it became such a dominant part of those early songs?

BW: That was my brother Dennis's idea, for a surf song. It was his idea to write surf songs.

PM: What about the ocean? Does the ocean mean anything to you?

BW: The ocean doesn't do it for me, no. I'm scared of the ocean.

PM: Scared of the ocean?

BW: Yes, I'm scared of the waves and the ocean.

PM: You know, it must be hard to describe that to millions of fans who grew up listening to you as the Beach Boys—the surf songs, all about the ocean.

BW: And yet I don't like the ocean.

PM: You don't surf, you don't like the ocean.

BW: I like playing on the beach and getting a tan, but I don't like going in the water. I think the ocean is very beautiful and the sand is beautiful, but the shore, the waves are too scary for me, so I never did it.

PM: What was that music saying to that generation?

BW: It was saying, "Get going, get out, surf and be happy, and get some California sunshine." That's what it meant.

PM: Do you like touring? I mean, you're back touring now.

BW: I like touring because it's fun work. You can both work and have fun on tour.

PM: But there was that period in the sixties that lasted for some time where you said you didn't want to tour.

BW: I didn't want to tour at all. Oh, yeah. I didn't tour from 1965 to 1978. Then I toured through the eighties and then I stopped touring completely. Then in 1998 I started a solo career, which was my wife's idea. I owe her all my love for that. She gave me my solo career.

PM: There were the years when you were troubled with depression, alcohol, drugs. Some would describe them as kind of the "lost years." Maybe you wouldn't. I'm not sure how you best describe it.

BW: It was alcohol and drugs, yeah, that messed me up.

PM: And that was from the lifestyle on the road?

BW: Just at home. When I went on the road I didn't drink. At home I was an alcoholic.

PM: And what did that do to you?

BW: It made me not want to work. Made me lazy and made me drugged out.

PM: But you were still creative during that period, were you not?

BW: I was creative, yeah, but not as creative as when I was off the booze, you know.

PM: How long did that last?

BW: About ten years.

PM: And that was a period where, for the most part, you just stayed in your house.

BW: Right.

PM: And were you totally disconnected from the world of music?

BW: I was. What I did was I took so much drugs that I sealed myself off from the business.

PM: What kind of drugs?

BW: LSD, marijuana, amphetamines, cocaine, Seconal—all kinds of drugs.

PM: Did that do anything for you in the creative world?

BW: Okay, you're right, it did help me to be more creative, but the price of taking the drugs was too heavy a price.

PM: And the price was what?

BW: The price was you have to come down off the drugs and be without drugs. Like a heroin addict: as soon as he kicks his heroin habit, he can't go back to drugs.

PM: And have you ever gone back?

BW: Have I? No.

PM: So you're off drugs, off alcohol.

BW: Yeah.

PM: I guess I was asking about this issue of the connection of drugs with being creative because you'll see with some of the great artists—whether it's music or painting, acting—they're troubled by something, and some of them draw strength from that trouble.

BW: That's what I went through, exactly what I went through.

PM: Not depression, though?

BW: No, depression is something that comes and goes. I've had periods of two years with no depression. I really was depressed in the 1990s, and about 1999, when I started my solo career, I felt a lot better and I didn't feel as depressed.

PM: That period when you were disconnected from the real world because of drugs—how has that period changed your music?

BW: It made me write songs like "'Til I Die." It made me write very deep songs. I wrote about what I was going through.

PM: Tell me about that.

BW: I was going through a lot of mental, emotional fear because of auditory hallucinations that I have in my head.

PM: Hearing voices.

BW: Right. And it bummed me out to hear the voices telling me they're going to kill me, I'm going to get murdered and all that stuff. It bummed me out.

PM: You still hear those voices?

BW: Yeah, I still do.

PM: And how do they explain that to you? Or how do you explain it to yourself?

BW: I just say, look, I took drugs, and the drugs created some auditory hallucinations. That's all I can tell you.

PM: And when does this happen? When you're alone, or—

BW: Mostly when I'm alone, yeah.

PM: But does it happen when you're playing music?

BW: No, not at all, no, no.

PM: So music is the release then?

BW: Music is my saviour, yeah.

PM: What's it like being on the road, on tour now compared with the Beach Boys?

BW: I'm much happier because my band is so heavy and it's such a great band to play with. And they sing better than the Beach Boys. They're superior musicians. They're an eclectic bunch of people that I have.

PM: Better than the Beach Boys?

BW: Better than the Beach Boys will ever be, absolutely.

PM: Do you say that because you've lost that name now?

BW: No, I'm telling you the truth. We're way better than the Beach Boys. I go out as Brian Wilson, you know, with my band.

PM: Do you ever miss those days at all?

BW: Not at all, no. I don't miss them at all. I never talk to Mike Love or Bruce Johnston, haven't talked to them for eight years. When my brother Carl died, it kind of screwed things up between us, so we stopped talking.

PM: But Mike Love was the person you wrote many of those early songs with.

BW: I wrote some of the early surfing songs with Mike. Then I started working with Tony Asher and Van Dyke Parks, you know.

PM: Does it hurt not to be able to talk to somebody you started with so long ago?

BW: It hurts me because I feel like there's a bad vibe that came between us because of all that time not talking. Otherwise, now I still have good memories to think about.

PM: When you look back at your catalogue of songs.

BW: Right.

PM: What are the ones at the top for you?

BW: Okay. I'll tell you my top Beach Boy songs that I like.

PM: Good.

BW: First, "California Girls."

PM: Because?

BW: Because it's happy and it's got a shuffle beat. I like the shuffle beat. And I like "Surfer Girl" because it's a sweet ballad, and "God Only Knows" because it makes people cry, and "'Til I Die" because it's a very, very, very heavy record about how you feel so small in the universe. And "In My Room" because it's a spiritual idea about being in your room and you don't have to be afraid at night. So those are my favourites.

PM: So do you not count "Good Vibrations"?

BW: "Good Vibrations" doesn't count because it drives me crazy every time I sing it.

PM: No!

BW: I'm getting tired of "Good Vibrations," I really am. It brings back so many memories I don't want to think about.

PM: But it's on this album.

BW: I know it is. It was my wife's idea to put it on the album, to finish the album with it. Otherwise I wouldn't have done it.

PM: But it brings back difficult memories?

BW: Difficult memories, yes.

PM: Because it's not an issue of singing the same song over again.

BW: No, I could sing the song and do it without fucking screwing up. But I can't deal with the memories. So I have to go *through* "Good Vibrations" rather than have a good time with "Good Vibrations."

PM: So what happens on stage when you sing it now?

BW: Nothing. People love it. They think it's a great record.

PM: It is a great record. But is it hard for you to do it?

BW: No, not at all. I get the memories while I'm doing it, but I can get over those after I'm through with it.

PM: What do you think of modern pop music?

BW: I don't like it. You mean like of the '90s and the 2000s? I don't like it. You like it?

PM: You know, we're of a same similar age. Do you think it's because we're just too old?

BW: We're not too old. It's just I don't agree with all that rap music. I think it's not a positive thing.

PM: So there's nothing you see in modern pop music?

BW: Nothing. There's nothing that I would even listen to. I gave it a real good chance. I would listen to TV, MTV, listen to the radio, go to concerts. And my final opinion was, it's not for me. Not for me.

PM: Because it's not music or—

BW: It's destructive, negative, unpleasant music. That's the only way to describe it.

PM: Now when you look out at audiences, you're not just seeing old Beach Boys fans, are you? They're obviously all Brian Wilson fans, but are you seeing some of the young people that you think perhaps are not being well served by that kind of pop music?

BW: I see some young people enjoying the *SMiLE* album. I do see some people enjoying it.

PM: But it's mainly people who are our generation, or are you seeing a mix?

BW: I see a mix, a little bit of mix, but mostly our generation, yeah.

PM: And how do you feel about that?

BW: I'm right in my right place. I love my generation, I love all those guys. I grew up with all those people.

PM: They grew up with you.

BW: Right, they grew up with me.

PM: Is it hard sometimes when you're standing up there, when you look out at the audience and you see them mouthing all the words to your song?

BW: They know my music, which makes me feel proud. I feel pretty proud, and that's about it for me. . . . You are a good interview. You are a good interview, sir.

PM: We're having a good time.

BW: You are a good interview.

PM: So can I now go up on stage with you?

BW: You can sing "Good Vibrations" with me.

PM: "Good Vibrations"!

BW: You can sit in my seat and sing "Vibrations" for an hour.

—

ON BOTH OCCASIONS WHEN WE BROKE for commercials, Wilson started to get up as if the interview was over. I pleaded with him to hang on: "Just a few more minutes to go." At one point I looked over at my producer, Jasmin, for guidance, but she offered me nothing in return, not even a glance. She was afraid she'd burst out laughing—or start crying. I was on my own.

At the end of it all, another surprise. We stood up and Brian Wilson, my rock idol, looked at me and said, "Give me a hug, Peter." And there we were, two old guys in the balcony of Massey Hall, hugging. For the record, our shoelaces were tied.

BILL CLINTON

I FIRST TOLD MY BILL CLINTON story in a *Maclean's* magazine column in 2004. It's one of my favourites because it was such an honest moment in a business that, let's face it, can come across as so staged.

While thousands of people waited outside a downtown Toronto bookstore for his arrival, I waited for my allotted fifteen minutes with the former president on the fifteenth floor of one of the city's finest hotels. Clinton, notorious in office for keeping people waiting, has retained that trait. Our cameras had been ready for more than an hour, wedged into a suite that had the beds shuffled out of the way to give the room the appearance of a colonial living room.

Suddenly, with a half-dozen or so Secret Service agents at his side, out of the elevator stepped the forty-second president of the United States, running about an hour late. Understandably, the arrival caused a commotion. A Michigan couple and their daughter, visiting Toronto, had been standing in their doorway, and Clinton stopped to chat, allowed pictures to be taken and signed some copies of the book he was hustling while in town. Then came one of those unscripted moments you always hope for but rarely see.

The door of the room immediately next to the Michigan family's slowly opened and out stepped a thirty-something guy in his underpants, with bed-head and morning beard, fingers rubbing his eyes, mumbling, "What's all the racket about?"—followed by the jaw-dropping exclamation, "That's Bill Clinton!" The Secret Service agents weren't sure whether to smile or reach for whatever they had on their belts, while the man who used to be the most powerful person in the world simply bellowed with laughter, stuck out his hand and shook the poor chap completely awake. Clinton looked totally in his element and treated the guy like he was a long-lost college roommate.

Later I tapped on the fellow's door and asked what his story was. He'd flown in from Boston late the night before and had a big business meeting scheduled for the afternoon, so he had been sleeping late. When he woke to the racket outside his room, he got up and peeked through the little spy-hole in the door. He could see only camera flashes, the backs of heads, and heard what he thought was a familiar voice. So he opened the door.

As for Clinton, when we eventually sat down for our chat, and before the cameras rolled, I asked whether he'd ever before been confronted with anything quite like that. He shook his head, laughed and said that moment was a first. Then the interview started and it was on to Iraq, Bush and bin Laden.

2004-09-11

Peter Mansbridge: Mr. President, welcome to Canada. Latest stop on the book tour—is your signing hand getting a little sore yet?

Bill Clinton: Not yet. Every now and then I have to ice it down, but it's doing all right.

PM: They tell me you handwrote the book.

BC: I did.

PM: So the long-lost art of handwriting is not a problem for Bill Clinton.

BC: I wrote it in twenty-one notebooks, something like that.

PM: In our time together I want to ask you about a couple of things you mention in the book. I'm going to start with a story you told about when you were ten years old. It was 1956. Your family got its first television set. You talk about the different things you watched, including the political conventions that summer. And you were, I think the word you used was "transfixed," by watching the political dynamic on television.

BC: I was.

PM: What I wonder is, now, almost fifty years later, are young Americans, and young Canadians for that matter, transfixed by the political process?

BC: I don't know. I think that there's a lot more competition for their interests. They have a lot more sources of information. And the press coverage tends to be a lot more critical today. But I would hope they would be. One of the reasons I wrote this book is to show people that politics is an honourable vocation, that most people, whatever their political views, honestly believe what they say, and try to do what they say they're going to do. And that there are significant consequences to the way we live. I got that, but I grew up after World War II. There was not much cynicism. We believed in the system, we believed in our leaders. And the press coverage was less cynical. Everything was different. But I was thrilled as a ten-year-old boy watching those conventions, both the Republican and the Democratic conventions. And interested in it.

And one of the reasons I wrote this book, and one of the reasons I do interviews and do book signings, is to try to inspire young people to believe that freedom is a responsibility as well as a gift, and a great opportunity to have a more interesting life. But you have to be aware. You have to know what's going on and you have to participate.

PM: But why don't you think they seem to be buying in to that? Your country's seen a drop in the voter turnout rate. So has this country.

BC: Yeah.

PM: A significant drop.

BC: I think part of it is the success of our countries, you know? People think things are going to be all right regardless, and so that doesn't matter as much as if they vote. And part of it is a growing sense of cynicism. People think they believe the politicians aren't all that different, may not be straight and there are no consequences. That's largely a function of changing press coverage. All I can tell you is, in my country, I think politics is more honest than it was thirty or forty years ago, but people think it's less honest.

PM: Why is that?

BC: The different press coverage—basically, the atomization of the press in America. You know, we don't have just three big networks now. We have four big networks and lots of cable networks, and lots of different competition. When you balkanize the press coverage, you cut it up and everybody's trying to get a little angle, a little this, a little of that. And if you're not careful it becomes more negative because it's necessary to be more sharp to get your segment of the market to listen to your view.

PM: Is it fair to blame the messenger on this one?

BC: No. Actually, I'm not blaming them. I don't think there's any way they can avoid it. I think that Vietnam and Watergate and all that tended to make the media sceptical of people in power and the prospect of abuse of power. But I think it got overdone in my country. I think largely it's been the changing nature of the competition. The increasing segmentation of the media has led to greater competition and has required a certain sharpness that may be entertaining in the moment. But the cumulative impact of it may be for people to think either that politicians are less honest or less committed or less hard-working than they are, or that the work itself is less serious than it is.

Though I actually believe it's shifting back. I think the media in America since 9/11, for example, has tended to be—it's not that they're never critical anymore. Sometimes they're critical of President Bush; sometimes they're critical of things I did as president. But there's a more serious tone to it, you know, a certain sense that shows that politics matters again. And there's been a lot of interest amongst citizens in this campaign in our country. When I ran in '92, I felt this. It was the only time since the eighteen-year-olds got to vote in America that a majority of eighteen- to twenty-one-year-olds voted. I believe that in this election [2004] a majority of young people will vote again. So I'm hopeful that the combined effect of all these events has convinced people politics matters again.

PM: Let me talk about the election underway in your country now. We just finished one, as you know. And the ballot question seemed to be "Who do you trust? Who do you trust to protect the values that you see as important to your country?" in our case. What's the ballot question that's shaping up for this fall in your country? Is it Iraq?

BC: It is, but I think the real question is, what are we going to do now? I disagreed with attacking them before the U.N. inspectors had finished their jobs.

PM: That's not to say that you wouldn't have attacked?

BC: Well— No, no. If Hans Blix, the U.N. inspector, had said, "Saddam Hussein has weapons of mass destruction and won't give them up," or if Hans Blix had said, "I will never be able to certify him because he won't co-operate," then I would have supported attacking. Strongly. So I would have voted for that resolution in the Senate to give them the authority.

But the whole idea was, the whole premise for those of us who cared about weapons of mass destruction was that we didn't know. Keep in mind, I bombed Saddam Hussein for four days in '98. I didn't know whether we got rid of that stuff or not, but I thought there was a serious chance he had weapons of mass destruction. He did in '95 when his sons-in-law defected—they told us what he had. We uncovered huge stashes of this stuff. So I would have supported that.

PM: But what if Hans Blix had said, "I can't see any evidence of weapons of mass destruction." Would you have believed him over your own intelligence agencies?

BC: Yeah, I would have. It's not a question of believing him over the intelligence agencies, but that the intelligence was ambiguous on the point, really. The British intelligence had all that business about him having yellowcake to use to make a nuclear weapon from Niger, but the CIA told the White House that wasn't true. I certainly would have believed it enough to put it off and try to build more support. What was the hurry? Look where we are now. Who's the threat from? Iraq? Saddam Hussein? No, from bin Laden and al Qaeda. How do we know about the threat? Because the Pakistanis got this computer and gave it to us so it could be analyzed. Why did we put our number-one security threat in the hands of the Pakistanis, with us playing a supporting role, and put all of our military resources into Iraq—which was, I think, at best our number-five security threat? In other words, how did we get to the point where we have 130,000 troops in Iraq and 15,000 in Afghanistan? We now know that al Qaeda is an ongoing, continuing threat, even though when I was president, we took down over twenty of their cells. They still had enough left to do 9/11. And since then, in the Bush years, they've taken out over twenty of their cells. But they're operating with impunity in that mountainous region, going back and forth between Pakistan and Afghanistan. And we have only 15,000 troops in that country.

PM: Is that why bin Laden and al-Zawahiri haven't been caught?

BC: We don't know. But we know one thing: we'd have a better chance of catching him if we had 150,000 troops there than if we had 15,000.

PM: Why is it so hard, for not just America, but—this country's had a couple of thousand people in Afghanistan in support of that operation—why has it been so hard to find bin Laden?

BC: First of all, he is a very smart, well-funded, well-organized man with fanatical followers. Secondly, Afghanistan is a big, rough, mountainous, remote country. You know, a lot of the best-laid plans of humanity have been buried in Afghanistan. The point I'm trying to make is, we'll never know if we could have gotten him, 'cause we didn't make it a priority. Because we basically have said to President Musharraf now, in Pakistan, "Please help us." He said okay. He has changed sides, in effect. He's no longer ambivalent; he's clearly trying to help us.

PM: That concern you had about Pakistan is no longer?

BC: No. I think he's plainly on our side. He's risked his life. He's survived two assassination attempts. But the fact that he's survived two assassination attempts shows you that there are still Pakistanis who are sympathetic with the Taliban and al Qaeda. But we basically are dependent on him to find bin Laden, to find al-Zawahiri, to break in and find the computer people and give it to us, because we've got all our resources somewhere else—in Iraq.

PM: I just want to ask one last question, as it relates to this and it touches back to a story, an anecdotal tale in the book about your early years in Washington, when you were working as an aide to Senator Fulbright. You talk about moving material back and forth to the Foreign Relations Committee—the envelopes marked "secret and confidential." I wanted to ask you whether you were allowed to open those, but you did open them and read them.

BC: I did. I had a security clearance, so it was permissible for me to read them. I didn't open them in the middle of transporting them, but when I loaded them I sometimes read them, and I was permitted to do so because I had a clearance.

PM: They made a great impact on you, because what you read was not what the American people were hearing about the Vietnam War.

BC: That's right.

PM: I'm wondering now how much the American people really know about 9/11, how much they really know about what happened in Iraq, and what continues to happen in Iraq, and the fight on bin Laden. Is the same situation possible now as was possible that you saw yourself in 1968?

BC: First of all, what I saw in those classified documents that I carried showed that the war in Vietnam was not going as well as the government was asserting. However, fairly close on the heels of that information there were American journalists and global journalists in the field in Vietnam saying exactly what the material I saw said. Now, I believe if you read the 9/11 Commission report, it appeared to me to be factually accurate about what was going on. We've seen a book by Richard Clarke, the man who was responsible for a lot of our anti-terror efforts during the first President Bush's administration and at the beginning of my administration. I read his book with some care. As far as I know, it is factually accurate. So I do think we know more.

I was disturbed that, just a couple of months ago, half the American people still believed that Saddam Hussein had something to do with 9/11. Now, that bothered me. I think that there was a brief period of time after 9/11 when the press coverage went from being super-cynical and negative to super-supportive and uncritical, from that period, in effect, through the early stages of the conflict in Iraq. But my own view is that it's completely understandable. Our country, in fact the whole free world, was in a period of psychological shock. It was disorientating. We all wanted to be strong. We wanted to be united. We wanted to defend freedom, including the freedom of the press. We wanted to stand against fanaticism and the senseless murder of innocent civilians, including in New York, over two hundred of them Muslims. So I think there was a period where we didn't know, and we just suspended critical judgment. I did too. We all do it. And I'm not ashamed of it. But we're sort of back to normal now, and I think people have kind of got it.

I think that the job of politicians in elections is to present clear choices to people as honestly as they can. Obviously you would make the argument so it works for you, but you still don't want to slander your adversary. You want to say, "We had these honest differences. Here's the way I see it. You choose." And if that's done in this election, then I think people will have a feel for where we are in Iraq and a feel for where we are in Afghanistan.

PM: Mr. President, you remain an optimistic person about the future at a time when it can be easy to be pessimistic.

BC: Yeah, that's the one thing I'll say. I cannot look you in the eye and tell you there'll never be a big terrorist attack in Toronto or that there'll never be another one in America, because we have open societies with people from everywhere. It's that our great joy is our great vulnerability, so I can't say that. But I can tell you that every day there are people in Canada and the United States working together, notwithstanding all our political differences—there are security people, law enforcement people—they're working together and they're making headway on this. No terrorist movement has ever toppled a nation or is capable of toppling freedom in general. It won't happen.

So the most important thing is that we keep our heads about us and we keep going forward. And we don't do anything dumb to compromise the future of our children or the character of our nations as free societies. But I am very optimistic over the long run. Eventually we're going to prevail. I have no doubt about it.

—

EARLIER I MENTIONED THAT THE AGREED-UPON time for my interview was fifteen minutes. While it's rare for a guest to leave exactly when the time expires, funny things often happen. In Clinton's case, first it was a staffer standing just outside the room with his cellphone, which had been silent for fifteen minutes but started ringing in the sixteenth. Then, as we moved past the twenty-minute mark (and clearly Clinton wanted to keep going—no wonder he's always late), his communications person, who was sitting behind me, started coughing—and coughing—and coughing. It almost ruined a great answer, and it did bring things to an end. Coincidence? You decide.

Oh yes, one final note on our visiting businessman from Massachusetts: they were boxers, not briefs. Clearly not a Clinton man.

PAUL WATSON

IN MY EARLY DAYS OF JOURNALISM I mainly covered traffic accidents, fires and school board meetings. They were challenging stories, and ones that are the staple of all young journalists looking to make their way in the profession. Nonetheless I was always searching beyond the city limits, fascinated by some of the great international stories of the time. And there were few bigger in the late sixties and early seventies than the Vietnam War. I'd watch the coverage on every network possible, in both Canada and the United States, marvelling at how close up the cameras could get to the conflict, closer than in any previous war. When one of our cameramen, Ernie Einarson, was asked to fill in for the CBC's regular Hong Kong–based crew, he leapt at the chance. He was gone for about a month, saw lots of action and couldn't wait to talk about it.

One thing had always fascinated me. How, with firefights breaking out all around them, could people like Ernie keep their cameras focused on the combat and not dive for cover? Everyone operates differently, but I've never forgotten how Ernie answered that question. He said, "It's like watching television, not recording it." What he meant was that for him, the experience of looking through the eyepiece of his camera made it feel like he wasn't even there. Instead he was simply viewing the scene on a monitor from afar. Now I doubt that many seasoned veterans would call that smart; in fact I've had many tell me that's a sure-fire way to get yourself hurt. But on that assignment and at that time, it worked for Ernie.

Paul Watson knew exactly where he was, what was in his camera's sights, the impact it would •have and the potential danger it placed him in as he started clicking away in Somalia on October 4, 1993. He'd gone to that African nation to cover the United States' attempt to bring order to a country in chaos, a land run by warlords and drug lords who were constantly fighting each other while the Somali people suffered from extreme starvation. Watson was working for the *Toronto Star*, and the pictures he snapped that day would change the course of U.S. foreign policy and win Watson worldwide recognition and a Pulitzer Prize. They would also haunt him for years afterwards.

The pictures were graphic and shocking. The body of a U.S. soldier, Staff Sergeant William David Cleveland Jr., stripped almost completely naked, was being dragged by ropes through the streets of the country's capital, Mogadishu.

2007-09-08

Peter Mansbridge: I want to start with the photograph that you took in October of '93. Anyone who looks at that picture is haunted by it. You took it, and in your book you concede that you're very much still haunted by it.

Paul Watson: Just to hear you describe it takes me back to that place. It's with me, he's with me almost all the time. In stronger moments I can fight him back. In weaker moments I have to beg him, "Please, just leave me alone." I feel guilt for a whole bunch of complex reasons. One, I stole his dignity. The people who beat him and desecrated his corpse did it, but I captured it and amplified it. And I begged him as I was about to do it, when I heard a voice—I'm sure it was his voice—that said, "If you do this I will own you forever." I begged him in reply, "Forgive me, but understand why I have to do this." And I don't— You know, I've tried to free myself from it, but it's still there.

PM: You say in the prologue to your book that the right photo can stop the most powerful army in the world. And that's what happened here.

PW: Right.

PM: So was it the right photo?

PW: It was the right photo in the sense that it proved truth against a lie. You know, I didn't kill Cleveland. I didn't drag his corpse around. All I wanted to do was tell the truth. It seems to me that it's up to the political leaders and the military commanders to have the courage to lead the public. We learned that in Vietnam and seem to have forgotten that, and then suddenly we're learning it all over again. If the public isn't firmly behind the operation, it cannot succeed. It's impossible. Because a few things are going to go wrong; they always go wrong. The bodies are going to mount; over long conflicts they always mount. And then when people figure out they were lied to, support evaporates. So who do you blame for that? Reporters who told the truth, or the political leaders and the commanders who didn't build the support with a strong foundation of truth in the first place? If they had told the truth in mid-September, maybe, you know, what happened on October fourth that I captured never would have happened.

PM: Well, it did happen, and it had significant consequences. Within days the Clinton administration decided that they were going to start withdrawing from Somalia. And as you point out in the book, it took on much bigger proportions, not only in the days and months later, but in the years later, for somebody named Osama bin Laden.

PW: Right. You know, I didn't know it at the time, and I don't think most people did, including intelligence people, that bin Laden himself has bragged about it—they participated in the attacks on U.S. and on foreign forces in Somalia. The burden that I carry now is that it seems to me, if you take eighteen American dead without the photograph of Cleveland being dragged through the streets, you've got a political problem, but it's one that could have been managed. Add the photo to the equation—[Clinton] couldn't stand the heat. He withdrew from Somalia, and then Osama bin Laden can say not only to his followers but to his strategists, "Do you see that we can defeat the world's most powerful army with just the right propaganda picture?" Now, I wasn't led to Cleveland's corpse. I went looking for it for my own reasons. It wasn't a setup event but I fear that they learned something from that. And if I did contribute in any way to their understanding of the power of propaganda, I am deeply sorry for it.

PM: You talked to us about ten years ago for a CBC documentary and you talked about how, if you had the opportunity to talk to the Cleveland family, you would like to do that. Here's what you said back in the 1990s.

> WATSON CLIP: *This is very difficult to say, but if I ever met his family, I don't know if, if I could apologize enough. I don't know if they would ever understand why I did it, and why others in my position would have done it.*

Well, you tried to make that possibility happen.

PW: I did. I made a trip to Arizona, where his mother lives in a trailer home in a compound. And I had this fantasy that I was going to find her in an open field or something and could just knock on her door and introduce myself, and we would embrace and cry on each other's shoulders and make our peace. Anyone who reads the book will find out that my life at least is not quite that fantasy. She refused to see me; she didn't and couldn't speak to me directly because I left a message on her answering machine, which was a mistake. When she heard who I was and why I was there, it just all came flooding back, and she had an emotional breakdown. Her son phoned me. He was angry and said, "Just leave my mother, my family alone. Don't try to contact us."

And I begged him, "Give me ten minutes in a coffee shop of your choosing just to hear me out, to understand who I am." And he said, "I don't want to understand who you are. I don't care who you are. You were somebody doing your job." And that was like a knife to my heart, because the whole reason I'd come there was in hope that they would see me as a human being, just as their son was. Not as somebody—some machine—doing his job, but someone who had reasons to do what he did. I deeply wanted him to understand those reasons and to forgive me in the end. I wanted to be forgiven.

PM: You talk in graphic detail about what happened that day, the day that you first saw Cleveland in the streets. There's one moment of many that I latch on to, and it's when you got back to your hotel and you ran to your room, put the film under the mattress and lay on the bed, listening to the air conditioner whirring. It's almost reminiscent of that scene at the beginning of *Apocalypse Now* where the fellow's lying in his hotel room in Saigon and the fan above is turning, and he's being tortured by the things that he's seen. Did you realize then, that day—just minutes, hours after the event—that this was going to be the beginning of a long journey for you?

PW: I was really very much in the moment, and I remember distinctly saying to myself, "Who the hell do you think you are?" I'd just gotten away with something I shouldn't have gotten away with. And it was such an intense experience that when I hit that bed with the door locked and put the air conditioner on, I just— I lost it. But the fact was, I couldn't lose it for long because I had to get that film out. I didn't have the processing equipment. I didn't have the transmission equipment. All of the regular bureaus had been evacuated weeks earlier. I had to get that film to the airport by going back out into the anarchy, get it onto a United Nations plane and then persuade someone in Nairobi, Kenya, to meet that plane and get it processed and transmitted. Just getting the picture was half a war, and then getting it out was a whole new one.

PM: We tend to forget that these are normal people who live in these cities that we watch getting blown up on the screens and on the front pages of newspapers. Do you still feel that way about them, having seen what you've seen after all this time?

PW: I do. And you know, having heard that clip, it scares me. Because I can hear, even in my voice then, that I liked it too much.

PM: Do you still like it?

PW: Not anymore. I hate it. But I still need it. It's like a drug. It came to define me. And if I don't do just a little of it, just to say I can still do it, I feel like I've failed, like it beat me.

PM: It is tough to read this book. You know, I've seen a few bad things during my career, but nothing compared with what you've seen, page after page here. And you're really left wondering at the end of it—not only the things you've seen but the situations you've put yourself in, the danger that you've been in yourself, personally. Why do you keep doing it?

PW: I don't know if it's arrogance or what it is. But again, I don't really get the pleasure that I once got from it. I hate it now. But I know that there are things that I understand that other people don't, and that if I can get through it safely then I can contribute. I have something important to say. And when you ask about people who live in these cities, in Afghanistan, it just breaks my heart to know the goodness of those people. And the images we get, the stories that I write—I'm guilty of the same thing. I tend to focus on the people who are causing problems. But by far the majority of Afghans are good people who just want the same things we do: better life for their children, security.

In Iraq my life was saved by about a dozen people who formed a circle around me in a mob. And it occurred to me only recently that they were part of that mob in the first place that was stoning, kicking, beating me. And then something clicked in their brains that said, "We've got to save this guy. This is going too far." And then they risked their lives to save mine. That's another thing, frankly, that is part of the addiction. Sure, you see a lot of bad things in these places, but you see the most powerful good. You can't believe the strength of the human spirit that you see in places like that. And as I sit here now trying to figure it out in my mind, I'm sure that's one of the things that draws me back. Because you can see the pettiness in our societies. You know, this is part of what I'm writing about—the war within. The things we do in our day-to-day lives.

PM: I want your thoughts on modern-day war. You say in your book that war is organized killing, and for centuries writers and reporters have been trying to put some kind of meaning to that. You've covered, perhaps, as much of modern-day warfare as anyone else in the last two decades, through Rwanda and Kosovo and Somalia, Iraq, Afghanistan. What is your sense of war today?

PW: I was one of those reporters in Somalia, Rwanda, Kosovo, banging the drum, saying, "Where are the foreign troops? Why aren't they intervening?" And it was in Kosovo that I realized that when we work that way, we're easily fooled. I reached a point in the Kosovo conflict where I thought, the moral lines here are not as clear as I thought they were. You know, can we be tricked by guerrilla armies that aren't strong enough to fight their own fight, who can provoke retaliations against civilians and use that, through us, to get NATO to bomb their enemy? That's a scary thought, and I really think there was an element of that going on in Kosovo. And I wonder if there's an element of that going on in Darfur right now. I don't pretend to know enough about Darfur to even suggest that, but I ask the question because I've seen it happen before. There's just so much evil in war. To me it's a poison, and it toxifies anyone it touches. I found it very hard to find any good intentions in any kind of warfare. I understand that it's necessary sometimes—we're attacked, we have to defend ourselves—but it's a necessary evil. You know, we can't make it any better than that.

PM: Here's the tough one, as if the things you deal with aren't difficult enough already. You have a young child, seven years old, eight years old?

PW: Yes.

PM: What do you say to that child, when you're going off to Iraq or going to Afghanistan, about what it is you're doing? And I ask you that because when you read your book and you see the things you've seen, so often it's young kids that age who are being blown to bits in the streets.

PW: Yeah. I want to keep him innocent as long as he can be innocent. And all I want him to know is that his father loves him. I tell him that a thousand times a day. If something happens to me, I just want him to know that even without me he can have that sense of love. That as long as I was here, he was everything to me. And the rest, I just don't tell him. I don't. I'm naively hoping that he doesn't understand what I do. But maybe that's wrong of me.

PM: Do you see in him any of those kids you've seen?

PW: I do. And the scariest thing is I see some of myself in him. I see distant stares out of car windows when he looks angry.

And I've actually asked him, "What are you angry about?" And he says, "I'm not angry. I'm just thinking." And you know, it's just—it's me speaking. It scares the hell out of me.

—

PAUL WATSON'S BESTSELLING BOOK, *Where War Lives*, chronicles his constant reflection on that day in October 1993. He made a major career-altering decision in the summer of 2009. From covering the wars and conflicts of the Third World, Watson chose to come home, back to Canada, to report for the *Toronto Star* on a very different frontier—the Arctic.

ELLEN JOHNSON-SIRLEAF

EVER SINCE THAT DISASTROUS 1993 interview with Margaret Thatcher that I mentioned at the beginning of this book, I've looked forward to a kind of redemption through the challenge of interviewing other powerful women. A banner day in that personal voyage was September 5, 2002, when over the span of a few hours, in Washington and in Ottawa, I sat down with two of the most powerful women in North America.

The interviews were part of our coverage of the first anniversary of the 9/11 attacks. In Washington the talk was with Condoleezza Rice, George W. Bush's national security advisor. At one point I asked her what moment in that day she remembered most. Her answer was surprising and made a few headlines: she talked about how, after the initial attacks on the World Trade Center and the Pentagon, she and Dick Cheney had been rushed to a White House underground "situation room"; there they learned of United Airlines Flight 93 and how it had just torpedoed into the ground in Pennsylvania. For a few moments, Rice explained to me, everyone in the room was frozen by the possibility that U.S. Air Force jets, scrambled to prevent yet another attack, might have shot down the passenger jet in an effort to protect the city the hijacked plane seemed to be heading towards—Washington. As we all soon learned, that was not what happened; instead, a fight between passengers and hijackers had sent the plane hurtling towards its fate.

As interesting as the Rice conversation was, it was the first interview I did that day that I found even more rewarding. Margaret Bloodworth was far less well-known, but on September 11, 2001, as Canada's Deputy Minister of Transport, she made some of this country's most difficult decisions. Her actions helped establish the defence of Canada during the minutes when no one knew with any certainty exactly what was unfolding in the skies above North America. She convinced her political boss, transport minister David Collenette, to shut down all air traffic over the country. She had dozens of aircraft, destined for the heavily populated cities of central and western Canada, diverted to smaller locations in Atlantic and northern Canada. It was gut-check time in those minutes immediately after the planes flew into the World Trade Center, when no one was sure how many more aircraft might be involved in the plot, where they might be heading or what chaos and destruction they might cause. Margaret Bloodworth didn't flinch when the tough calls had to be made.

She did flinch, though, when I asked to interview her about her decisions. She didn't want to go public with her story and instead wanted to stay anonymous, as most public servants do. I kept trying though, because I wanted Canadians to know who had really made some of the critical decisions that day. Finally I managed to persuade her, but only after enlisting the persuasive powers of the prime minister of the day, Jean Chrétien.

Neither the Rice nor the Bloodworth interview was for *One on One*, so they're not included in this book, but almost five years later I met their match with another powerful woman who does belong here. She was not unelected, as they had been, but was someone "the people" had brought to power, and in that lies the key to her remarkable story.

Ellen Johnson-Sirleaf is the president of Liberia, and those who understand Africa see her as that continent's best example of real democracy. Born in Liberia, educated at Harvard,

Johnson-Sirleaf's rise to power has not been easy. In fact, her determination to achieve democracy has faced constant challenges, including a jail cell where, while she won't admit it, she was almost certainly tortured. Our conversation focused on the struggle all African countries continue to face in trying to determine their own future and the sense that that challenge must be met now, or it may very quickly become too late. But we started on a more personal note.

2007-03-31

Peter Mansbridge: Whenever I read about you or when I see you introduced by other world leaders, there's always a phrase attached to your name: "the first democratically elected woman president of an African nation." What does it mean to you when you hear that?

Ellen Johnson-Sirleaf: I think about the thousands and thousands of women—first in my own country, Liberia, and then in Africa, and I dare say sometimes the world—those thousands who have not had the opportunity to reach their full potential, those whose aspirations and expectations I represent. And I get very humbled, because I know that for them I must succeed.

PM: There must be a great sense of pressure because of that.

EJS: Indeed there is. Because I am the leader of a country that's very complicated, where the challenges are so enormous, and we've got to do a whole lot to succeed. I sometimes just get so overwhelmed. And I think of all those thousands of women out there just watching, monitoring, praying for me. I'm humbled, but on the other hand that rejuvenates me, because I get motivated, I get excited, I get passionate in addressing the tasks that I have to undertake. As I said, they're always in my mind. Everything I do, I know I must do it right for them.

PM: I want to talk about the role of women, not only in your country, but in Africa at large. It has historically been such a male-dominated, chauvinistic society. And for young girls growing up, even considering what you've been able to achieve, the struggle is still so incredibly great in your country. Half the children—boys or girls—only half go to school. Only a quarter of that number are girls. So the odds are stacked against them right from the beginning, are they not?

EJS: Yes, they are. And that's what we're trying to address. In Africa, in traditional societies, even though men dominated through the chieftain system, women had a role. All the leaders gather at a place we call the palaver hut. There have always been the old women who were part of this, whose wisdom was shared with the society. In the resolution of disputes, their voices were heard. Of course, as society modernized and education became a major endeavour, and with resources so scarce, boys got the preference and the girls got left behind. By that I mean they stayed with their mothers. They were forced into early marriages. And that's why today we have the statistic you just quoted. That's our challenge: to reverse it. In Liberia we've tried to do so. We've got a special program supported by individuals and institutions in the United States and other places where we've placed an emphasis on giving scholarships to young girls and training teachers who would go out into rural areas. We've enforced compulsory primary education in public schools and reduced the fees in secondary schools. And as a result of that, enrolment has increased by some 48 percent. And I tell you, much of the increase comes from girls, because before parents couldn't afford to send both girls and boys to school. There's much more to be done, though.

PM: I guess there's also an attempt to change a mindset amongst men and boys. I was reading a quote from a senior United Nations official who talked about rape as a "national pastime" in your country. And your country's not alone on this in Africa. But in your country, how do you go about trying to change that mindset of the role of women?

EJS: That's a tough one. And I must say that I'm saddened when that subject comes up, because much of it is true. Rape is increasingly a big problem in our society. And they're children, they're young girls who are victimized in this way. The Association of Liberian Women Lawyers has tried to address it by making sure they got a very tough law passed against rape, one that makes it a crime against humanity in which the penalties are very severe—you can even get life imprisonment. The problem is enforcing those laws, because our court system is still dominated by men who don't see this as a very serious crime. We've got to find ways to address it. Women's organizations are very active, demonstrating, educating, sensitizing. Of course, as you know, rape is something where silence is a big problem. Young girls, their mothers, their families don't want this to come into the open about what it does to their child or their young girls.

PM: You know, when Canadians listen to your story and hear you talking with the passion you do about this, they will at the same time get a sense of what life must be like for a woman in your country. They've got to be asking, "How did she become president? How did she get through that maze to be where she is now?" Is there a simple answer to that?

EJS: There's no simple answer to that. It's been a long road. Sometimes along that road I wondered if I were going to ever make it to where I am today. I didn't start off wanting to be president as a young girl. My mother was a preacher and a teacher. I thought I'd follow in her footsteps and be an English teacher. You know, I came from a family that, in a way, represented the best and the worst of all in our country—indigenous family, settler family. And I had mothers and fathers who never forgot their roots. My two grandmothers were illiterate. So I came with such a strong sense of the need for equity and the need for change.

And as I went through school, I took a very strong position. I spoke out very vocally on issues, and as I became a young professional I did the same. I happened to have been lucky. I married at seventeen years old, right after high school, and had four boys before I went back to school. My life, I say, was turned upside down. But that gave me a special drive and a special motivation to succeed. And one thing followed another.

I paid a heavy price on this road. I spoke out. I was jailed; I came close to death one or two times in prison. I was exiled so many times. But every obstacle just seemed to restore my commitment and my faith that there had to be something different in our country, that our people did deserve better. I guess in the end I got lucky, because the Liberian people finally said, "She's done enough; she's paid the price. Let's see if a woman will make a difference." And I think, in large measure, that was the conviction of women, and they made it happen.

PM: I want to ask about the challenges that you know you face and how you're dealing with them. I've watched you at a number of conferences where you talk about the pressure to deliver in a post-conflict country like yours. Canadians are aware of this watching the situation in Afghanistan, because so many Canadian troops are there. It's one thing to end the conflict; it's another to deliver for the people their hopes and dreams, or at least to show a possibility for a better world. Talk to me for a moment about that pressure in a post-conflict country and how much time you really have to make a difference.

EJS: I tell you, in a post-conflict situation, when you've just won an election, the expectations of people are raised. And in my case, with the many international contacts and positions I have, those expectations are quite high. Hope is raised and they expect that you're going to do things that transform their lives in the shortest period of time. All the kids will be in school, they'll have a square meal every night, the roads will be fixed and the hospitals and the schools and the clinics will all be functioning again.

Even though you get the support from partners, it doesn't happen that quickly. The records show in Africa that post-conflict countries have a very good chance of slipping back into conflict when those expectations are not met. In our case, I tell people we've got about two years to make a difference. We're already fourteen months into the two years.

We've been a bit lucky. We've gotten a lot of international support, and we've been able to take some very important first steps. And because of that, I think our people are a little more patient. They see things like electricity turned on for the first time in fifteen years—not much of it: a few street lights, a few hospitals. Things like water turning on from a tap, something kids fifteen to twenty years old had never seen—they thought water just came from a bucket. I think that has given them a bit more patience and has stretched out their hope. But we're not out of the woods.

PM: Not out of the woods, for sure. When you look at it, your capital, Monrovia, a city that I understand was built for a population of about half a million, now has almost one and a half million living there, and an unemployment rate of 80 percent. Now, most people would say, "Eighty percent—what can we do about that?" But that has to change.

EJS: That has to and is changing. We've started some emergency employment programs, such as the reconstruction of our infrastructure. We have built them around labour-intensive programs so that we put people to work instead of using machines. To dig the ditches and clear the roads we use labour, to put these young people to work. What we are trying to do is to get our private sector functioning again: our mines, our forestry, our agriculture. Because that's where the major efforts will be in resolving our unemployment problem. Again, that takes some time.

PM: And it takes a belief that the country's going to be stable, so that private companies want to invest that kind of money in the future.

EJS: That is very true. And you know, that's why investment has been a bit slow, because it takes confidence and it takes consistency. It doesn't happen in a year, building the confidence that security will be sustained. But again we've been lucky. One of the major world companies, ArcelorMittal Steel, has recently concluded a renegotiation with us on an investment of $1 billion over a seven-year period in one of our major iron ore mines. And that sends good signals.

As I said, we're not there yet. Many, many investors are still on the fence waiting to see if we'll get past a second year, and a third year. We still have U.N. peacekeeping forces in the country, and that's not a good signal. It's good on the one hand, because it provides protection while we try to train our security forces, but it does tell people that the country's not yet fully secure.

PM: Your country is also one of those African countries that is crippled by debt. The issue of debt relief has dominated so many G-7 and then G-8 meetings about what should be done about this—should we forgive debt? I find it fascinating when you talk about the debt your country has because three-quarters of it is paying interest on the original debt incurred by past governments that were basically spending money on weapons. Now when you make that argument to international groups, looking for relief, what do they say back?

EJS: They express sympathy. "Yes, we know those are the circumstances, but you know," the hard-nosed ones will say, "a debt is a debt is a debt." And there's nothing we can particularly do about that. We're dealing with the major financial institutions whose own viability depends upon them resolving the debt issue without being paid. That's why you have to go through these special arrangements with bilateral partners supporting the repayment of this debt through special facilities. That's what we're trying to do right now. But everybody says and knows that it's not sustainable. It hasn't been serviced since the early 1980s. That's why we have the accumulated interest you referred to.

But again, we're very lucky. We have had some good responses. The United States has played a key leading role in working with us on debt relief under the Heavily Indebted Poor Countries Initiative. The U.K. and Germany have come behind. I walk away with a promise that Canada will work with other partners on our debt issue, and that's very important in the G-8. And I walk away with the hope that we continue to perform the way we are, so that we will get Canada as a strong, bilateral partner.

—

IN THE PERIOD SINCE THAT CONVERSATION a new crisis has settled on Africa, one it shares with the world. The global economic situation has thrown millions of the continent's citizens out of work and threatens the progress that has been made, worrying all African leaders and especially Ellen Johnson-Sirleaf. She says that the very stability of post-conflict countries like hers is at risk and that it makes sense for the world's richest countries to help now, or they may have to spend considerably more on peacekeeping operations later.

DULEEP de CHICKERA

WALKING ALONG A BEAUTIFUL SRI LANKAN beach in January 2005, it was hard to imagine that only days before the waves coming ashore were six metres high and carried enough force to wipe out whole communities. I was in Kalmunai, on the country's eastern coast, a city of about a hundred thousand, where hundreds had been swept away by the tsunami that devastated much of the Indian Ocean basin. One hospital worker told me that corpses had been stacked three or four deep in the small garden area outside the operating room when the hospital finally ordered arriving bodies to be sent elsewhere to be processed.

But strange things happen in places of such devastation, and one was unfolding in front of me. Amidst the ruins of the coastal neighbourhood, a group of young children was playing soccer. They'd been watching me record a "stand-up," a short talk to camera for that night's *National*, and when I'd finished I joined them by kicking the ball around a bit. Suddenly a young girl— she couldn't have been more than eight—noticed I was wearing a Canadian flag pin on my jacket. She pointed at it and said in halting English, "Ca-na-da good." I asked our translator to find out more, and the answer involved a vaccination the children had received earlier that day from a group of Canadian nurses who were hoping to prevent the kind of problems, from dysentery to cholera, that often flourish in post-disaster conditions.

It took us a while, but we tracked the nurses down. Within days of the tsunami they'd taken time off from work, flown from Vancouver to Sri Lanka on their own tab and volunteered to go anywhere, do anything to help. As a result one little girl will, for the rest of her life, I'm sure, associate Canada with good. And how lucky are we for that?

Finding a nice story in a wash of horror is always heartening, and there's no doubt we do try to find them. Viewers can take the pain of watching tragedy for only so long before they become desperate to see solutions that can lift the human spirit. If not, they simply switch off. I'm convinced that stories such as the one about the Vancouver nurses, and similar pieces concerning help from aid groups and military assistance units, helped do that. However, all that good doesn't fix the reality that events such as the tsunami are dominated by death and destruction. Not for the first time, a disaster story was making me question my belief in a greater being, one that is supposed to protect the helpless and the innocent. Standing amidst the rubble, it's hard to be a believer. So, before I left Sri Lanka, I wanted to interview a person of faith who could try to explain the contradiction.

While I was off packaging the day's news for *The National*, I asked *One on One* producer Jasmin Tuffaha, who was back in Toronto, to work the phones to try to find someone who could fill that bill. She did just that when she found a gentle and thoughtful man, Duleep de Chickera, the bishop of Sri Lanka's capital city, Colombo. We met in the quiet stillness of a weekday morning in the front-row pews of his church.

2005-01-22

Peter Mansbridge: I want to talk about faith, and how it's tested at a time like this. Where was God on December 26?

Duleep de Chickera: Well, that's a question we've been asking. It's not a new question. You may be aware that we are a people who have faced a great deal of violence and conflict and division. But this was a question that has come up with some new intensity. It affected all communities, and people of faith have been struggling with this question. How does a god of love, the creator God— how does one explain such a god in circumstances like this? There's no easy answer. It calls for reflection. Conversation and dialogue amongst people within the community of faith helps, and this is something that our churches have now asked for: a dialogue, trying to find answers to the very question that you raised.

PM: How do you answer it when someone comes to you and says, "How can a god allow this to happen?"

DC: This is certainly not God's doing, but it happened, and for some reason it was allowed to happen. Now that's the focal point of your question. And we need to press on with this quest. It's a quest of faith, but it must be a quest of faith in which you have your feet rooted on the ground.

PM: Does it not seem so unfair not only that incredible numbers of people lost their lives, but that the overwhelming majority who lost their lives were the poor, the dispossessed? How does one explain that?

DC: This is a recurring question. It's a question that people asked in Psalms as well: the question of evil; the question of suffering; who's responsible; why do the evil prosper; why do the righteous suffer; why do the poor suffer; why are the poor exploited. One catches a glimpse of an answer to this question in the life and death of Jesus. The incarnation teaches that God was in Jesus. And in circumstances of hardship and inconvenience and suffering, God walks likewise, God does likewise. And I think that's the starting part of the spirituality, which leads from there to a theology. That God identified God's self not simply with people, but with the lowly, the poor, the exploited. So you have this incarnation of God becoming human, human becoming servant and servant dying as a criminal. It's as if from step to step, God in Jesus is stepping further away from privilege and dominance into vulnerability, saying to the whole world, "I am present when this kind of suffering takes place." Now that's the message the Church has got to understand and reinterpret.

PM: How much trouble have you had trying to explain it to yourself? You're from this country. You grew up in Hikadua. There was a terrible, terrible train derailment there as a result of the tsunami. Has it been a struggle for you personally, even as Bishop of Colombo?

DC: Indeed. I've had my share of sleepless nights like lots of others. This is a challenge that brings people together. One has got to learn to do one's personal reflection but also come together with other persons of faith so that God will give us some shared light in these circumstances.

PM: You talked earlier about how the different faiths have been very much trying to talk together to deal with this situation, and that's unusual here, in a country that's had such deep differences on the political level and on the religious level. Could it be that this happened to try and encourage that new kind of unity on so many different levels?

DC: That it happened for a new unity, I'm not so sure. Now that it has happened, can a new unity emerge out of it? I hope so, and I hope so very dearly.

PM: Tell me about those hopes and those dreams that you have. What would you see in a new Sri Lanka?

DC: I would see a growth of trust among communities, a sharing of that which is best in one's ethnic or religious tradition with others, enriching the other because of what I am. I would also like to see the strong reach out to the vulnerable, regardless of one's culture or ethnic background. I would like to see a change of lifestyle for the poor, who have been forgotten and who have been extremely patient. I would like to see them living with a sense of dignity. And I would like to see all communities enjoying equal rights. I know this is very much an idea, but what I'm really suggesting is that we walk towards this. There will be recurring crises—that's what history teaches—but if we can learn from each of these crises then I think the sharing and the interdependence that we long for is going to be slightly more possible.

PM: So we may, we just may be looking at a turning point here.

DC: Yes, we're beginning to see signs of a turning point, but it's too early. My fear is that we can very easily return to our prejudices and our differences, and this is where we need the leadership that can anticipate that and prevent that. This is also where we need a vibrant people's spirituality and movement to prevent that from happening.

—

WHEN THOSE WHO DO THE COUNTING and the adding had finished their work, it was determined that 225,000 people in eleven different countries lost their lives because of the tsunami. It was one of the deadliest natural disasters in recorded history.

Many critics of television news suggest that we rush to the scene of disasters because we're ghouls, that we subscribe to the "if it bleeds it leads" style of journalism. I reject that. If we wanted gory stories every night, believe me, the material exists and is available all day, every day. In the case of the tsunami, though, intensive media coverage helped rather than hurt. It helped drive the people of the world to donate billions of dollars in aid, much of it going to help communities across the region, like Kalmunai, Sri Lanka, to recover and rebuild.

BILL GATES

MUCH HAS BEEN SAID ABOUT the spectacular home Bill and Melinda Gates have built into the side of a hill just outside Seattle, Washington. The building is massive and so is the acreage it sits on, so much so that the annual property taxes alone are said to be just under a million dollars. As I was flying to Seattle to interview Gates at his Microsoft headquarters, I read how there were dozens of plasma televisions on walls throughout his home, not to view programming but to display images of famous works of art. My first thought on that was not flattering—it somehow seemed rather cheap to me. After all, this is the richest guy in the world. Why doesn't he just buy the real thing?

A few hours later I was sitting in a comfy chair in a room Microsoft uses for its senior executives to conduct interviews. It was set up to look like a living room, and from the decor I surmised it was probably the closest I was ever going to get to sitting in Gates's actual living room. There on the wall was a plasma television with a famous Monet on the screen. And, I must admit, it looked fantastic. Perhaps Gates was right about this televised artwork thing.

Then the man himself entered the room, the trademark rumpled sweater over his open-necked button-down shirt. Usually in these sessions it takes a few minutes for the crew to get things ready for the cameras to roll: microphones have to be pinned on shirts or sweaters, the lighting has to be adjusted and backgrounds have to be checked. This is where a degree of small talk enters the atmospheric equation. Weather gets a bit boring, so I chose to talk about how surprised I was that the Monet image came off looking so striking on the plasma screen. He nodded and said, "Yes, they are fantastic monitors." But he clearly wanted to add something else, so he leaned towards me and ventured, "And they've really come down in price." It's true, of course, and therefore a perfectly reasonable thing to say, but somehow it sounded odd coming from the richest man in the world, whose estimated worth at the time was $58 billion. I sat there staring at him, imagining Bill Gates doing a Sunday afternoon price check at the local Costco.

When we started the interview, though, it wasn't how he spent his money personally that I wanted to focus on, but how he and his wife were using a significant portion of it for the greater good of the planet. Sounds easy, but as I discovered, giving money away has its challenges.

2007-02-10

Peter Mansbridge: I want to start by talking about the Bill & Melinda Gates Foundation that you and your wife have set up, and the billions of dollars that you're putting aside for work in global health and fighting poverty. I read somewhere—I think it might have been your friend Warren Buffett—that it's actually easier to make money than it is to give it away. He was talking about giving money away in a responsible way, looking for a result. Is that true?

Bill Gates: Well, there's a way of looking at it that makes that true, which is that when you make money, you're always getting feedback—you know, which products don't sell, which ones are selling more than you expect. And so you have constant market signals that are showing you where the best path may lie. In the case of giving money away, you start on something like designing a new medicine to cure malaria or to cure AIDS and you're not certain if that'll work or not, and you'll often have difficulties delivering it in countries where the people are very poor or the government infrastructure's not there or there are not many doctors. And so you have to be a bit careful. I guess it'd be easier to be fooled in philanthropy, but I don't think in the final analysis it's really any harder than in innovation.

PM: How do you try not to be fooled? I assume you go about this, as you hint, the same way you've gone about business: you're looking for results, you're looking for successes. And there must be a certain degree of accountability associated with that. How do you do that?

BG: The Foundation for Global Health is looking to save millions and millions of lives. There are a number of diseases, like AIDS and malaria, that the world does not put much money into, because there isn't the market for a vaccine for diseases that in the rich world either don't exist or they have other ways of being dealt with. So that's where we've stepped in. With those kinds of advances we'll have a huge impact, because when you improve health in a country, then population growth actually goes down and the ability to feed and educate and all those good things start to come together. So we feel we picked the right priorities. We're working with the best scientists, giving them lots of resources. It's still a risky business, but we have our strategy.

PM: What's realistic within your lifetime? Obviously it would be wonderful if a vaccine could be developed for HIV. But what's realistic to you? I ask that because there's always this concern for those who set up foundations that things charge along when they're directing them, but when they're gone they become a kind of bloated bureaucracy, where nothing is accomplished because

the focus on them from the head—whether it's you or your wife—
is no longer there. What's your hope for what happens within
your lifetime?

BG: Our foundation won't last in perpetuity. It'll only last at most
a few decades, when Melinda and I are there to run it. So you
know this money is going to be spent on some very important
causes in this century. And of the top twenty diseases that create
the inequity, we will have either drugs or vaccines to virtually
eliminate most of those within our lifetime. Even now we're on
the verge of polio elimination. There are a lot of new good drug
leads in the malaria area. AIDS is the toughest, but certainly in
my lifetime, I'd be very surprised if we don't have a vaccine.

PM: Part of that strategy is backed obviously by an awful lot of
money—billions of dollars. I think fifty to sixty billion is the
latest figure, when you count both yours and Warren Buffett's
and others who've contributed. But you've also said that's kind
of a drop in the bucket compared to what you're trying to accomplish, saying that to try and provoke others, mainly governments,
to be more involved.

BG: That's right. The scale of these problems in delivering the
drugs and allowing poor countries to have equal opportunity is
going to require more generosity and development aid. Whether
it's Canada, the U.S., the U.K., we're making these global health
issues more visible, and so people really do want to reach out.
The governments have got to play the central role.

PM: Are they responding?

BG: There have been some increases and some new innovative
ways of getting governments to come forward and help out. The
U.S. has stepped up from a very low point, but with some new
things like an AIDS program. Canada's done some new things,
in fact working with my foundation in a couple of areas. So there

are improvements, but we're going to have to get it up by another factor of three almost to be able to meet what are called the millennium development goals, where by 2015 we want to see a big reduction in the disparities going on. So it's a big challenge. I meet with government leaders, and hopefully their voters will think of these as a priority for some spending.

PM: You mentioned the pressure that voters have to apply when they see this as a major issue. I want to read you a couple of quotes from two people whom you know. The first one's from Ted Turner: "the single greatest challenge that humanity has ever faced." And the second one is from Al Gore, so you're going to know where this is heading: "Never before has all of civilization been threatened." Now they're not talking about your issue here. They're talking about climate change, global warming, which seems to have become the issue for a lot of voters as well. I'm wondering, is there room for two great causes, where two great causes can be dealt with? Do you see them as two great causes? Are these in competition with each other—global warming and climate change versus the end of poverty and major progress on global health issues?

BG: They're both important. If you look at the scale of the tragedy of these health disasters, they're dramatically more imminent and of greater magnitude. A projection for the environment for even fifty years from now means we have to start to shift our energy economy in certain ways. But there's a ton of innovation that can drive that. It would be tragic if that took away from these cases where we're saving lives—literally for $100 each—and allowing countries to have the vicious cycle that we all take for granted.

PM: I guess what I was getting at is whether you worry about the focus suddenly shifting to environmental issues. You're seeing George W. Bush talking about climate change. In our country we've seen the Prime Minister change his view considerably on how much of an issue it is. And you see the data from citizens at large that they see it as the top concern. You know what happens with politicians who are driven often by public concerns through polling data: they shift attention. At a time when you're focusing on governments to become more involved in the issues that matter so much to you, is this a competing issue?

BG: Governments have to be able to deal with more than one thing at a time. Governments have to think about education; they have to think about retirement programs; they have to think about justice. And governments face complex problems. The portion of government budget that's going to go to this very effective aid to let these countries get out of their poverty trap, that's going to go up. The amount of the research budget that goes to global health and global warming, that's going to go up as well. And you know, countries can afford to take on these things. Certainly the U.S. and Canada should have no problem. In fact, the opportunity for the scientists to do fun and interesting work and have breakthroughs here really ought to draw more people into science. We have a shortage of people going into science, but these are both areas where people should say, "Wow, I'd love to be the one who helps advance either one of those causes."

PM: I want to shift to technology and where we stand at the moment. On the flight here I was sitting on the plane with my laptop looking back at a number of interviews that we have done with you over the last fifteen years. Many of the predictions you made, the hopes and dreams you had for the immediate future, clearly have been recognized. The things that you talked about that were going to happen, happened. There's one that seems to be a constant: you talk about the advanced form of the tablet. And you talk about how voice recognition is just around the corner, how you can literally have this machine working simply by voice command. Is that still just around the corner, or has it not happened as fast as clearly you had hoped?

BG: Oh, we're big believers that that tablet form factor, as it gets lighter, cheaper and better, will become just a common sense thing—in fact, that all students will have one. They won't have to have paper textbooks, but rather, on this tablet-like device, they'll be able to write their notes, be able to see what the teacher wants to present, go out to the Internet, get in-depth information. The teacher can customize things more than they can when it's just a fixed textbook. So, absolutely, we're investing very heavily in that. The number of tablets has gone up a lot, but it's still not a mainstream thing. We still have to get out there.

PM: When you first started playing around with computers— that would be what, late sixties?

BG: Right.

PM: As a teenager, thirteen, fourteen years old, did you have an image of where we'd be now? You must have had certain dreams, hopes—call them whatever you wish—that the relationship between people and computers would have taken us to a certain spot by now. Are we at that spot?

BG: The dreams we had included some of these frontiers we're still working on, like the natural interface. But by and large, you know, we thought about the machine we'd personally like to use, that would let us find information or find little video clips or communicate with people who are far away or create documents that look as good as what any big company can create. That has happened, and it's an amazing thing to have a dream when you're quite young and not only see it happen but actually get a chance to be a part of it—bringing in this vision of a software industry and creating literally hundreds of thousands of companies that have success providing software for the Windows PC. So, you know, it's been phenomenal.

PM: You're coming up on your last year as chairman.

BG: I'll stay as chairman. I'm eighteen months away from my switch away from full-time.

PM: When one's at a point like that, they tend to look back. Your successes are extremely well-known. Where did you miss?

BG: Well, Microsoft just had so much opportunity. It's not like we'd say, "Jeez, if we could only have changed one thing." Some things we were way ahead on, like putting TV on the Internet— we were way early on that. Tablet computers—you can say we were early on that. There are one or two things about the direction the Internet took where we weren't ahead on those things. The search function is the one people look at right now and say, "Hey, Google's doing such a great job on that." What does that mean for Microsoft? You know, we've had that throughout our history. Most of the things we're doing, we're in the forefront, like the video or handwriting area.

And then we'll have some area where people say, "How can they do that?" In video games and phones people have seen us come in and do quite well. Phones, they've seen that. And search—there they'll be surprised, I think. It's a very fast-moving business. Now, I wouldn't pick any one thing, because the key thing we got right was hiring smart people, creating success for our partners and believing that software was this magical thing that would create empowerment. And on all of that we were absolutely right. It's even more true today. When you think about the future of communications or photography or creativity, technology/software is playing a stronger role in every one of those things than ever before.

PM: Do your kids teach you things while on the computer?

BG: Sure. My oldest is ten, and she goes to a school where they use a tablet machine all the time. It's been great to see her mess around with it. And you know, it's just so natural when you start from the beginning that way.

PM: Just a last question, and it's about where you see yourself in terms of the big picture. Are you the Ford, the Rockefeller—the combination of both—of our time?

BG: No, I wouldn't say that. I've been extremely lucky to be involved in one of the big changes. When you see kids learning and you see blind people able to access information, you see the medical advances that were enabled by this—you know, nothing has been a change agent like the computer and software. And this partnership model has worked very well. So I'd say I'm one of the luckiest people alive today. And I have this big responsibility now to take the wealth that that's created and work with my wife to make sure it goes back to society in the best way.

PM: Why did you feel that you had that responsibility?

BG: I think there are so many things, including my education in an environment that supported innovation, and letting a young person start a company and hire tons of other people. That framework in North America allowed for my success. So I don't think giving the money to our kids would be good for them or good for society. And so now I have to say, "Okay, what are the great inequities?" And most of that's global health. Some is seeing how education can be improved as well. Anyone who's in the kind of position I am should put their energies into giving back.

PM: But haven't you just kind of defined the two things? The Ford of the day—you can call it luck, whatever—in terms of how you've changed our world. And the Rockefeller of the day in terms of giving back. So aren't you exactly them?

BG: No, I don't think so. What they did was unique, and there are lessons to be learned. Rockefeller in his giving was amazingly adept. Schools for blacks, medicine, even Beijing University—he helped fund that. He was a great thinker, and kind of a lone thinker on some of those issues. So I want to make sure I benefit from what they've done, but I think they'll always stand as unique examples.

PM: But you clearly learned from them, especially from Rockefeller.

BG: I'd say that's fair. You know, people talk about philanthropy being new. Well, there's lots still to be learned from the Carnegies and Rockefellers of the past.

PM: Both the hits and the misses.

BG: Yup.

—

ACCORDING TO THE *Forbes* magazine scoreboard of who the richest people in the world are, Bill Gates sits at the top. But in their latest list (2009), it's interesting to note that Gates's net worth is considerably less than it was when we chatted in early 2007. *Forbes* estimated that Gates was worth $40 billion when it did its counting, a drop of $18 billion as a result of the global economic turmoil. That's a lot of plasma screens.

SOUTH AFRICA:
DESMOND TUTU AND THABO MBEKI

IT'S ALWAYS INTERESTING TO WATCH how the studio crew reacts when guests arrive for their *One on One* taping. The floor director, camera operators and lighting personnel are all experienced professionals. Most have been at it for more than a few years and they've met a lot of famous people. So when someone well-known comes in for an interview, they're polite and respectful but they're not easily dazzled. Prime ministers come and go, rock stars rise and fall, authors hit and miss, so the crews rarely get too excited. But some guests do break through that wall of "been there, done that." The day Desmond Tutu walked into the studio, people were falling over themselves to catch a glimpse, snag a hello and offer any help they could to make his visit as pleasant as possible: "Are you happy with that chair, sir?" "Is that enough water?" I was waiting for "Would you like someone other than Peter to do the interview?" but no one went that far.

The reception was no small wonder. After all, Nobel Peace Prize winners don't walk into your workplace every day, especially one who had impressed the world as he courageously stood up to the decades-long oppression and brutality of South African apartheid. Before Nelson Mandela was released from his lengthy imprisonment, Tutu, the Anglican archbishop of Cape Town, was the most visible face of the anti-apartheid movement. People everywhere watched him plead with the international community to pressure South Africa while at the same time taunting his own government with bold challenges demanding change.

With Mandela in prison and his African National Congress (ANC) party outlawed, other supporters had to operate in exile to lobby for an end to apartheid. I first met Thabo Mbeki in London in 1986. As the ANC's representative, he was trying to influence the Margaret Thatcher government to offer its clout, as the Mulroney government in Canada was already doing, to implement sanctions against the South African government. Mbeki was little known internationally but you could sense this guy was an up-and-comer, one of the potential leaders of a post-Mandela generation in training.

In the late eighties the anti-apartheid campaign remained a tough sell, but slowly Mbeki and Tutu, coming from two very different angles, helped engineer success for the lobby against the white South African government. After apartheid was outlawed, Mandela was released and players such as Mbeki went home. Life in South Africa changed very quickly and mostly for the good. Mandela became president for three years and then watched as Mbeki, the man he had engineered to be his deputy, replaced him. Tutu never got directly into the political game but remained as an international watchdog of sorts over what happened to his beloved country.

Desmond Tutu and Thabo Mbeki: two historic figures in the South African story, and two guests we were proud to host in the first decade of *One on One*.

Desmond Tutu

2002-09-02

Peter Mansbridge: I want to talk about the big picture of

international events. When you look at the world right now, what worries you?

Desmond Tutu: That we are taking a heck of a long time learning one lesson that God seems to be wanting to teach us: that we are family. There are so many ways in which that lesson has to be driven home. You look at, say, the environment. When somebody pollutes in one part of the world, we wish it could be quarantined and that they pay the price alone. But it isn't. It's the whole globe that has to run the gauntlet and pay the price. Terrorism: you discover in fact that you can't hope for one country, however powerful, to be able to combat terrorism. It is the basic element that we are refusing to learn, that our survival is going to happen the day we recognize we're made for one another. That we are made for family. That it's not just obscene to spend huge amounts of money on instruments of death and destruction when a small percentage of that would enable children everywhere to have clean water, enough to eat, et cetera—it makes the world so wholly unstable.

PM: Prime Minister Chrétien has talked about that a number of times over these past few months—that perhaps the Western world still doesn't quite get it, that the West is quite self-satisfied, greedy. That we don't understand that there are other parts of the world that clearly have problems, and if we don't address them we're going to have to deal with them in different ways, perhaps even terrorism.

DT: Yes. I don't want to be so harsh in the generalization, because I have also been wonderfully exhilarated by the fact that there are many people who care, many people who are concerned. You see some of those demonstrations when the World Trade Organization meets—those are people who care. Some of them may go overboard, but the truth of the matter is that if the gap between the haves and the have-nots is not dramatically narrowed, then we have a recipe for all kinds of mayhem. As long as we have conditions in the world that can make people desperate—poverty, hunger, disease, ignorance—making them more vulnerable to being used by unscrupulous people, we are unlikely to win the war against terrorism. Because there is another kind of terrorism: a terrorism of poverty, of disease. And it isn't as if people in the so-called Third World are all looking for hand-outs. Many are wonderful people, people with an incredible sense of dignity, who have the odds stacked against them.

It's okay if we think that this is not a moral universe. But I don't. I believe fervently, passionately that God cares and that this is a moral universe, that right will eventually prevail. And God is saying, "Please, for goodness sake, my dear children, can't you wake up before it is too late?"

PM: You've just spent some time in the United States after the first anniversary of September 11. Do you think that many Americans are still having trouble understanding how God could care, to allow something like that to happen?

DT: Yes, I think that it was one of the most devastating things to have happened anywhere in the world, and it deserves to be condemned outright as a horrendous outrage. I think for a very long time those people have not had things of that kind happen on their soil, have often watched it happen to other people on television—smart bombs heading out to faraway places. They have not understood that the vulnerability they experienced, the fragility, the sense of weakness is in fact of the essence of our world. Only God is invulnerable. And fragility and vulnerability are something actually to celebrate, because they say, "All that you are, all that I am, all that we have is a gift."

PM: Turning to South Africa now, we were so focused throughout the 1980s on the struggle to end apartheid. That struggle was won; Nelson Mandela was freed. One person, one vote came into being. Our focus is no longer on South Africa. How is your country doing now?

DT: One of the things we've got to say is thank you, all of you, for having helped us to become free. What has changed is, we're free! That is something that you can't in a way compute. That is something you can't describe. It's almost like trying to describe colour to a blind person. If you've never been unfree and you are now free, it's something ineffable.

We face very, very many problems. Many of those are the legacy of apartheid. And that is part of why some of us have started to put forward a case that, just as you had a Marshall Plan to help Europe after the devastation of World War II, so too a very good case could be made for something similar to help not just South Africa but southern Africa, which was devastated by apartheid. We have unemployment. We have a huge backlog in housing. We have poor educational and health facilities still for very, very many of our children. And a lot of these are problems that were created artificially by the apartheid government's misapplication of resources. I think that our government has to deal first of all with that backlog, and also with the current problems. We face a huge, huge problem relating to HIV/AIDS in nearly four million of our people in South Africa. One in ten have been affected, and that is just devastating.

PM: In spite of those problems, have the black and the white populations of South Africa achieved a marriage of some sort since all this?

DT: One of the wonderful things is saying that we're nearly ten years down the line since our election, and the level of stability is remarkable when you look at and compare it with what's happening in Russia, for instance. But you've got to bear in mind, look at what's happening in Germany, the reunification of Germans— white Germans, speaking one language—reconciliation is still ongoing. Imagine now with us, where we have eleven official languages, and therefore the thought that we might achieve reconciliation overnight would be unrealistic. We are getting there. We have problems. But it is indeed surprising that nowadays you can see a mixed couple walking down the street when that was previously prohibited by law. When I became archbishop, I couldn't live in the official residence of the archbishop because it was in a white area. Now you can live anywhere. It's wonderful. It couldn't be better.

PM: What about Desmond Tutu? What is the challenge that's left for Desmond Tutu?

DT: To learn and to know that he has retired! (laughter)

PM: You can't stop, can you?

DT: At least I'm not as crazy as Nelson Mandela. He's eighty-four and—whew, when you look at his schedule—he leaves me breathless. He's a remarkable phenomenon.

PM: And you? Are you well?

DT: I'm well. Sometimes I say, "God said, 'I'm getting too many prayers about this guy. It's a nuisance, let's make him better.'" (laughter)

Thabo Mbeki

2003-11-08

Peter Mansbridge: I want to spend a couple of minutes talking about the change and the evolution that you've witnessed in the last twenty years, since I first met you when you were in London, in exile, speaking on behalf of the African National Congress. So much has changed since then. I'm wondering if the hopes and dreams you had then, of what it could be like, are met at all by the reality of having power.

Thabo Mbeki: Not all of them. There's been the important political change. We've got a democratic country, which is fine, but I think we underestimated the depth of the problem with regard to the issues of poverty and underdevelopment. There was a general view that there would be a post-apartheid dividend, that if you ended the system of apartheid it would release enormous resources, that you could quickly put to bed these great racial disparities that are part of our legacy. Well, it didn't. The end of the apartheid system did not release enormous resources we assumed would be there. And so I think the pace of change with regard to change in the lives of the people for the better hasn't been as fast as we thought it would be.

PM: How frustrating has that been?

TM: It's not frustrating, but I think it provides a very important learning experience when we grapple in a practical way with the question of everything the people need. They need a school, they need a clinic, they need a road, they need a job—they need everything, and all at the same time.

PM: They want it now.

TM: You can't say, "No, no, let's postpone giving you a loaf of bread because there isn't enough money for that," and then attend to something else instead. You can't deal with all of them simultaneously. It has been a very important and interesting challenge. Not frustrating but challenging, because you've got to think quite seriously and practically and produce results. And you can't say, "Look, wait until Friday because I'm still thinking," because people must respond to very, very pressing needs. The people are very badly disadvantaged.

PM: How difficult has it been for you personally? You achieved the presidency after Nelson Mandela, who had achieved it himself with a certain glow, both domestically and internationally, because of the focus on him while he was in prison. You arrived back from exile, worked in the Mandela administration and ended up taking over. Is that glow still attached to these post-apartheid days? How much more difficult is it for you?

TM: It hasn't been a problem. The focus hasn't been so much on the personalities but on the question "Are we getting to where we need to get to?" The glow hasn't gone, and I think the basic reason for that is that people can see change: "Here we were living in a shack six months ago. Now I'm still in a shack, but my neighbour is now in a proper house." Before, none of the people in the village had access to clean water. Now it's, "Our village still doesn't have access to water, but the village next door has access, and it's coming to us"—that kind of thing. So there's a sustained hope among the people for change. And I think it's driven essentially by visible change, even if that change hasn't touched "me" yet. But it's coming, so the enthusiasm for the democratic order hasn't dimmed.

PM: Your father was in prison for all those years during the apartheid era, many of them with Nelson Mandela. Your father passed away just a couple of years ago, but he fought long and hard for freedom in your country and he saw it achieved. He saw that you became president. And, I guess, he also saw the problems that still existed. What do you think would be the one thing now that he would want to see addressed more than any other?

TM: That's a generation that would include my father; it would include the late Walter Sisulu* and of course Nelson Mandela. What that generation always says to me is, "Persist in what you are doing. Don't get discouraged. We are getting there." Perhaps more than anything else they would call for stamina, and a refusal to be tempted by sliding into an easy life, as it were, because the

* *Walter Sisulu (1912–2003) was an anti-apartheid activist and leader in the African National Congress.*

temptations are many. For a person who sits in my position—
staying in a comfortable house, moving in comfortable cars, surrounded by security—you can forget that there are millions of
people out there who are in a very, very different position.

———

THABO MBEKI WAS SIXTY-EIGHT years old in the fall of
2008 when his nine-year presidency came to an end. It wasn't a
flattering finish. His own party forced him out after a string of
controversies and questionable decisions that provoked even
Desmond Tutu to say Mbeki was an elitist who protected his
friends while leaving the poor with nothing.

As for Tutu, he continues to inspire the kind of reverence
reserved for only a few in our world. He retired from the Church
in the late nineties and has successfully fought cancer. As he
approaches his eightieth birthday he remains a passionate
defender of human rights and a continuing critic of governments,
especially his own, for not doing enough to look after the disadvantaged in society.

In many ways South Africa has fallen from international attention. With the end of apartheid it's generally assumed by many
outside the country that all must now be well. Much is better,
but for many of South Africa's blacks, the poorest especially, the
struggle remains. In retirement Tutu remains their greatest advocate, and Mbeki perhaps their greatest disappointment.

THE DALAI LAMA

THERE ARE SOME PEOPLE WHO HAVE a quality that draws
everybody and everything towards them. These are people who
simply by their presence can dominate a scene. Pope John Paul II
was like that. Pierre Trudeau, love him or hate him—and a significant number of Canadians held one of those views—still
managed to steal the spotlight when he walked into a room.

And then there's the Queen, of course. My mother found that
out when she attended a reception for Elizabeth II in Victoria in
the early 1990s. My mother, although British by birth, was not
what one would call a fan of the royal family, and she was never
shy about launching into verbal assaults on the Queen's choice of
clothing or her annual Christmas address to the Commonwealth.
So I was more than surprised to hear that Mother had gone to
the reception.

She was deep in conversation with a friend when suddenly she
felt someone else join them. She turned and discovered she was
face to face with Elizabeth R. And damned if the Queen didn't
look her straight in the eye and say, "Such a pleasant evening, isn't
it?" Now all that required in response was a simple "Yes, Your
Majesty," but it was simply too much for Brenda Mansbridge.
She just stood there, mouth agape, dumbfounded, incapable of

uttering a word. After an awkward pause of a few seconds, the monarch gave up and moved on to seek conversation elsewhere.

Which brings me to the Dalai Lama, who is so much more than just a spiritual and political leader. His cause of cultural freedom and a degree of self-government for Tibet is something that has attracted the support of millions, from prime ministers to movie stars. The Tibet discussion is actually a lot more complicated than many people accept, because at its root is a fundamental disagreement over the history of Tibet and China. Simply put, it comes down to who did what to whom and when they did it.

But when the Dalai Lama comes into a room, his presence seems to overwhelm the debate. It's quite amazing, actually. His spiritual nature precedes him and an aura of calm takes over the space. When we talked in the spring of 2008, he was an even more sought-after interview than usual. The Beijing Olympics were approaching, and constant demonstrations in favour of an independent Tibet were leading to a difficult pre-Games tour of the world for those carrying the Olympic torch. Tibet was our focus for the interview, trying to determine where his bottom line is and, after fifty years of struggling to return to Tibet, whether he can ever see a resolution to the differences with China.

2008-04-18

Peter Mansbridge: When you say "Tibetan nation," I want to try to understand. What does Tibet mean to you? Obviously it's your home. But is it a province of China, is it a region of China, is it a country of its own? What is it in your mind?

Dalai Lama: There are four traditional Tibetan areas in Chinese provinces.* Then there is the Tibetan Autonomous Region, which was liberated by the Chinese government through peaceful

---

* *Tibetans traditionally lived in the provinces of Qinghai, Gansu, Sichuan and Yunnan in China, as well as in the Tibetan region.*

means. So Tibet is an autonomous region of the People's Republic of China. That's been the right description since the Seventeen Point Agreement was signed in 1951. Eventually they set up the autonomous region. So it is very clear. We are not seeking separation.

PM: Why do the Chinese not believe you on that? They say that you want independence and that you haven't clearly renounced full independence.

DL: This is difficult to understand. The Chinese government is always repeating the same thing, that Tibet has been a part of China since the seventh century. In the 1960s and 1970s they said that. In the 1980s, perhaps, they didn't mention that part, but they said instead that Tibet has been a part of China since the thirteenth century. So throughout history there have been different versions, different viewpoints. So you see, my position is not to talk about past history. Past is past. We cannot change past history. This is not a political decision. The political decision is the future. As far as that is concerned, we are fully committed to having Tibet remain within the People's Republic of China, because that's in our own interest.

Tibet is materially very, very backward, and every Tibetan wants a more modernized Tibet. So for that reason, remaining within the People's Republic of China will give us greater benefits, provided we have our own cultural heritage and our very rich Buddhist tradition and Tibetan language. We should have meaningful autonomy. That is our belief, and the majority of Tibetans also feel that approach is realistic and appropriate. Of course, some Tibetans, inside and outside, are very critical about that sort of approach.

PM: You've been in the struggle for autonomy for half a century.

DL: Yes.

PM: We look at the situation today in Tibet: people being arrested, people killed, none of the rights that you want or the Tibetan people want for themselves. How do you tell your supporters that this is the way to do it? You've cited Mao saying "Power comes from the barrel of the gun," but, quoting you, "Power comes from the heart."

DL: Ultimately. (laughs)

PM: Ultimately, yes, ultimately. How can you still maintain that?

DL: Not at this moment. Now the power of the gun is up ahead! (raises arm to head level)

PM: Quite a bit ahead.

DL: It's true. Not only in the Tibet case, but unfortunately there are many other cases also.

PM: But how do you make that argument to them? Because you've spent your whole life losing to the power of the gun.

DL: It's the truth. We have to stand for the truth. Whether it materializes or not, whether it is achieved within our lifetime or not, that's a different question. That's our principle. In 1959, when we became·refugees, some of our friends told me, "Now Tibet is finished." They may have been right. But we are determined to be granted our own rights, for our own struggle is truthful. And also, from the Chinese viewpoint, many patriotic Chinese are supportive of our stand. So meaningful autonomy is the best guarantee for the preservation of Tibetan Buddhist cultural heritage. It is also an immense benefit to the millions of Chinese.

PM: But I was rereading a part of one of your books this morning where you talked about past struggles with China on the Tibet issue. You said that one of the lessons you'd learned is that every time you push, they come back harder, which seems to be what's happening now.

DL: Yes, yes.

PM: So what good is any of it doing—the public protests, the comments from other governments? Is there any evidence that China is listening in any way?

DL: It is very difficult to say. But it is right—what people feel, what they believe should be expressed. I've always believed that if we look at the situation about Tibet locally, then it's hopeless. But if you look from a wider perspective, then there's hope, because the People's Republic of China is actually in a moment of transition. Things are changing. Much has changed in today's China compared to twenty, thirty, forty years ago. So this change will still continue. Now, for example, my picture is prohibited in Tibet itself and also in areas surrounding Tibet. But in China proper, in China's big cities, there are some Chinese businessmen selling my picture. So there are differences.

PM: Do you think people will be buying them and wearing them in the Olympic stadium?

DL: (laughs) I don't know, I don't know.

PM: Is there any possibility that there can be a door opened between you and the Chinese leadership to talk about Tibet's place within China? You said before that there are always back-channel discussions of some sort going on. How possible could it be that we could see you sitting at a table with a Chinese leader?

DL: I feel it's very possible. But now the Chinese method has been a crackdown; you see what they've done in the name of law and order. But it's possible that now the Chinese leadership will have to think seriously about what is wrong. They've spent a lot of money and there's a new generation. This new generation was born in and grew up under the Communists' so-called "happy days." There's an artificial expression that maintains, "Now, under communism, we're really happy." If that expression represents the reality, then an uprising would be impossible. But in spite of some superficial stability and harmony, deep inside there's something wrong. Now, what is the cause of that? Hopefully the leadership will take the opportunity to review their policy from the past fifty or sixty years. Hu Jintao has very much emphasized the importance of genuine harmony, and his slogan is about building a harmonious society. We'll fully support that. But a real harmonious society under the gun is impossible. Real harmony must come from the heart.

PM: What is your message to the people inside Tibet? As you mentioned earlier, there were demonstrations in areas of Tibet where there's been no record of demonstrations over the last fifty years. It's new to them, and a new generation, as you say. What do you say to them as they're standing there holding your picture, shouting slogans about human rights?

DL: That basically I'm a person who is really, fully committed to democracy and freedom of expression. Now I'm in India. And in India and outside India there are people who criticize me directly. That's okay—I welcome that. Some people criticize Buddhism. I have no right to say, "Shut up." They use their own individual freedom of expression. So too, inside Tibet, generally we also have the right to express ourselves. In spite of that there are some suggestions that they are provoking violence. That must be avoided. I tell Tibetans, as far as our spiritual Buddhist tradition is concerned, we are very rich. But this is not sufficient. We must build our own country.

PM: "Build our own country." Are you talking of Tibet or all of China?

DL: All of China, yes.

PM: What do you tell them about coming home? Should they expect to see you in Tibet one day?

DL: Yes, I have always been eager to visit.

PM: But do you believe you will?

DL: I do believe. I think this is a political matter. So if a few leaders' minds become more realistic, then within a few hours it can change. But as far as my own future is concerned, no problem! As I always say, I'm a simple Buddhist monk. I have a lot of friends. I am already an honorary citizen of Canada, so I can settle in Canada peacefully. (laughs)

As a matter of fact, in the early 1980s the Chinese government made a proposal for my return. They said, "You'll get all the privileges which the Dalai Lama had before 1959, all these things we will restore and everything. We will have a high official go to India to receive you." And at that time I responded, "This is not the issue. The issue is six million Tibetan people's well-being, their rights."

So I'm still the longest guest of the Indian government. For almost half a century I've been there and I remain homeless. But it doesn't matter, you see; it doesn't matter. The important thing is for one's own life to be purposeful or meaningful. My number-one commitment, above all, is the promotion of human values and trying to bring inner peace. Now we have six billion human beings. Different nationalities, different religious faiths, different colours, different social backgrounds—these are secondary issues. What's important is that we're all human beings. Everyone wants a happy life. Everyone has the same potential to bring inner peace.

FIRST NATIONS:
PHIL FONTAINE AND HARRY LaFORME

WHEN I WORKED IN CHURCHILL, Manitoba, in the late 1960s I lived face to face with the squalor that was life then, and still is now, for so many of Canada's First Nations people. I'm not proud to admit that I did next to little to try to change that.

Churchill was at that time a microcosm of the Canadian aboriginal story. The population was mixed: Cree, Chipewyan, Métis, Inuit and non-native. What made it so volatile at times was the simple fact that each group lived in their own settlement. The total population was less than two thousand, yet virtually no one lived side by side on the same street. Segregated communities? You bet. And some were awful, the Chipewyan area especially. Dragged out of a relatively peaceful life in the remote northern Manitoba bush by a government that felt they needed to assimilate, they now lived in an area called Dene Village, on the outskirts of Churchill. Fuelled as they were by unemployment, liquor and despair, rarely a month would go by without the village facing some form of terrible tragedy— a car crash, a brutal rape, a suicide, a family burned to death in a home fire.

In 1970, my last year in Churchill, I tried to make a small difference in the lives of a few young Dene teenagers. We offered to help make an obstacle course in the bush for an upcoming Boy Scout jamboree, and the idea was accepted. It was a challenge because none of us had ever organized something like this before, but it was great fun. While I was the leader, in the end I think they taught me more than I ever taught them. I'll never forget working on an area we'd built up with pine branches, a kind of hurdle that the Scouts would have to jump over and then immediately leap across a small creek. As we chopped wood and beat off the flies, one of the Dene boys suddenly held up his hand to command silence. Everyone stopped. I heard nothing, and I was about to ask what the halt was all about when my young companion held a finger to his lips. Sure enough, within minutes a huge flock of birds flew overhead—ducks, I think. We looked at each other and smiled, and in those days smiles didn't come easily on those young people's faces.

I was puzzled then, and remain puzzled today, about how he had heard wings flapping amidst the commotion we were making in the bush, while I heard nothing even in those forced moments of silence. It wasn't until the birds were directly overhead that I had any idea of what was going on. There is so much that we in the non-native community do not understand about our first citizens, whether it's their culture, their traditions or the suffering they have faced, often from the actions of our non-native predecessors. I constantly find myself asking native leaders and non-native leaders responsible for action on this issue the same question: why do things never seem to change?

One on One has focused on that question more than a few times, but for this book I'm relying on the thoughts of just two of our guests: Justice Harry LaForme, himself native, who has had a distinguished legal career and was, until his resignation, chair of the Residential Schools Truth and Reconciliation Commission; and Phil Fontaine, a former residential school student and long-time leader of the Assembly of First Nations. In different ways both men have been focused on a similar goal: trying to reconcile the pain, inequalities and unfairness of parts of our country's past in hopes of providing a more united future. It is an honourable goal, but success, as our discussions revealed, is elusive.

Phil Fontaine

2005-01-01

Peter Mansbridge: Here we are, still describing it as a struggle. It's the year 2005, this country's been around for a long time and yet there's still this struggle for the aboriginal people of this country. Why is that?

Phil Fontaine: I think it has to do with history and the fact that too many Canadians don't know the true history of this country.

PM: They don't know it, or they don't care about it?

PF: They don't know it. I think if they knew their history better they would come to care more deeply about all of the issues that matter to the country, including the issues related to the people I represent.

PM: On that score, on the history of the people you represent, what is it that the average Canadian doesn't understand?

PF: They don't know that we've been a positive influence in the way this country has been shaped. And we've been real contributors to the well-being of Canada, starting from treaty negotiations that helped shape Canada. Because treaties weren't just real estate transactions; they were about coexistence and the sharing of the resources and the riches of the land. And that's what, in our view, made it possible for Canada to become one of the richest countries in the world.

PM: But it's got to be more than just not knowing our history. Why haven't aboriginal groups and governments—whether they're federal or provincial—been able to come to some real movement on the struggle that your people face?

PF: It's not due to any lack of effort by the parties that are affected by this challenge. And first of all, it would be wrong to suggest that things haven't changed, because there have been some important positive changes.

PM: Like?

PF: One of the obvious significant achievements is in education. In 1952 we had two First Nations students in two universities, one in McGill, one at UBC. By 1969, when Jean Chrétien was minister of Indian affairs, we had approximately a hundred. Today we have close to thirty thousand. And we have now judges—twenty; we have a Court of Appeal judge, Justice Harry LaForme. We have close to four hundred lawyers. We have doctors, dentists. You name the discipline, you name the profession, we have First Nations people there that excel. And so there have been some real positive changes.

But of course there are challenges. And so many people have spoken out about the fact that there are too many First Nation communities in crisis. The most recent has to do with the Auditor General's report on the housing crisis of First Nation communities. It seems that we can't come to grips with what to do about the situation. The fact is, the current system has delivered the results that we're living, and that's completely unacceptable. So we have to do it some other way, and some other way is really through our governments, and our communities, and our people.

PM: You know, when you look at some of the challenges—like, for example, as you're saying about education—that's where the statistics really do tell a story of some success. When you look at some of the other challenges, there are a considerable number, whether it's the delivery of health care, whether it's the high rate of suicide among young people, whether it's the housing problems. I found it interesting when you were speaking a couple of weeks ago in Ottawa; let me just read one sentence. When you were talking about all the issues confronting the aboriginal people of this country, you picked residential schools. You said, "There is nothing that's more important for the relationship between First Nations and Canada than the resolution of this problem— residential schools." Is that the most important issue right now confronting that relationship?

PF: It is indeed of fundamental importance. Because the policy on residential schools was really an attempt to eradicate any sense of Indianness in the country. It was an attack on our cultures; it was an attack on our languages; it was an attack on our families—indeed, our place in this country. They were designed to mould us into something we could never be. And so we're still living the results of this terrible and tragic experiment. We have to come to grips with this. We've called on Canada, the federal government, to sit with us and resolve this so that we can conclude this chapter, this tragic chapter that's like a plague on our communities.

PM: Resolution in terms of what? In terms of a financial settlement? An apology?

PF: We would like nothing less than what the Japanese Canadians achieved. It was an apology in Parliament delivered by then–prime minister the Right Honourable Brian Mulroney. There was a very efficient process to secure compensation, to pay compensation to the Japanese Canadians. And we're suggesting something not much different than that particular situation: an apology in Parliament by the prime minister, compensation, a lump-sum payment to every First Nation student that's living. We shouldn't forget that 150,000 of our people attended these industrial schools, boarding schools, residential schools. Today there are 87,000 still living.

PM: And you're one of them.

PF: I'm one of them, absolutely.

PM: Clearly, for you it's a page that has to be turned—before addressing the deeper aspects of the relationship.

PF: Absolutely. It speaks about respect, mutual respect. It speaks to the importance of the acceptance of our place here in Canada, that we matter, that we're significant, and that before Canada can truly represent itself as it has—the great defender of human rights, the protector of human rights wherever there has been violation of human rights in this part of the world or that part of the world— it has to fix this particular human rights violation.

Harry LaForme

2008-05-30

Peter Mansbridge: I want to talk about the Residential Schools Truth and Reconciliation Commission and how it's going to operate. Why was it necessary?

Harry LaForme: Oh, it's necessary, I think, for a lot of reasons, but the most significant reason is so that Canada knows what's been described many times as a dark period of history. This occurred out of government policy to remove the Indian from the cultural fabric of Canada. That's the policy that was set up. "We are not going to have an Indian problem, because we're not going to have Indians. How do we do that? Kill the Indian in the child." And they did that through education, removal of their language, removal of their cultures, teaching them Christianity. In my view that would have been horrific enough, except that these environments then bred all of this horrendous conduct that these children ultimately had to endure. So it's all of these layers that are so important.

But beyond that, you move into the equally important reconciliation component to it. I believe that that missing chapter
of history, in all its layers—once it gets learned and the Canadian
public know it as the truth and accept it as the truth—I believe
we will all then be in a better position to identify this relationship which currently exists between aboriginal people and
Canada. It's a relationship I describe as unhealthy, fractured, faulty.
It's based on mistrust. It's one that just can't succeed. And we
know that. History's told us—this relationship doesn't succeed. I
think part of the problem is that we look at it in socio-economic
terms. We always talk about the poverty of these communities:
"Build them more houses; build them more schools; make their
water clean and fresh." All of that's important, that's true.

But in my view, even if you corrected all of that, you're still
missing one very, very serious component which can be defined
through that history of residential schools. It's about the rights
of aboriginal people. It's about how those rights blend in with
the framework of Canada. If we do that, if we get to define that
and say, "Gosh, now I know why this is such a terrible relationship that we have with each other—Canada and aboriginal
people," then I think maybe we can figure out a way to fix this
in the future.

PM: What's more important to you—hearing the stories of the
former students or hearing the stories of those who are on the other
side of this issue? I ask that because to some degree we know
the former students' story. But we really don't know the story on
the other side, whether it's used as a confessional or whether
it's used as trying to explain an issue that seems unexplainable.
We haven't heard that. So doesn't that make that more
important?

HL: I don't know about it being more important. I could never
say that, to be honest with you. I could never say it's more
important because—

PM: You know what I mean.

HL: I do.

PM: In trying to understand the bigger picture, and in no way trying to take anything away from the former students' situation.

HL: You might be suggesting that maybe the focus has to be on collecting those testimonies because we know so much about the other side, and that ought to be at least part of the focus. I would say it's important because it's part of the truth. That's the first thing. But it's also important because of the reconciliation component. I mean, this is truth and reconciliation. It's so easy to get caught up in wanting to focus it on the stories of abuse, which we all know is there. You're right, but it is all about reconciliation. I would think we want to take this horrific experience that some of these survivors went through and be able to say to them, "I wish it had never happened, but you know, maybe you can feel good that this had some positive effect for the future, and this can work to make it better for the aboriginal people in Canada."

PM: Boy, how do you sell that?

HL: I don't know. I don't know. But somebody's got to believe that their suffering wasn't for nothing. I think that's the best you can hope for. You can never take away the pain and you can never take away the scars. But that other side—there is a reconciliation component there too that one has to recognize. Church leaders today, they need to know this history and they need to reconcile themselves with that past. Not just with the aboriginal people but with their Church, with what their Church engaged in. And that's a part of the reconciliation process also.

PM: I'm going to paraphrase a quote from a speech you gave a few years ago: "People will be shocked if there's another Oka. But aboriginal people will tell you that there will be." Why'd you say that?

HL: Because we're not dealing with aboriginal problems the way that they need to be dealt with to be resolved. Land claims take too long. I don't know if people would put Ipperwash in the same category as Oka—I certainly would—but Ipperwash happened after Oka. There are constantly moods of unrest out west, and all over Canada, with aboriginal communities. We deal with these issues of aboriginal unrest as they arise. The water rises and floods the land of a First Nation community, so we move them out, even though we knew that flood was going to happen. That's not addressing the problem. If all you're going to do is put out brush fires over and over—every time an issue arose we would go in and resolve it, thinking we were resolving the issue, when we weren't. We weren't resolving the issue. And that still seems to be the way these issues are approached and dealt with, and the frustrations are there with young people.

I remember when I first started out in law; I had a difficult time with aboriginal clients because we were the first wave of aboriginal lawyers. They would say, "I don't know. Are you a real lawyer?" So you had to re-establish your credentials and credibility all over again. And they would say, "Okay, we've got a lawyer now. Now we can fight these battles in the same arenas as everybody else." Well, it doesn't work that way. After a while these young people start observing and saying, "You know, you're trying it your way, but I don't see anything changing. We'll give you a chance, but—" And that's what I meant by that speech at that time. They will give us a chance and they will give negotiation a chance; they'll give any other forum that avoids violence a chance. But young people run out of patience, and especially if it's a third-, fourth-generation person tackling the same issue, I can't imagine anybody that wouldn't be frustrated in those circumstances.

That's why I think this commission, again, is a good way to really face that underlying issue, which is the relationship issue. It's the relationship of aboriginal people and Canada. Why do we mistrust each other so much? And what is at the root of it? If we can get there, then we can plan that future a little better.

—

JUSTICE HARRY LaFORME RESIGNED as chair of the Truth and Reconciliation Commission in the fall of 2008. He gave no interviews but instead issued a statement saying, ironically, that he couldn't reconcile the differences between himself and his fellow commissioners, who a few months later signalled that they too were stepping down.

Since his *One on One* appearance, Phil Fontaine has succeeded in receiving some very high profile apologies for native Canadians affected by the residential school issue. The Parliament of Canada in 2008 and the Pope in 2009.

ISRAELI PMs:
EHUD OLMERT, BENJAMIN NETANYAHU
AND SHIMON PERES

EVERY FEW YEARS WE BRING ALL of our foreign correspondents home for meetings and a very special public session. Nine or ten of them sit at the front of a hall, with me in the middle moderating a question-and-answer period with what is always a large group of very bright people. The questions are about world affairs, and our correspondents describe what they see going on in places like Washington, Moscow, Beijing, Nairobi, Kandahar, Beirut, London and Jerusalem. It's a fascinating look at the planet through Canadian eyes.

I remember one session about ten years ago when someone asked Patrick Brown how the rest of the world sees Canada. Now Patrick, who has covered the globe for us for decades, has seen more than anyone should see of war, famine, disaster, brutality, poverty and general misery and mayhem. His answer was very frank and went something like this: "The world barely notices Canada." Before anyone's feelings could be hurt, he added, "And for that you should get on your knees every night and thank whatever god you pray to, and beg him that the world never notices Canada." What Patrick was saying, of course, is that when a country makes headlines, it's almost always because bad things are happening.

So where are there more foreign correspondents per square inch than anywhere else on Earth? The answer is Israel. Israel is a country not even half the size of Nova Scotia and with fewer inhabitants than Ontario, yet every major news organization in the world has a bureau there. Since it was founded in 1948, Israel has fought five full-scale wars and has been part of incursions, invasions, uprisings and other violent clashes that have never given it one real day of complete peace.

Canadians care deeply about what happens, not just in Israel but in the surrounding Arab countries as well. To three major religions, Christianity, Judaism and Islam—which happen to be the top three in Canada—the Middle East is the Holy Land. Even Canadians who don't consider themselves particularly religious have some sort of cultural ties to the area. This means that anytime we do a story on the Middle East, it seems that someone is unhappy about what we say. There's nothing too surprising about that. Israelis and Arabs, and those who support them, often see the world very differently. For example, Israelis see May 15, 1948, as Independence Day, while many Arabs see it as *al Nakba*, "the day of the catastrophe." We get a lot of mail and a lot of phone calls accusing us of being biased against one side or the other. Usually the accusation is that we are intentionally slanting the news, but sometimes people say we just "don't understand" or that we "don't know the history."

I try to understand, and to know the history. I remember being in Washington, on a rooftop overlooking the White House lawn, when Yitzhak Rabin shook hands with Yasser Arafat—that was history. We dared to hope that we were seeing the start of a new Middle East. We were wrong. It's just been impossible, it seems, for either side to get past all the bitterness.

I also try to understand by seeing for myself. I get to the Middle East as often as I can, and when I'm there I talk to people who are well connected. That has included three Israeli prime ministers. The prime minister is the most powerful political figure in this tiny nation that looms so large on the international stage. The following men are in a select group—only twelve individuals so far have held the office (some on more than one occasion) over the sixty-one-year history of Israel.

Ehud Olmert

I INTERVIEWED EHUD OLMERT (Prime Minister Number Twelve) in his office at a time when the rumour mill was alive with talk that he was engaged in secret negotiations to get the peace process back on track. Cynics argued that it was just talk, an attempt to get his own leadership back on track.

What surprised me was how small his office was. When you see the spacious Oval Office in the White House or the Parliament Hill offices (there are two) of Canada's prime minister, you start to equate size with power. Not in Jerusalem. There was barely room for Olmert's desk, a few chairs and a small couch. But as small as it was and as limited as the options were for how to shoot the interview, much time was taken up by his image consultant concerning where the cameras would be placed and at what angle they would be capturing the prime minister's image. When he finally arrived, he seemed ready for the conversation, but a little surprised that so many people were crawling all over his furniture in order to stay out of the shot.

2007-03-21

Peter Mansbridge: Prime Minister, there seems to be an awful lot going on in what we call the peace process in North America. You're meeting with President Mahmoud Abbas on the Saudi initiative, with discussions on the part of the Arab League. Yet at the same time the fundamental core differences between the Israelis and the Palestinians remain. So I'm wondering, in general terms, is it right to be optimistic at this point that significant movement could be happening in this process?

Ehud Olmert: At this point it is essential to be optimistic. You cannot deal with anything unless you are optimistic, because if you don't, you have plenty of reasons every day why it is not good to be optimistic. But that's not the way to create momentum, and I want to create momentum. Therefore I force myself to be optimistic, even when there is not always a reason for it. I do think that there are currently some good reasons. I now have a regular pattern of meetings between me and the head of the Palestinian Authority. This may seem very normal in other parts of the world, but here it's a great breakthrough. It has never happened before. And next time I am going to try and meet with him in Jericho.

PM: When you sit across the table from him, do you feel you're dealing with someone who can effect change? We all know his political position.

EO: That's the more difficult part. But let's talk about the reasons for optimism. This is one thing: we have our meetings, my staff meets his staff, and that will continue to take place. I think that it's very important to talk. You're less inclined to fight. The problem with the Palestinians is that Abbas talks to me and all the rest continue to fight against us. We have to somehow find a way to continue the discussions with the moderate parts and to somehow stop the more extreme elements from continuing their terrorist tactics. Now there is what you called the Saudi initiative, and I'm looking at it very favourably. I am ready to sit down with the Saudis and talk to them about their initiative and to listen to them, learn their perspectives and their perceptions and their desires.

PM: Let me follow that up. When you say you're ready to sit with the Saudis, what does that mean? Have you talked with the Saudis yet?

EO: I don't want to go into that. They are not always direct talks. But, you know, the Saudis are not that distant, and there are countries that we talk to and they talk to. There are always ministers and leaders that come here and they go there. So there are ways of passing messages, even when you don't have formal talks or direct contacts.

PM: So is that the message that you've passed through them?

EO: I've said it publicly that I look at the Saudis as a key to the progress in the Middle East. The Saudis have enormous influence over the Arab countries and the Palestinians. They are a central force in the moderate Arab world. And I think that they now understand something which was not so easy for them and not so natural for them to understand in the past, and that is that Israel is not the worst thing that ever happened to the world. Some worse things may be the radicalism of the extremist fundamentalist forces amongst the Shiites, which can shatter the foundations of that part of the world in a very serious way.

PM: You say you're just waiting for them to respond to your response to them. What are we short of here—a phone call? Is it a matter of somebody calling you or you calling somebody? I don't understand the process.

EO: (laughs) Telephones can reach almost any person on Earth, so I don't think there is a problem of our telecommunication. It's a process; it takes time. It took some of the countries we are dealing with a lot of time before they were prepared to be recognized publicly. What was going on beneath the surface, on a quieter level, between us and them—that takes time. Remember, rebel forces threaten some of the moderate Arab societies. Therefore they have to calculate how they will ultimately deal with us publicly with some awareness of the influence of these forces. I understand that, and yet I think the time has come for the moderate Arab forces in the world to make a statement of courage and of leadership that will send a message across the Middle East that the days of the extremists are over. And the Saudis can play a major, vital role in this direction.

PM: And you want to see them send that message at a meeting with you?

EO: Maybe. Or maybe one of the ways to send such a message will be—oh, it's not such a personal matter for me, it's the public recognition of the existence of Israel as a legitimate force in the Middle East, and a force you want to reckon with rather than to fight with.

PM: Do you think that's hopeful for this year?

EO: I think it's hopeful even for this month. I know it's something which is on the agenda. It is something which can surface overnight, or it can take years.

—

NOTHING EVER CAME OF OLMERT'S push for peace and, as it turns out, not much came of his prime ministership either. He lost his party's leadership and eventually handed over power to Benjamin Netanyahu.

Benjamin Netanyahu

IN THE SPRING OF 2009, Benjamin Netanyahu (Number Nine, for his 1996 election victory) became prime minister again after the collapse of the Olmert government and a request to Netanyahu's party, Likud, to form a coalition government. He is always interesting to interview because he's totally no-nonsense— always in a hurry, always ready with a direct, straightforward quote. When I last interviewed him, in 2003, he was Israel's foreign minister and his country was waiting with anticipation for the Iraq war.

2003-01-25

Peter Mansbridge: You've not only been a successful politician, you've also been a successful diplomat, as an ambassador to the United Nations. When you see the United States' efforts to build the coalition to go into Iraq, as we're seeing now, does that leave you with the impression that they may have to act alone on this?

Benjamin Netanyahu: I hope not. I think that there are many fair-minded people around the world. We can't lose sight of what is truly important here. It is very, very difficult to take pre-emptive action. But sometimes true leadership and true statesmanship mean taking the action that will prevent a future disaster, despite the slings and arrows and vilification that accompany such action. I am absolutely convinced that preventing Saddam Hussein's regime from acquiring weapons of mass destruction is in the interest of everybody—the interest of Europeans, the interest of America, the interests of Israelis and Arabs alike, the interest of the Iraqis. It is not in the interest of Saddam Hussein.

PM: You mentioned the Arab world. What about those who are fearful of what could happen in the Arab world with an attack? Especially if that attack is conducted by the United States alone, or almost alone, could it inflame the Arab world?

BN: I constantly hear that, and I always fall back on the question I was asked in the late eighties, when the United States and Britain bombed Libyan leader Muammar Qaddafi after he initiated terrorist action against American forces in Germany. People said this would enrage the Arab world, that American embassies would be burned and so on. I think Dan Rather interviewed me, and he asked me what would happen and I said nothing would happen—American embassies would not be burned and the Arab masses would not rise, and if they did, it would be for some prearranged and limited demonstrations. In fact, nothing did happen.

PM: Do you think nothing has changed since then?

BN: Yes, I think something has changed enormously. There is one superpower today and that superpower understands that it has a responsibility to prevent the arming of such regimes. In the past, however, it was easier to prevent, because the Soviet Union, for all its ills, prevented the seepage of nuclear and ballistic technology to these regimes, so you didn't really have this problem of rogue states. But you do now, and that has changed. And what has also changed since September 11 is the understanding that if the civilized world does not take action against the savagery, then it's just a question of time when these regions or the organizations that they sponsor will eventually obliterate New York or Washington or Toronto.

PM: I want to draw you back to 1991, at the time of the last Gulf War. We remember seeing you at times sitting with a gas mask on in the TV studio.

BN: That wasn't my most eloquent interview.

PM: I guess the issue that arises from that experience is that Israel had to make a very difficult decision, and that was not to retaliate at the time when Scud missiles were coming into Israel from Iraq. How difficult was that for a country that prides itself in defending itself when under attack?

BN: It was very difficult. Thirty-nine Scud missiles hit Israel, but miraculously no one was hurt. There was also the issue of an Arab coalition at the time that we didn't want to see frayed and unravelled. I don't think that is the case now. Of course, we will have to see what happens. We reserve the indisputable and elementary right, which is every obligation of any government, to take whatever action is needed to defend our people and defend our state.

PM: There's an election unfolding in this country in just a few days. When President Sharon was elected here two years ago, he ran on a ticket that was about peace and security. You know the line in American politics—if an opposition party asked today, "Are you more secure, more at peace than you were two years ago?" what would the answer be?

BN: You're not more at peace but you're definitely more secure. The fear of terror attacks has dropped significantly because the government has actually taken action to strike at the basis of terror. People said that you can't stop terror militarily. Of course you can. Terror is a particular kind of physical assault. It requires first a breeding ground and then it requires a base, and then it requires dispatchers, and then it requires people who themselves don't want to die but want to find and nurture and cultivate these qualities in others. Suicides guarantee the perpetrators' families money and so on. So if you strike at that infrastructure and you create actual physical barriers, the rate of terror attacks and suicide attacks drops precipitously. That's exactly what is happening.

PM: So you're more secure but not necessarily more at peace.

BN: No, because to achieve peace you have to do two things. First of all, you have to have a level of security to stop these rampant attacks. But the second thing is, you need a partner for peace. The reason we could make peace with the late Egyptian president Anwar Sadat or with the Jordanian leader, King Hussein, is because they wanted peace. You can only make peace with an enemy that wants peace. An enemy that uses the proverbial peace process as a stepping stone to simply get more territories is not a partner for peace.

If you want the best illustration of the difference between the two, between Arafat and King Hussein, I remember, when I was prime minister, six Israeli schoolgirls were gunned down by a Jordanian soldier. King Hussein flew to Jerusalem. He went with me to the families of these schoolgirls, he knelt before their grieving parents, with tears streaming down from his eyes, and he said, "Please forgive me." Arafat, by contrast, calls public celebrations in honour of these killers. There was a football tournament in one of the schools in Arafat's police state yesterday, in Tolkarem, and the teams are named after suicide killers, including the one involved in the Passover evening massacre. A team of kids! So what do you expect? So these kids will go to suicide kindergarten camps, suicide schools, suicide tournaments, Suicide University?

PM: Do you see leadership in the Palestinian community reaching out at this time?

BN: They're afraid, because are there any leaders inside Iraq right now? They could be eliminated in two minutes, and the same is true of Arafat. But are there people there waiting in the wings? The answer is yes, without a doubt. I don't think it's important to name them. The Palestinian dictatorship, just like the Iraq dictatorship, has to be replaced by democracy. It will take time to build democratic institutions, to ventilate these societies, to draw out the toxins that teach children to become suicide bombers. But this has to be done. This is the crucial step towards peace.

PM: If one accepts that step has to happen on the Palestinian side, then what has to happen on the Israeli side? There are reasonable people within the debate in this country who feel the major step that has to happen is withdrawal, or at least a stopping of some of the settlement programs.

BN: I think they're wrong. Not because I don't think that the territorial issue, including the settlements, will be on the table, but I think they're wrong to think this is the cause of the problem.

PM: I'm not saying it's the cause of the problem. I'm saying that it has to be part of the solution.

BN: It will be a part of a negotiated solution, there's no question. There will be negotiations about this. They will put forward their claims and we'll put forward our claims. These are not occupied territories; they are territories in dispute. Our claim only goes back 3,500 years. But we know they have a claim, so we'll negotiate it. But that is something that can only be done with someone who says, "I want to live next to you. I want a political entity or a state next to Israel," but not a state *instead* of Israel. That's why we could solve it with Jordan. That's why we could solve it with Egypt. The reason why we can't solve it with Arafat's Palestinian dictatorship is because they don't want to live next to us—they want to replace us.

I think we need a different leadership to deal with. Once we have that cooling-off period, once we have a Marshall Plan, once we have political and educational reforms in Palestinian society, then we can see free elections. And a freely elected, more moderate, more responsible Palestinian leadership could negotiate with us. They don't have to accept our position on where to draw the line on the map, but neither do we have to accept theirs. They do have to accept the fact that we're here to stay. We're not going to disappear as a people, as a country, as a state. I think that will produce peace. And I think that's the right order of things. If we were to say today, "No, let's just walk out," as we did in Lebanon, what you'd get is another Lebanon. And that's wrong, because retreating from terrorist fire just produces more terrorism.

Shimon Peres

ISRAEL'S PRIME MINISTER NUMBER EIGHT remains my favourite, not for his policies or his actions but for his longevity and his style. Shimon Peres has been there in one role or another since the creation of Israel in 1948. He has known all the players, big and small, from David Ben-Gurion (Number One) to Ariel Sharon (Number Eleven) and everyone in between—and he remembers them all.

We last met in his office in Tel Aviv in 2006. He was vice–prime minister at that point but it was really a title in name only; his role had become more symbolic than substantial. But his experience was, and still is, unquestioned, and he's constantly sought after—while I was there the Italian prime minister, Romano Prodi, called for advice. Later, as he told stories about the moments captured in the pictures that filled every conceivable space on his office walls, his bookcase shelves and his very cluttered desk, I had the sense that I was walking through history. Peres with Arafat, Peres with Clinton, Peres in Oslo accepting the Nobel Peace Prize, and many, many more moments frozen by a camera lens and dating back as far as seven decades ago.

2006-04-08

Peter Mansbridge: Yesterday I spoke with Aziz Dweik, a senior member of Hamas and speaker of the Palestinian parliament. One of the things he said was that while Hamas doesn't feel it's in a position to sit at a table with Israel, it has no problem with Mahmoud Abbas sitting at the table with Israel. You've spoken of him with respect. Is he someone you can deal with?

Shimon Peres: Yes, provided he isn't overpowered by Hamas. He has some constitutional rights and obligations. I don't have any problems talking with him. I met with him quite recently; we had a very thorough discussion. And as I said, I have respect for him.

PM: So they have to allow him to talk freely about the issues.

SP: Yes. I told him, "Look, I can talk. If you say I don't respect the agreements, I don't recognize Israel, I don't renounce terrorists, what do we have to speak about? Change your platform;

otherwise nothing can be done." That's the problem.

PM: You don't see any pause in the angry rhetoric of Hamas during this period?

SP: You know the saying in politics: never say never. But it's like moving from a very orthodox religious position to a secular society; it's the same distance. If you ask me about somebody who's very religious, is there a chance of him becoming secular? Maybe. But I must admit it doesn't happen often, and surely it doesn't happen quickly.

PM: When I look at your library, many of the books are focused on leadership. Some of the great leaders of the past hundred years in different parts of the world, some of the not-so-great leaders—they're all reflected here.

SP: Well, yes. I know the strengths of leaders because of their weakness. If you think that a leader can stop the winds of history, that's an exaggeration. If you think a leader can run with the wind and affect it a little bit, that may be the case.

PM: And great leaders sometimes change their position.

SP: Yes. They have to.

PM: You can call it compromise, whatever. Ariel Sharon changed his position.

SP: Yes.

PM: And Hamas?

SP: You see, Sharon is a single man and Hamas is a religious movement. That's what worries me. They have a double leadership: one here, the other in Syria.

PM: But doesn't it come down to whether or not they want a
relationship, whether they want peace, whether they want a
better life for their people? It seems history has taught us that
sometimes it's the extremists that are the ones that can make
those kinds of deals. Whether it was Reagan with Gorbachev,
whether it was—

SP: Sometimes it happens, sometimes not. It sometimes happens
clearly, but usually it's being forced by outside forces. There are
leaders who change or else changes are forced by circumstances.
And Sharon is a good example of it, yes. But there are others who
are adamant not to move.

PM: That document behind your desk recognizes your Nobel
Peace Prize that you shared with Arafat in 1994. That's twelve
years ago now—still no peace here.

SP: No. Many things happened. Twelve years ago the Palestinians
didn't have any recognition. It was a Palestinian personality but
not a Palestinian state in being. They didn't have any authority.
We, on the other hand, are not recognized by them. There has
been profound change in public opinion. But alas, it takes time.
I wish it would happen quicker. What this span of time feels like
for an individual man is great, but for collective history it's still
reasonable. I don't think this is the end.

PM: The last time we talked, you said that you're an optimistic
person by nature.

SP: Yes.

PM: Are you still that way?

SP: One hundred percent. I say jokingly that though the optimist and the pessimist are dying the same way, they live differently. So why shouldn't I live as an optimist? And when I look

back, so many optimistic things happened to our country. First of all, consider the wars won and most of the dangers overcome over fifty-eight years: four intifadas and five wars. Then I saw peace with Egypt and peace with Jordan, and I'm sure we shall make peace with the Palestinians as well.

PM: You are eighty-two now. Do you think your dreams can be fulfilled within your lifetime?

SP: I'm eighty-two and I have one advantage over other politicians. I am free to dream. I can imagine. I don't have to be careful with all the political limitations. I'm still fighting for a different Middle East: four hundred kilometres of peace instead of four hundred kilometres of confrontation. Now I can do it because, first of all, they suspect that I'm a dreamer anyway, and I'm an unpaid dreamer, so I'm not dangerous and I don't cost too much. But I think basically I'm right. I think great things are happening.

—

SHIMON PERES IS NOW PRESIDENT of Israel. It seems as if he has occupied every possible position in the country's government since 1948, when it all started.

DIANA BUTTU

TRYING TO REPORT FAIRLY on the Middle East, especially the Israeli–Palestinian issue, is one of our greatest challenges. It seems that no matter what we say on the daily developments of this story, one side or the other, and often both, criticizes us. On nights when our email inbox is crammed with outrage, it usually means we've upset someone in our coverage of this issue, and our ombudsman is constantly fielding concerns from viewers and writing reports on the same subject. To be fair, I imagine the same goes for most of our colleagues in other media organizations. Feelings run deep on this issue, and no one is shy about making those feelings clear.

All that puts the onus on us to try to find people who can marshal their arguments in an informative way and with passion, yet with the understanding that there are at least two very different views on what needs to happen to solve the Middle East dilemma. It doesn't always work. In fact, I've moderated panels on this story that have dissolved into impossible verbal slugfests where no one comes out looking good and we conclude that it's impossible to ever have a meaningful conversation on the subject. But every once in a while you connect with someone who gives you an insight you may not have had before into how the process is unfolding.

Diana Buttu is one of those people. She lives in Ramallah, on the West Bank, and has worked with and for many of the big names in the Palestinian leadership, from Yasser Arafat to Mahmoud Abbas. She's been the Palestinian Authority's communications director and also one of its legal advisors, and she has been deeply involved in peace negotiations with Israel. Oh yes, and she's Canadian. When we talked in the fall of 2003, the Palestinian Authority's Ramallah compound had been heavily damaged by Israeli attacks and its leaders were confined to a few rooms, with no ability to leave. We did discuss that, but the subject of her Canadian roots was where we started.

2003-10-10

Peter Mansbridge: There's lots to talk about. But I guess, first of all, we want to try to understand how someone who was born and grew up in Scarborough ends up in Ramallah. How does that work?

Diana Buttu: My parents are Palestinian, and Canada ended up providing a home to my parents. And growing up as a Canadian, I learned values of equality and justice. I remember as a child telling my parents that they had to forget about the fact that they were Palestinian, forget that they were refugees, and simply move on in life. It wasn't until I went back to Israel and saw the conditions they had lived under that I realized there was inequality and injustice, and that I, as a Canadian and as a Palestinian, owed a responsibility and had to do something to change that.

PM: How old were you when you made that trip?

DB: I was seventeen years old.

PM: So, growing up, you weren't focused on this issue. This wasn't something that you thought was your mission in life.

DB: Not at all. I was more focused on Girl Guides and on soft-ball and on other issues. Certainly not with respect to the Palestinians. Not at all.

PM: So how did you take that interest that you developed when you were seventeen and turn it into actual work now?

DB: It's actually very funny, because before that time I wanted to become a physician. I used to keep a diary all the time. And when I came back from that trip in 1987, after having witnessed what life was like for Palestinians living inside Israel, I immedi-ately decided that I was going to become a lawyer and that I was going to represent the Palestinians. I remember writing that down in my diary. My mother recently showed me my diary and said to me, "Don't you remember exactly what you said in 1987?" So I became involved in campus activities with respect to Palestine and Israel and started studying a lot. I hadn't spoken Arabic before that. So I learned Arabic and learned a lot about the history of the area after studying at the University of Toronto, and then did exactly as I said I was going to do, which was go on to law school.

PM: What did your friends think of your decision to move over there, get right involved in this process that seems, from this side of the world, like a process that can never find a solution?

DB: My friends and my family—I should include my parents in this—they all thought I was crazy. My father specifically said to me, "You know, we left for a reason, so why are you going to go back?" But I did feel compelled and I still do feel com-pelled to be there. Because I think that when people really understand what's happening over there, then people become moved, and they become moved to change things.

PM: I guess it's one thing to say you're going to go over and do this; it's another to actually get there and be able to insert yourself at the kind of levels you have managed to. How did you do that?

DB: It was, ironically enough, following a conversation with an Israeli friend of mine. We were both studying in the United States at the time, and it was immediately after Camp David that my friend turned to me and sort of threw up his hands and said, "What is wrong with the Palestinians? What is wrong with you people?" That conversation fuelled me to try to reach out and to try to not only figure out what was going on with respect to Camp David and what had happened during the peace process, but also to try to reach out to Israelis. So I basically went to Ramallah and knocked on a few doors and found some doors that were receptive. They were looking for lawyers who had experience in international law and international human rights law, so the match fit.

PM: And now you really are in that inner circle? You can find yourself briefing Arafat or the prime minister?

DB: Yes, definitely. All of the Palestinians in the leadership, the members of the negotiations team, including President Arafat and Mahmoud Abbas. They're all individuals with whom I speak.

PM: What's that like? Obviously we have an image of Arafat that's almost solely based on what we see on television. We don't have the view that you have. What is he like, especially now? Because he seems so frail and—literally—under the gun.

DB: Frail is definitely the word to describe his state right now. He's basically been confined to two rooms. Each room is probably about ten feet by ten feet. One has a window, the other does not. And he's been living under these conditions now for two years. If anybody has ever lived under these conditions or in prison, you can begin to get a sense of feeling completely confined, completely cut off from the rest of the world. It certainly has an impact on the way that you act, the way that you speak, the way that you react. This is definitely something from which he is now suffering.

PM: To some degree he really is cut off from the rest of the world.

DB: Yeah.

PM: Those who considered him not necessarily a friend but somebody whom they would deal with won't have anything to do with him anymore.

DB: That's right.

PM: What impact does that have on the kind of work you're trying to do?

DB: It makes it very, very difficult. Palestinians view it with a bit of hostility when the United States talks about establishing democracy in the Middle East and at the same time basically ignores perhaps the only democratically elected leader in the Arab world— and won't allow him freedom of movement. And yet they're constantly pointing the finger at him as though he has the ability to do something, as though he's the ruler of a monolithic mass of people who have no means of thought, no means of expression. So it doesn't really sit well with Palestinians, particularly when I tell them that I'm trying to reach out to countries all around the world. They look at me ironically and say, "What's the point if our leader can't even leave two rooms that are ten by ten?"

PM: And how do you answer that?

DB: I really am at a loss for words, because the strategy that the United States and Israel have both employed seems to be backfiring, and will constantly backfire. Again, they may not like him and people may not like him, and I myself, if I were voting tomorrow, I would not vote for him for a whole plethora of reasons, but that doesn't mean I don't respect democracy. And if one respects democracy, then one has to respect the democratically elected ruler. The United States and Israel must allow the Palestinians to have elections, which is something that civil society has been calling for now for the past three years, but has been blocked every step of the way by Israel or the United States.

PM: But you do paint a world that in some way coincides with the view that many people outside of the area have: that the Palestinian leadership is in some chaos—a leader who's frail and cut off; prime ministers who are constantly changing, who have no power and can't accomplish anything.

DB: That's right.

PM: Is it that chaotic right now?

DB: It absolutely is. One of the things that Israel first did when this uprising started was to attack the Palestinian Authority security forces. It was very systematic at attacking all the security forces yet at the same time demanding that the Palestinian Authority provide security, which is a kind of perverse logic. They want the Palestinians, who are the occupied, to provide security to a state that's the occupier. But apart from that, what they did was systematically destroy the security forces and they've systematically destroyed the Palestinian Authority. So what's left is simply a shell at this point in time. And until people begin to realize that it's not the shell that's going to lead the Palestinians out of occupation, that it really is the occupation itself, then I think we're going to be stuck in this conflict for many, many years to come.

PM: You know, while the big-picture negotiations aren't happening, you mentioned that part of your job, as determined by you, would be to constantly reach out to Israelis.

DB: Yes.

PM: Are you still able to reach out to Israelis?

DB: Yes, definitely. Part of the work I do is to quite literally go into Israeli homes to talk to them so that they can get a perspective on what's happening on the other side of the Green Line, what's happening to the Palestinians apart from what they see on television or read in the papers.

PM: And how generally accepted is that? Are you really just talking to those who would be considered on the left of the Israeli spectrum, or is it a broad range?

DB: It's very broad. We've spoken with everybody from the left wing to the ultra-left wing, to the centre, to the right, to the religious right and basically every shade in between. They're difficult sessions. They're not easy. Sometimes people yell; oftentimes they shout. Sometimes we've been attacked. But by and large I think people walk away with a sense that they have heard something, something that they hadn't learned about before. Many people end up calling us back and saying, "Look, I don't agree with everything you said, but I want you to talk to my neighbours," or "I want you to talk to my relatives." So it's been, you know, small-scale. I can't really say if it's successful or not, but it's certainly been an interesting experience for me.

PM: Is the reverse true? Do you hear things and suddenly accept things that you hadn't thought of before, from their side?

DB: Definitely. One thing that was very interesting was when I first started, I thought that I was going to be educating Israelis. And I've since learned a lot about Israel and about Israelis through this process. So it's not at all been a one-way street. It's been a two-way street.

PM: So is this now the life ambition? How long are you going to stay there?

DB: I originally went for simply one year, and I thought that, you know, I'll do my service and after a year I'll go back to Canada. It's been three years now. I don't know if I'll stay. It's difficult, it's very difficult to live under occupation. I've witnessed it all. I've seen people killed. I've been taken out of my apartment at gunpoint and sent into a gun battle. I've been shot at, tear-gassed, everything. But I always ask myself, "Am I making a difference?" And if I can continue to say yes, then I'll stay, but it's getting increasingly difficult to say yes.

PM: What is the major difference going to be from both sides, if there's any reason for anyone here to feel a sense of optimism that things can be resolved?

DB: I think it's going to require a lot of intervention and a change of thinking. I think what's been missing throughout the period of Oslo and continues to be missing today is this idea of equality, the idea that we're both equal, we both have equal right to be there, both Palestinians and Israelis. I think that's something that wasn't fostered during Oslo and continues not to be fostered today. And that's where I believe Canadians can help, working on this idea of equality.

—

DIANA BUTTU IS STILL LIVING in Ramallah but has decided to take a break from the politics of the Middle East. Instead she's studying and writing a book on her experiences. In a recent email she told me that it would be fair to say she's been disillusioned of late by the actions of those on both sides. That doesn't mean she's given up on the prospects for peace, but she now thinks that international pressure is more likely to succeed in achieving that goal than the kind of direct discussions she herself has witnessed.

REX MURPHY

"WHAT'S REX MURPHY REALLY LIKE?" I get asked that a lot when I travel the country. Many of our viewers wonder whether Rex is anything like his persona on television during his regular Point of View commentaries or every Sunday afternoon on CBC Radio's *Cross Country Checkup*. Invariably I say that he really is the way he appears.

For starters, I don't think I have ever seen him dressed in anything other than a jacket and tie. That may seem odd coming from me, because viewers probably assume that I wear a suit most of the time. Wrong—I'm usually wearing jeans and a golf shirt or a turtleneck around the office during the day. (I often wear shorts in the summer. In the old days, before we had an air-conditioned studio, I'd even wear shorts on the half you don't see on *The National*!) The tie is one of the last things I look for before heading to the studio each night. Not Rex—one of the smartest all-day, every-day dressers in the building.

And does he really talk that way all the time? The accent, of course, is permanent, but it's Rex's vocabulary that strikes most people. Where do those words come from? And are they even real words at all? Surely he makes them up. If so, we haven't caught him out yet.

Rex loves to talk politics and politicians. Whenever I see him in the halls of the CBC, he pulls me over and wants to know what I'm hearing. "Is it really true?" he'll ask about the latest rumour wafting down from Parliament Hill. "We have to have lunch and talk about this," he'll pronounce. And believe me, if you think he's colourful on the air, you should see him in action at lunch. We try to stay away from the usual CBC haunts. When I buy, it might be the reasonable Royal Canadian Military Institute; when Rex is opening his wallet, we go whole hog at the Four Seasons or Canoe. Wherever it may be, I'm constantly looking around to see who's watching, or worse, listening—Rex saves some of his really special words just for lunch.

There's no doubt that we all turn to Rex for his wisdom on a lot of things, not just politics and not just Newfoundland. He seems to capture the spirit of the country in a way that few people do. And more than a few times on *One on One* we've all been richer for the experience, or could have been. (Keep in mind that some of Rex's comments transcribed here are from 2000. Read carefully, and take note of what he said back then about the stock markets.)

2000-01-16

Peter Mansbridge: Sometimes what you have to say makes us smile, sometimes it makes us mad, but it always makes us think. So, have you always been opinionated?

Rex Murphy: Oh, I think it was launched somewhere within the scattered strands of a mad DNA. I'm from Newfoundland, and there's an Irish tinge in there somewhere, and that—allied with a fairly genuine passion for certain kinds of writing and stuff— that began rather early. People like Mark Twain, Ambrose Bierce, Flann O'Brien, H.L. Mencken and these types. I've always had an affection for people who had the seeming unutterable gift of saying things so precisely and, in some cases, with such lethal force. And there are a great number of them out there. I think it's declined a lot, unfortunately.

PM: When you say "early," what are we talking about? Was little five-year-old Rex Murphy—?

RM: Well, not five, but I can say honestly—without affectation, because there's no glory or neither is there any blame to it—I was thinking about this when I was about ten or eleven. Looking for certain kinds of things. One of the reasons that I particularly like poetry so much is that in poetry you get the greatest compression, and if the word really matches the noun or if the image is really fine, in the greatest of poets and in the best of poets the marriage of the word and the thing is so fine. And that's all poetry. There's a subdivision of wit, in one sense, finding that exact term when it really, really fits. Even in a lyric poem, seventeenth-century or twentieth-century poetry, it's this precision. Yeats has it, and if you go really far back in a different kind of sense, you'll find it in Milton. I always liked that, and I tried to figure out how it was that they found that precision. The other thing is, you always read to see how other people do things. If you ever have a chance, read Vladimir Nabokov's autobiography, *Speak, Memory*. That's probably the most precisely and yet affectionately written book that we've seen in this world in fifty years. But it's the high example of what I'm trying to say and obviously not doing! (laughs)

PM: Now, this attained knowledge and experience and use of language that you picked up through this reading became something you used in arguing and debating in your early days in school in Newfoundland. They tell me you even got into a public argument with Joey Smallwood when you were seventeen.

RM: Oh, absolutely. I got into university, and the only thing I found that I was any good at was picking arguments. I was pathologically reserved and shy, and I decided the way to get out of that was to start debating. And then I found that actually it was a lot of fun, this business of debating or giving speeches.

I slipped out of Newfoundland for the first time at sixteen, because the president of the student council failed that year. I was the only one hanging around during the summer—probably stealing library books—and they had to send someone up to the student delegation. Smallwood had announced some great policy about free first-year tuition, and I got into this huge gathering of students from across the country. I remember the phrase I used: I said it was either a fraud or halfway between a fraud and a lie. Joey didn't like that description. He exploded back home and went on television for half an hour and told me not to come home, which put my mother to bed for a week. I didn't know about it, but when I came back, of course, I discovered all these things had gone on. Actually the speech went over very well, but I didn't realize the potency of the particular phrase right then. But it got picked up and Joey went thermonuclear—that's a spectacle you don't want to see even now.

PM: Now this is a person who was, and still is, a hero of yours.

RM: Oh, Joey was a magnificent creation. I think Joey was more of a phenomenon than a human being, and I really did like him, even though there were times when I was scared to death of him. He gave me the best calling-down I've ever had in my life, ever. No one else can bawl me out, because it's been done by the master. There was also something extremely attractive about him. In a serious sense, he had fundamental energies; he was almost like a natural phenomenon. His affection for Newfoundland was not feigned. He became a desperate politician, by the way—don't whitewash him. He was tyrannical; he was mean; he could be petty.

But on the other side of it, he had large ideas. He was an amateur who knew he was an amateur, as opposed to some of the more fanatical politicians we have at the end of this particular period of time. I used to have the idea that Joey Smallwood would take a day once a week to put things in perspective. He knew that all this was a joke and was willing to laugh even at himself. Now we have premiers, prime ministers and cabinet ministers across this country who are more sober than Joey and may technically be more educated, but I don't think that they have that "day off" in the way that I'm speaking about it. And secondly, I'm not sure that their fundamental commitment to where they are or the people that they are truly representing is as honest or authentic as his was. So in that sense, he was a natural lava vent of words and invention.

PM: You've raised something that makes me think about our current leaders, and I wonder whether it's a product of our age as opposed to what our leaders of this current era are really like. There did seem to be a character and a style of leadership through the Pearson, Diefenbaker, Smallwood days into the seventies, with Trudeau and the premiers of that era, whether they were Blakeney or Lougheed or Davis. There was a style, a character of leadership then that we don't see—or at least I don't see—anymore. And I wonder, is it us? Is it our older eyes, or is there really a difference?

RM: No, it isn't. There's one contribution to it that's a result of where you are placed in history. They've become more familiar today, so they're not as godlike. I know that when Joey Smallwood walked down a main street in Newfoundland in, let's say, the late 1950s, this was like a visitation by some sultan in the Middle Ages. People were shocked because this was someone they had heard and talked about, maybe heard as a voice on the radio.

But there's a bigger reason, and it's not just that they've become more familiar to us. They're not, in the main, as authentic. Whatever personality was in there then with all those you listed, Trudeau is probably the only modern example who retained it. They kept a large part of their character, and they weren't afraid of exhibiting it. They didn't have this trainload, this wagon train of executive assistants, speech writers, consultants and pollsters who constructed a public persona and put it out in either all its blandness or all its calculation. The Lévesques, the Smallwoods, the Hatfields—those types of people—they kind of gambled more or less in the raw.

PM: You take the pulse of the nation every week on *Cross Country Checkup*. Whether it's fish or farming, what's happening to this country?

RM: Oh, that is the question. There are a couple of things that are happening. One of them is that we've become more discrete and separated. I don't think the real dynamic of this country, by the way, is clarity legislation or the Quebec referendum. I think that that's a dynamic that is spent. It still has life; in other words, it has to go a certain course, but the vital things that gave rise to the moments of Quebec's awakening in the 1960s and the 1970s, when it had a real animation—they're gone. This is an inertial machine going to its predestined end.

The real areas of fracture, of disunity in this country—and they're not acerbic, they're not exaggerated yet—are things that are going on in the Prairies, in B.C. and, in a different kind of way, in the Atlantic provinces. The intensity of regional identification is as great as it's ever been. There's no continuity of consciousness about this whole country. So when the Prairies had a problem, when the crisis became manifest and people made very decorous complaints about their situation, there wasn't a broad-scale national response, and also not a broad-scale political response. And you heard people like Premier Romanow, the most unlikely person, saying, "We may have to retest our understanding of this arrangement if we have such an assembly of people— honest, ordinary, decent types of people—in a dramatic collective crisis and it isn't the business of the rest of the country."

People should never mistake Ottawa for the country, but the dynamics between Ottawa and provincial capitals often come to stand for it. So you have provinces, I don't say politically, but psychologically hiving off. We'll have a millennium broadcast or we'll have some great hockey game, and once in a flash moment we have a country. But it just spirals into view and does a kind of strobe moment of high-intensity existence and then it's gone. We don't have that series of continuities and intense shared moments that constitutes a dynamic twenty-first-century place.

PM: So who does?

RM: Oh, the Americans. They have it right down to their genes. You can have an episode in a Boston neighbourhood and it's a Boston story, but it's already integrated into the whole American psyche. They have a basket of symbols, and also a more frenetic way of doing it. I think they overdo it. But in our case (I speak of Newfoundland, and I've got such a core idea of it), Cape Breton, Manitoba, British Columbia, the North—all of these areas are intense, vital, civic. They're alive, but the capital, and the Canadian presence, is not present enough. It isn't as vigorous as it should be. It's fine in ordinary times. In times that are relatively speaking prosperous, it doesn't matter that much. But I think we are already a fairly fragmented bunch of people. And if we get a new torsion, a new twist of politics that changes, if there is some desperate run on the stock markets now that so many people are in them, if some new kind of challenge intrudes in here, then suddenly I don't think we've framed enough, emotionally, psychologically or civically, to give us much of a backup when the need arises. I'm being serious.

PM: That's scary. And that's happening at the same time as we're rushing headlong into huge technological and workforce change that is disrupting a lot of people. The other day a couple of those Cape Breton miners who are losing their mine were down at the bottom of the mine on a hunger strike, and one of them phoned up the message as to why they were there: "I'm forty-eight years old, I'm losing my job, I've been a miner all my life—who's going to hire me?"

RM: That's a direct quotation—change maybe a word, change only the location—from when I did the story on a Newfoundland fishery seven years ago. I don't think he said forty-eight, I think he said fifty. "Who's going to hire me?" And it's the same quotation—change another word or two—as the story from the Saskatchewan farmers. And do you know what's at the bottom of all three statements? "I'm this, I'm this"—and there's no reference that there's some sort of national community. I'm not talking about the Liberal Party or the Tory Party or the NDP, but that there's no national community. When something of that force hits a part of our whole community and we see that kind of particularized anxiety—the anxiety of a man or a woman heading a family who hasn't got a damn job anymore and also realizes with the swift march of change, "I'm not going to be part of that game"—those people can't be chopped off. I'm sorry, they really can't be.

And when you don't have a response or you have a sluggish response to an entire province or an entire region like the Prairies, and when it seems that the collective, the nation doesn't want to give a response—the thing that Canadians say we're all about is that we intertexture our lives, we support each other on the normal plane of things. But it's always these people in primary industries. It's farming, it's fishing, it's mining—those are the historical and heritage ones, by which I mean not that you should glamorize them but that they reach into the way we nursed our values, how we built ourselves. Now, they may have to go over time, but we should be conscious that they're going, and those that are caught in the change should be spoken to by all of us. That's the function of government and it's the function of the nation.

2004-11-13

PM: I want to talk to you about the *The Greatest Canadian*, because you're the advocate for—who was that guy?

RM: The only one. (smiles)

PM: He used to be a prime minister. What was his name?

RM: The only one, my friend.

PM: You are the advocate, as they call it, for one of the ten Great Canadians, and it's Trudeau.

RM: It is Trudeau.

PM: I don't want you to make the case here, because it's not fair to the other nine.

RM: No, it wouldn't be fair, I assure you.

PM: You obviously had to do a lot of work on this to get ready for your one-hour opportunity. What did you learn about this guy that we don't already know?

RM: Well, I always admired him. But after I spent about two and a half months in the archives, I learned that when this guy arrived as prime minister, he had done the one thing that's necessary. He had articulated the various forces at play in Canada: region, identity, histories, all those things. And he had a map for the most important things that we have to do as a country, as a totality, and for what will keep the civility that we have, what will extend and enhance the values and the sense of nationhood. The key sentence that came out of Pierre Trudeau's mouth was "Who speaks for Canada?" When he was there in 1968, he actually—this is what startled me—he actually had thought it out. He had about a ten-year map in his head. This was a strategic prime minister. And from bilingualism to the Charter of Rights, once you follow him through you actually start to see that this guy is moving almost as if it's a game of chess. Boil it down into simple terms, it comes to this: that at least one person who sought high office had studied the nature of the country, articulated for himself a vision, tried to persuade a number of people to it, but kept the whole, the totality, the dynamic of a country that is always changing in his mind.

Our deficiency at the present time, which is at work in provincial and federal politics, is that the minds are not as large as the country, and the various forces at play are not being attended to and are not being paid attention to. We're a country that's very casual about our own existence. And if we're ever deeply, deeply stressed, those continuities that we're ignoring will have faded away and we'll be in a circumstance of some jeopardy.

—

REX TRULY BELIEVED THAT PIERRE TRUDEAU was the "Greatest Canadian," but the judges for the CBC television special—the people of Canada—didn't. When all the counting was done, Saskatchewan's Tommy Douglas, the father of medicare, was the winner. Don't mention it to Rex—he's got a whole new set of words to explain the loss.

THE HOCKEY PLAYERS:
SIDNEY CROSBY, JAROME IGINLA
AND HAYLEY WICKENHEISER

THE FIRST YEAR THAT I INTERVIEWED a professional hockey player was 1973—Bobby Hull, the Golden Jet. I'll admit I get more excited, nervous even, about interviewing hockey players than I do about politicians or captains of industry. It must be something about those nights lying in bed when I was nine years old, dreaming that someday I'd meet one of the players I was breaking curfew to listen to on the transistor radio hidden under my pillow.

Seventy-three was the first year of the Winnipeg Jets of the old World Hockey Association, and Bobby Hull and the boys had made it to the Avco Cup finals, the WHA's version of the Stanley Cup. It sounds pretty tacky now but it felt pretty important then. I managed to convince my bosses at CBC Winnipeg that I should go on a road trip with the Jets and do a profile of the one player who had made the league viable. Bobby Hull's on-ice prowess was unarguable. He was a prolific scorer and his slapshot was a thing to behold—even errant shots booming off the end boards would bring an arena to its feet. But he did more than just play the game. He sold it too.

I remember one Hull scene vividly. We were at the old Boston Gardens for a game against the New England Whalers. After it was over (the Jets lost), the players had all filed aboard the team bus headed for the hotel—except for Hull. He was out on the street with a throng of kids around him, all asking for autographs. Finally he waved the bus on and said he'd catch a taxi. I waited in the hotel lobby and, sure enough, about half an hour later he arrived. I asked him why he'd stayed. He told a wonderful story about his dad bringing him to Maple Leaf Gardens in the fifties to watch a Leafs–Red Wings game. Afterwards they'd stood outside the Wings' dressing room hoping to catch a glimpse of Gordie Howe. Sure enough Howe came by, paused for a second and then patted young Hull on the head, ruffling his hair. "I didn't sleep that night, and I never forgot what that moment meant for me."

Anyone who knows the full Bobby Hull story knows he is no saint, but that night in Boston, he was for me. These days our hockey stars seem much younger, much faster, much richer and much more media savvy. I've been lucky enough to meet three of our best on *One on One*.

Sidney Crosby

I TOOK MY SON, WILL, WHO WAS SEVEN years old at the time, along with me when I interviewed Sidney Crosby one Saturday in June 2007. We did the interview in Ottawa, and I didn't tell Will who the guest would be. Because it was Ottawa, he thought it was going to be a politician, and he was utterly bored by the prospect, but he put on a game face nonetheless. When the door opened and Crosby walked in, Will went into a trance, his jaw on the floor. In a way, I guess, it was his transistor-radio-under-the-pillow moment. We started the *One on One* by talking about how Crosby had just been named captain of the

Pittsburgh Penguins, even though he was still a teenager—a rarity in the NHL, even for an acknowledged superstar.

2007-09-29

Peter Mansbridge: You're now the captain of the Pittsburgh Penguins, and I find it interesting because clearly you've had to debate becoming captain within yourself, on whether to accept this. You'd already turned it down a couple of times. What's different now? Why did you say yes?

Sidney Crosby: I think I was just more comfortable around the guys. I think that's a big thing; you want to feel comfortable around the players. They're going to have to follow, so you have to make sure that you're ready to lead. Just getting to know the guys better, going through things with them, going through a round of playoffs and just knowing the responsibility that comes with it— I think you have to take all that into consideration. You have to be ready for that. It just really made me realize that I was ready to make this step. I definitely want to take on that role. Every night I'm going to lead by example and do my best to try to lead everyone in the right path.

PM: Now I know you've said that age is just a number, but you're nineteen, about to be twenty. Some of these guys who are on the team with you are well into their thirties. What's the challenge there, in leading people who are almost twice as old as you?

SC: I don't think a lot changes. You know, if you look at the guys being a little bit older, you might say, "Oh, maybe it's not the right fit." And that might be the case on another team, but I think on our team there's such a great relationship between all the guys, and the older guys care so much about the younger guys and they really want to see them do well. They're there for any questions or advice there is. So really I don't think my role's going to change a whole lot, besides the fact that I'm going to be taking on a bit more responsibility. It doesn't mean I lose respect for the guys who have played a lot longer and gone through a lot more. That's not the case at all. I've talked to guys who've been in the league for a long time, and after talking to them I really felt comfortable. And you know, they were all for it. There were guys who were really telling me to take this opportunity. It's a huge honour, and I think that it felt a lot better having heard that from them.

PM: I want to try to understand a little bit about you, because we have a lot of images of you, obviously, as a great hockey player. We've all seen that as you became a nationally known junior, and now in the NHL. But we also see you through some of the stories that are told about you. Even the ads you're in—in the Tim Hortons commercial you are that little guy who wouldn't come off the ice. You wanted to stay on the ice. Is that true? Were you really like that?

SC: Oh, yeah. And that's something you have to consider when you deal with endorsements and things like that: it has to be the right fit and it has to be *you*. That's the one thing I take very seriously when these things go out—that it is a true reflection of me. In the case of the Tim Hortons ad, it couldn't be more me! That's exactly how I was. I'm still like that now. My coaches were laughing about it after they'd seen that ad, because they said nothing's changed. It's just that passion I have, and I think that's an important part of what I do.

PM: You sometimes get the impression that hockey really is everything for you.

SC: I think so. I mean that it's something I love to do. For some people it's different things; for some people it's art, some people collect things. Hockey's my passion. I want to be good at it. But I think I've also realized there are other things, outside of hockey. Obviously family is very important.

PM: You know, we've talked to your mother. She talked about you and movies, and that you never watched any Disney movies when you were a kid.

SC: No.

PM: You were too busy playing hockey, getting ready for it.

SC: Yeah, well, I think that's true to a certain point. I loved to play. I wasn't happy with just sitting down on the couch and watching TV or watching a movie. That's not something I really enjoyed. I was competitive. I've always been competitive. And whether it was baseball or hockey, I played. I've always just loved to compete and be active. Like I said, some people like other things. Now you see a lot of kids into computers and PlayStations and things like that. That just wasn't for me, especially growing up.

PM: You've said before that life's pretty good for Sidney Crosby. How good is it?

SC: I'm doing something every day that I love to do, and not everyone gets that opportunity. For people who do, they'll tell you how enjoyable it is to work towards something. You're really getting a chance to explore your passion, and not everyone gets that opportunity.

PM: What is the ultimate goal? When you say you're working towards something, what is it?

SC: To win the Stanley Cup. From a team perspective, that's what you play for. That's why you play all those games—to get into the playoffs. You play the playoffs to get to the Stanley Cup. And every year that passes by, you know that maybe that's one year that you might not be able to do it. So for me, I'm lucky enough. I'm young. Hopefully I have a few more cracks at it, but it's still something you don't want to take for granted and don't want to overlook, because there's a lot of guys who play a long time and don't win it. So I'm just hoping that one day I get that opportunity.

PM: How much pressure is there on you? Is it hard to be Sidney Crosby?

SC: I don't think so. There is a lot of pressure—there's no hiding that—but I think the pressure that I put on myself is probably the pressure I take most seriously and probably the hardest to deal with. I'm pretty hard on myself and I expect a lot of myself. But as far as what other people put on me, I don't think it's something that really worries me a whole lot. I know what I'm capable of doing and I know if I'm being honest with myself. And that's the most important thing.

PM: Do you enjoy being chippy about it as well? You're not shy out there when you think something's gone wrong.

SC: To a certain point. I mean, that's not an act. That's my emotion, and I can't hide that. I can try to channel it, which I think I'm improving at doing, but—

PM: You think you need to?

SC: To a certain point. I think that you need to make sure that your focus is in the right areas. Sometimes it's easy to get frustrated because a guy's checking you well or maybe you think there was a call that should have been made. It's easy to lose your focus. The guys that are successful are the most tough mentally. If you talk about leaders, they're the guys who can channel that and make sure that it doesn't get in the way. I'm still learning and I'm still going to make mistakes, but I'm definitely going to try to learn from them.

PM: Do you love it as much as you thought you would?

SC: Yeah, I do. That level of competition is something that I really love. And with all the teams in the NHL being so tight, with the players being so good now, you have to push yourself if you want to survive. That's something I think drives everyone, but it drives me every day.

Jarome Iginla

AS A CHILD FAN OF THE ORIGINAL SIX, I never imagined a day when I'd be walking amongst palm trees to cover a Stanley Cup final. But there I was in 2004 in Tampa, Florida, spending time with the remarkably talented Calgary Flames player Jarome Iginla, whose team was playing the Tampa Bay Lightning for the Cup. Iginla is tough, never backing away from a physical challenge, but also smart, knowing that goals, not fights, win games. He loves to score and is brilliant at it, but he enjoys setting up others just as much. While most of the media attention goes to Sidney Crosby and the goal-scoring prowess and antics of the great Russian player Alexander Ovechkin, it is Iginla and his off-rink influence that may have more to say about the future of the game. He's a superb player, but it's his heritage and his conviction that players have to do more than just play that make him special. This is a guy who contributes $2,000 to charity every time he scores a goal. Here's part of the chat we had that day in Tampa.

2004-04-04

Peter Mansbridge: I've talked to quite a few people over the past few days, read a lot of things about you, and everybody says only great things about Jarome Iginla. Is there nothing bad about Jarome Iginla?

Jarome Iginla: Oh, that's very kind. Sure there is. You probably haven't talked to enough of my teammates, or I'm sure my mom—

I'm sure there are some bad childhood memories! She always said I was too hyper, things like that. Well, they're being very kind, and we have a very close team.

PM: I think they're pretty sincere. They talk about you not just as a player but as a leader and as a person who cares about the world he lives in, the community he lives in, the well-being of others. So let's take a little bit of a trip with Jarome Iginla. Tell me about the first time you can remember thinking that you could be in a Stanley Cup final. When did you first think about it?

JI: When I grew up playing hockey in St. Albert, a city just outside Edmonton. I started at age seven. I watched the Edmonton Oilers' and the Calgary Flames' battles. At the time I was an Oilers fan. I saw them winning the Stanley Cup, and I always dreamt of being in the NHL and, you know, never thought of the odds. My family was always so supportive and always wanted hockey to be fun, so I never thought of what it would take or anything like that. I just enjoyed the journey and the steps along the way.

PM: So whether it was on the rink or in road hockey or whatever, you were imagining those kinds of games?

JI: For sure, yeah.

PM: Little Jarome making the move on the minute for the Stanley Cup?

JI: Yup, I played a lot on the outdoor rink, and my first dream was to be in the NHL. Then you dream about a big game, then playing it and winning the Stanley Cup and hoisting it into the air.

PM: Who were the role models then for you? Who did you look to on that great Oilers team of the eighties?

JI: I had a lot of people I really looked up to. Everybody loved Wayne Gretzky. I loved Wayne Gretzky. Mark Messier—his intensity and his leadership. Loved him then, and still do. And Grant Fuhr, for a number of reasons.

PM: Tell me about those reasons, because I think some people can probably guess that you identified with him on more levels than just as a player.

JI: Yeah. When I started playing hockey, I was aware that I was the only black hockey player on my team. I dreamt of being an NHL player and kids would say—not in a mean way or anything—"There's not really many black players in the NHL." So other guys that I really looked up to were Grant Fuhr and Claude Vilgrain, who played in New Jersey, and Tony McKegney. They were black hockey players who meant a lot to me in following my dream, to be able to say to those kids, "Yeah, there are! Look, there's a few. There might not be that many, but they're there. Look at Grant Fuhr. He's winning Stanley Cups. He's an all-star. It is possible."

PM: Your heritage is from a Canadian mother and a Nigerian father, now Canadian.

JI: Yeah. My mom moved, actually. She's American; she moved from the States and she's been here since she was twelve. And my dad is Nigerian; he came when he was eighteen. I'm very proud of my parents. They've been awesome. They still are. I look back and I'm just so blessed to have them, and the support I had from my grandparents.

PM: You mentioned the challenge of being a black player when you were growing up. For a long time this has been a white Canadians' game. It's changed over time; there have been black players in the league, as you mentioned. But you're a little different in the sense that you also represent a new wave of immigrant

Canadians, through your father. And the game is changing out there. When you go to watch the young kids playing in Canada, you see Nigerian Canadians, you see Somali Canadians, Pakistani, Chinese, Indian Canadians. Do you sense that change? Do you see yourself as a kind of role model, somebody who can talk to these kids?

JI: I think hockey has been represented by a lot of nations, a lot of countries and a lot of heritages for a number of years, and that's been something special. It's great to be in a room and have people from Finland, Sweden, Slovakia and all around the world and be able to share stories. I think that's a great part of the game. As far as being a role model, it's something that I'd be honoured to be. It's hard to put into words, but I know what Claude Vilgrain, Grant Fuhr and Tony McKegney meant to me in following my dream and thinking it was possible. So if there are young kids, young minority kids who want to play, and they've got a lot more people to follow than when I was younger, I think it's great for the game and great for kids, whatever nationality they are. They should dream to do it, and not think of the obstacles but enjoy it and work at it and think anything's possible.

Hayley Wickenheiser

STRATFORD, ONTARIO, WHERE WE LIVE, is hockey-crazy. On cold January days they still clean off makeshift rinks on the Avon River, which cuts through town, and players of all ages quickly organize pickup games—and players of both sexes. Girls' and women's hockey is bigger than ever, in no small part, one assumes, because of the success and gold medal–winning ability of the national women's team. And while many of its players are international stars, one seems to grab most of the headlines, one who has become a role model for—and the envy of—young girls across Canada. Hayley Wickenheiser is an exceptional athlete. She was part of the gold medal–winning Olympic women's hockey team in both 2002 and 2006 and she's planning on Vancouver in 2010 as well. She also played for the women's softball team in the summer Olympics of 2000. How it all started is how we began our 2002 conversation on *One on One*.

2002-03-01

Peter Mansbridge: Let's talk about how you got into this in the first place. When did you start playing hockey?

Hayley Wickenheiser: I started playing hockey when I was about five years old. I grew up in a small town called Shaunavon, Saskatchewan. It was just a farming community where life was centred around the arena. My dad built an outdoor rink in our backyard and all the neighbourhood kids would play there, and that's where I got my start.

PM: Was it unusual at that time for girls to be playing local hockey, or was it something that happened regularly?

HW: I was often the only girl who played. I played boys' hockey up until I was about seventeen, eighteen, off and on. In Shaunavon there was no girls' hockey, so I had to play with the boys, and I was usually the only girl. I think I probably paved a road. When I was playing hockey, there weren't too many other girls, so it was tough at times, but I loved every minute of it.

PM: How was it tough?

HW: I think my parents probably heard more comments than I did about how girls shouldn't be playing hockey, they should be figure skating or doing ballet. Boys on other teams would try to come after me on the ice every once in a while because I was a pretty good player. So it was tough at times, but I look back and am really thankful for that experience, because it helped me develop a thick skin and it helped me to believe in myself when nobody else did.

PM: And what was it about the game that you loved so much that made you want to pursue it?

HW: I just loved the game. Probably some of my best memories outside of the Olympics are just being on the outdoor rink and playing hockey with all the other kids. I think it's such a great game. You have all the factors. It's physical, mental, emotional; the unexpected—it has so many factors and it's so much fun to play.

PM: How difficult was it when you wanted to take it beyond the hometown and play hockey at the kind of level that you're doing now? How hard was that?

HW: It was tough. I'd tried out for a midget triple-A team when I was fifteen, sixteen years old, here in Calgary. My first year I got cut, and the second year I went back and probably should have made the team, and I got cut again. The coach said, "I just can't handle having a girl on the team. It would be too difficult." It was really tough because I wanted to try to play at the highest level I could. It's a good thing that the women's national team was in existence. That became my home and where my career started.

PM: At one point you even played at the Philadelphia Flyers camp, did you not?

HW: I went to the Flyers rookie camp for two summers. Bob Clark had asked me after the '98 Olympics to come and train. I didn't go there with the intention of making the Flyers; I went there to get better, and I think I certainly did that. I saw what it took to play at that level. I owe Bob Clark a lot from that experience.

PM: How did the other players at the Flyers camp react to you?

HW: It was interesting, because the first day I went to the camp we had to sit around the dressing room and say who we were and where we were from. I was sitting in a corner where no one could see me, and I had a hat on and I had short hair. So when it came to be my turn, they heard a female voice, and heads turned—they just couldn't believe I was there. It took a couple of days, but eventually I think I earned their respect, and I had a lot of fun.

PM: There's talk of you wanting to go over to Europe and play for one of the European teams. Are you serious about that? If so, how do you pursue that?

HW: Oh, I'm very serious. I have an agent, Wade Arnett, and we're looking into finding the right fit where I could play. I'd want to go and be able to play and not just be a spectacle. I've played with the women's national team now for eight years, since I was fifteen years old. I think that it's now time for me to maybe have a change of pace and try to raise the level of my game another notch.

PM: What does that say, then, about the state of women's hockey and the future of women's hockey, that for you to raise it to the next level you're going to have to play with men? Do you see this eventually as the way hockey has to go—that there has to be a mixed league?

HW: No, absolutely not. I think that the future of the women's game is in great hands, and the next step for the women's game is the professional league. But I see it being another three or four years before something happens there, because I think we need more talent from the European countries to come and help make the league a success. So until that point, it'll be tough to find competition. There are great Canadian club teams in Ontario, Quebec and Alberta, but outside of that there's not the competition that we need. So it'll take a few more years, and until then I think you have to be creative.

PM: How will that competition come? Obviously there's got to be interest now when you look at the millions of viewers watching your Olympic gold win and the calibre of the hockey that was played. There has to be the interest. So what else has to happen to make this a reality?

HW: The interest is there, there's no question. I think a little more time is needed to get some of those younger players developed and into that elite pool. We have a great core of under-twenty-two-year-old female hockey players coming up in this country. They're the future of the game; that's really where the next skill level sits. But until maybe the next Olympics, it's going to need a little more time for development. We need leagues such as the National Women's Hockey League in Ontario and the Canadian Interuniversity Sport league to really come on board and help promote women's hockey.

PM: Is it a money thing as well? Is there a need for money to be involved in women's hockey?

HW: Oh, there's no question. There's always a need for money in sport, I think, but certainly in the women's game. We have had a lot more corporate support from groups such as the Royal Bank and Bauer and Nike that have come on board and helped out. But there's no question that if a professional league is to happen, we need that support from not only Canadian corporations but American ones too.

PM: The players that were on this women's team—obviously there were stars like yourself, but there were a lot of names that aren't familiar to Canadians. One assumes they had lives outside of hockey, they had jobs. Were they all able to take this kind of time off without any serious impact on their lives outside of hockey?

HW: I think it's a huge sacrifice to play on the women's team. But I don't look at it as a sacrifice because I love to do it, and

I think all the girls feel the same way. We moved out to Calgary in September and we spent six months there. A lot of the girls are from the Toronto and Montreal areas, and they left their families, they left their jobs, and some of them are going back to nothing right now because they had to leave their jobs. It is a full-time job for us in an Olympic year, but outside of an Olympic year there are girls who have to have jobs and go to school in order to make ends meet, for sure.

PM: Paint the picture for me of what you see if everything goes right. Five years down the road, what will women's hockey look like in this country?

HW: My dream world would be to have a professional league and a feeder system from the club system in Canada. The club teams act as a feeder to the professional teams, as well as the NCAA system in the U.S., which brings those junior-age players— twenty to twenty-three—into the pro league. This will probably end up being formed in eastern Canada and the eastern U.S. So that's what I see in the next five years, and I think it's a very realistic possibility now.

—

BOTH SIDNEY CROSBY AND JAROME IGINLA keep scoring goals, winning new fans and in Crosby's case, adding the 2009 Stanley Cup to his list of accomplishments. As for Hayley Wickenheiser's dreams beyond her dresser top stacked with gold medals, she has realized the one she mentioned about men's hockey. She became the first female player in history to register a point in a men's professional game, when she played a season for the Kirkkonummen Salumat in Finland's second division.

THE PRIME MINISTERS

I MET MY FIRST PRIME MINISTER in the fall of 1958. John Diefenbaker was the most popular politician in the country, having just won the largest majority in Canadian history. And there I was in his Parliament Hill office with my sister Wendy, shaking his hand while a photographer snapped away from across the room. My mother was there watching, proud as can be, as the National Film Board directed us in a production called *Michael and Mary Visit the Parliament Buildings*. Surprisingly, we had been picked as two typical Canadian schoolchildren, in spite of the fact that we were barely four years off the boat from Britain, and still had the accents to prove it.

Years later, in 1974, I asked the man affectionately known as "the Chief" if he would sign a photograph of that 1958 moment for me. I was a twenty-five-year-old reporter at CBC Winnipeg and a regular weekly assignment was to head out to the Winnipeg International Airport on Friday afternoons, when the former prime minister, still the sitting MP for Prince Albert, switched planes on his way home from Ottawa. He'd use the time to hold a news conference and the Winnipeg media would dutifully turn up to fire a few questions. It didn't matter much what was asked, because Dief would always answer with what he wanted to talk about. It was after one of those sessions that I made my move with the old snapshot of sister Wendy and me standing alongside the then new prime minister. I could only imagine how many pictures just like that he must have posed for over his many decades in public life. He looked at the photo for a few moments and then, his jowls shaking, said, "Ahhh, I remember that day. Your mother was there." Ever since, I have never doubted—nor allowed anyone else to doubt—the stories that the man from Prince Albert remembered everything.

I've interviewed every prime minister from Diefenbaker onwards, although both he and Lester Pearson were out of office by the time I had the chance. But from Pierre Trudeau on, I've sat across from all of them and opened the questioning with "Prime Minister . . ." *Mansbridge One on One* didn't begin until the Jean Chrétien era, and he and his successors Paul Martin and Stephen Harper have made appearances. Three former PMs have been on the program as well: Kim Campbell, John Turner and Joe Clark.

Joe Clark

I COVERED JOE CLARK IN THE MONTHS leading up to and through the 1979 election campaign, a time when he was described by some as incompetent because an airline lost his luggage, as awkward because he held his knife and fork so that he appeared to be eating steak from the inside out, and as bizarre because while on a world tour he questioned a South Asian farmer about the size of his farmland by asking, "What is the specificity of your acreage?" All that being said, Joe Clark beat Pierre Trudeau in an election campaign—something no one else will ever be able to claim.

2001-04-22

Peter Mansbridge: As a young reporter I followed you as a young MP, and as a young opposition leader and a young prime minister.

When things went against you in the 1980 election and in the 1983 leadership race, I was always convinced that you wanted to be prime minister again, and that if you ever got the opportunity you wouldn't step away from it. Do you want to be prime minister again?

Joe Clark: Yeah, I want to be prime minister, but that's not enough alone. You have to ask yourself two other questions. Do I want that more than some other things for myself and for my family? That, at my age, is a very real consideration. And secondly, am I in a position to lead my party to office? I made a decision in 1983 that put my interests—my personal interests—in conflict with my party's interests. I thought my party's interest was best served by a leadership campaign. And whether I was right or wrong about that, I think I've demonstrated that I'm not going to let my interest—anyone's interest—in being prime minister do all the running. I'm going to take other factors into account. But unquestionably, if we are in a position where we have been able to draw together an alternative in the country and been able to do some of the essential policy work that needs to be done before we can think seriously of being elected, and I am the only person who can do that, I'll think very seriously about that. All I'm saying is, I've got other factors I have to put into that equation.

John Turner

JOHN TURNER WAS THE DASHING DARLING of Canadian politics in the late sixties and the much talked-of Liberal leader-in-waiting in the seventies. By the time he became prime minister in the eighties, some of the old magic had gone and his time passed quickly. The Friday afternoon in 2000 when he came to record our *One on One*, he'd been at a late lunch where a few toasts had been the order of the day. We all agreed that coffee might be a good idea before we started recording. Eventually we went into the studio and the conversation that followed was wonderful, and quite enlightening about how he saw public service, the importance that should be placed upon it and who had helped inspire him to call for more of it. When we were finished and he headed for the exit, the lineup of adoring young well-wishers was something to behold. No magic missing on this day.

1999-12-12

Peter Mansbridge: At an appearance at Mount Allison University a few weeks ago, one of the students apparently said that you stood for a lot of things when you were head of the Liberal government, and that the current Liberal government seems to stand for things 180 degrees opposite to that day, whether it's the trade deal, whether it's the GST. How uncomfortable does that make you feel?

John Turner: It was a very sharp question. As I said to the student, "You've already answered your own question." I don't make a practice of intervening in the current political scene. People know where I stood and where I stand on these issues, whether it's trade or globalism or the national identity, Canadianism, patriotism, the environment, so I don't have to differentiate myself.

PM: However, you feel very strongly about these issues now, and you think we're at a critical point. So does your criticism not have to be more focused and more directed?

JT: It's not just a governmental matter. I'm worrying where Parliament is. I mean not just the Liberal government, but where is the Conservative Party? Where is the Reform Party? Where is the NDP, for God's sake, on a lot of these issues that they used to be very strong on? It's just that the issues are not being aired in the public forum. Parliament is just not a legislative machine. Parliament comes from the old Norman word *parler*, to speak.

Where are the issues being discussed? Where is the natural forum? The forum of oration is the House of Commons, and they are not being discussed on the floor of the House.

PM: Why do you think that is? The House of Commons has changed quite a bit, even in the short time since you've left, because of the regional nature of the parties that are there. Is that part of the problem here?

JT: It may be. As a matter of fact, I was asked about this down at Mount Allison. One of those students did a nice piece of research. They caught a speech that I'd made in the House of Commons in 1963—I was still in opposition, before Mr. Diefenbaker was defeated—on the subject of the role of a member of parliament. I said that a member of Parliament ought to be responsible to his or her own conscience, how he or she viewed the country, and responsible to the interests of his constituency, or constituents, and that the discipline of the party in Parliament—the whip— should be limited to budgetary matters or major issues of state. On legislation generally, a member should vote his or her conscience or the interests of the constituents.

PM: When did that fall apart? Because that hasn't happened for an awfully long time.

JT: Under Mr. Pearson it was pretty vibrant.

PM: Even through those minority governments?

JT: Oh, yeah, because, after all, we had to make deals with the other parties. So the members of Parliament had a lot of leverage, right? Under Mr. Trudeau it became very disciplined and there was a centralization of power.

PM: And that's never changed throughout the—

JT: Mr. Mulroney had the same feeling, and it's now very, very tight, very controlled from the Prime Minister's Office today. But eventually you're going to say to the members of Parliament, "Look, these are issues. Why does some has-been like John Turner have to bring them up? Why aren't you bringing them up in the House of Commons, for goodness sake? You know how we feel."

PM: Let me read a quote of yours. I guess this would be in the sixties, when you first went to Ottawa: "We came up here as young members of Parliament, and we thought it was an honour to serve. The generation following me in Toronto thought we were stupid." I guess you were talking about the 1970s–'80s generation.

JT: That phrase is perhaps a little extreme. What I was talking about there was—I had the honour of being a friend of Bobby Kennedy, and when he was running for attorney general [of the United States], I was attorney general [of Canada]. When he was running for the presidency of the United States, he asked me to do some bullet points for him—not essays, just points on U.S.–Canada that he could use in his presidential campaign.

PM: You mean he was going to talk about Canada in a presidential campaign?

JT: He certainly would want to know the answers if he was going to be asked the questions. So I went down to the University of Wisconsin in Madison, where he delivered a speech to fifteen thousand students. I listened to it and then we went to a steak house after, where I delivered my bullets on U.S.–Canada. Two weeks later he was assassinated. But at that speech he said to those students, "I want on behalf of the Democratic Party, and I want on behalf of America, the best and brightest of your generation." That was his phrase. David Halberstam, who's a great author and wrote the book, never gave Bobby credit for that phrase. That's why I said, "We need the best and brightest of the generation who now are in their thirties and forties to go into Parliament, go to the legislatures, go to the town councils, go to the school boards. We need a revival of public commitment such as Mr. Pearson and Walter Gordon were able to instill in us when we came into the Liberal Party in our early thirties." That was the best and the brightest I was talking about.

PM: So how do you get the best and the brightest back into Canadian politics?

JT: First of all, we've got to make it worthwhile if they are elected to whatever—the legislature or Parliament—that they have a free view. Take some of the discipline out of party politics. Let them speak representing their constituents. I think the media has got to understand the public service—that the ministry of God, the ministry of man and teaching are the three great vocations. And I think those who offer themselves up for public life ought to be encouraged to do so. None of us are saints. You know what I mean—I think the media has got to understand that human beings govern human beings.

PM: Earlier you called yourself a has-been. You don't really think that, do you?

JT: No, I'm still practising law 110 percent. Once every six weeks I'm out there because somebody wants me to be out there. I say no a lot more than I say yes. But do I have confidence in our young people, having said what I said? You're darn right! Those students four weeks ago at Mount Allison restored my faith.

Kim Campbell

KIM CAMPBELL REMAINS THE ONLY WOMAN to have headed a national government in North America. It may not have lasted long and it may well have been a bitter experience for both her and those who tried to help her, but no one can take the

"Right Honourable" away from her name. Ditto the splendid painting that hangs in Prime Ministers' Row outside the House of Commons chamber.

When Campbell entered the 1993 election campaign she was leading in the polls against Jean Chrétien. There was an excitement evident in many parts of the country that she was going to change politics as Canadians knew it at the time. But it didn't happen, and it was clear it wasn't going to happen almost from Day One. She was standing outside Government House, where she'd just visited the Governor General to ask for Parliament to be dissolved and an election called, and she invited questions from reporters. When one question came in about budgets, money and health care, Campbell brushed it off by implying that campaigns weren't the time for serious discussion about serious issues. It was a killer of a line—a Conservative campaign–killer, as it turned out. Campaigns should be exactly that, and most parties pretend they are, but Kim Campbell was probably right when she said what she said. History tends to prove that the party that goes deepest into policy ends up deepest in defeat—not always, but often. Think about it.

As for Kim Campbell, she's moved on and seems comfortable with her place in history and what it represents.

2004-05-07

Peter Mansbridge: When you ran in '93, you began a string of three elections in which there was always a woman leader. In the other two they were NDP leaders. There are none this time. Does that say something about our country?

Kim Campbell: It's pretty depressing. It's interesting—I just came back from Salzburg; I chaired a seminar for a week on democratic governance and women in power, and Canada and the United States are way behind other countries in terms of the percentage of women who are in national government. I know that an awful lot of Canadians got mad about that *National Geographic*

almanac that listed me as an important leader because the magazine thought it was significant that Canada had a female prime
minister. I would share their sense that it was kind of irrelevant
if I could stand on a platform with the second and the third woman
prime minister, but I don't see any in sight, and it does worry me.
I know there are a lot of Canadian women who are concerned about
it. There's a group that formed—Equal Voice—trying to find ways
of bringing more women into the process.

PM: Even the United States—let's face it, we always like to criticize them for various things, but they do consider a number of
women as potential future presidents.

KC: Yes, but they have fewer women in their national government than we do, only 13 percent.

PM: Okay, I hear you there. But in terms of even accepting the idea,
they seem to be further ahead than we are. Or am I wrong here?

KC: In 1993 I had the highest approval rating for a prime minister in thirty years, and it's interesting because Jim Blanchard,
who was the American ambassador, was sure I was going to win,
and his staff said, "But no, the party numbers aren't there." But
my approval ratings were in the seventies, and I think that shows
that Canadians were ready for a woman prime minister. They
were excited about it. What they needed were some women to
choose from. One of the big problems I have with the new
Conservative Party is that it has so few women candidates. I think
it has fewer than any of the other parties, around 10 percent.
But even Paul Martin hasn't really lived up to his promise to
bring more women in. Anne McLellan is his deputy prime minister now, and she's pretty competent; maybe she'll be a candidate next time around. But you look at the landscape: only two
women have ever done a G-7 summit. You look at those pictures and, unless Tony Blair puts a kilt on, you're not going to
see a skirt. You know, it's almost as if it's gone backwards from

the days when Margaret Thatcher loomed large over the horizon, and even Kim Campbell, in her fleeting time.

PM: Can you put a finger on why that is?

KC: I don't know. Maybe it's that we've gotten to the point where we're coming up hard against people's resistance. But I think it's also the structure. When you have a first-past-the-post system, it makes it difficult. The most successful systems are when parties have voluntary quotas, when they really try to make sure that at least 50 percent of their candidates are women. In a first-past-the-post system there's no guarantee that the seats where you're elected are the ones where the good candidates are going to be elected. So we need to think about our electoral system.

It's such a great thing, you know, when people sometimes say to me, "Do you miss politics?" I'll say, "I don't miss the mean parts, but I miss being at the centre of the action. That's always fun." You learn about your community. Whenever I meet somebody, man or woman, who wants to go into politics, I always encourage them. And yet it's as if people are worn out, or afraid of it, or they think it's too awful and terrible and mean and horrible and you guys make our lives miserable—and you do—but there are compensations.

PM: A moment ago you mentioned the *National Geographic* list— the fifty most influential leaders in history. You're on that list. You thought that some Canadians were making a big deal out of that. What did it mean to you?

KC: I only heard about it when I heard about the controversy in Canada. They didn't phone me up and say, "Hi, we're going to put your name on a list," so it took me quite by surprise. My assistant sent away for the almanac and it was only four bucks, so it was a pretty cheap date. I think they were just looking at people whose positions represented something in either change or development, and certainly my becoming prime minister of Canada did that. So that's fine.

PM: Pretty heavy list, though?

KC: Yeah, yeah. Attila the Hun—you know you've made it when you're on a list with Attila the Hun. Unlike Margaret Thatcher, who was known as "Attila the Hen," but that's another story.

Jean Chrétien

ONE DECEMBER, AFTER OUR ANNUAL year-end interview at Rideau Gate, the official government guest house, where the Christmastime prime ministerial interviews have taken place for at least the last thirty years, Jean Chrétien asked me to come across the street to 24 Sussex for a holiday drink. I'd covered him for twenty-five years, from back in the days when he was Indian and Northern Affairs minister in the 1970s. This was a first, and I accepted, thinking maybe I could actually learn something useful (the interview had produced predictable responses, as the year-enders usually do, no matter who is occupying the PM's office). When we sat down in the historic mansion's living room, he brought out a bottle of something he described as *special*. He said a Caribbean leader had given it to him during a summit they'd both attended. I could smell the rum from across the room as soon as he spun the lid off. It was powerful stuff—I was sure you could start a car with it. I stayed about an hour before heading out to catch my plane back to Toronto. I recall a lot of laughs, but to be honest, I don't remember what caused them. As I said, that special rum was powerful stuff.

2002-03-24

Peter Mansbridge: Prime Minister, last week George Bush said the campaign against terror would be—and these are his words— "a long war; tireless, relentless." What's your view? What's Canada's view about how long this war could take?

Jean Chrétien: The fight against terrorism will take a long time. It used to be that the fights were between countries. Now it looks like it's from movements that don't belong to one country, as the al Qaeda groups were from many, many countries. This is a new situation that needs attention on a constant basis. Of course, he is right on that. That's why we had to pass laws to cut off the financing of these movements as much as possible. It's a new phenomenon that is no more about one leader attacking the neighbour; it is of a different nature. We don't know exactly how long it will be there.

PM: But what would represent the end for Canada?

JC: The problem is there will probably never be an end. That there will always be terrorists is not an invention of yesterday. But suddenly terrorism has taken on a new dimension. Of course, when you look at it—the attack on September 11—it was unbelievable that terrorists could attack New York and Washington at the same moment with such an impact. Before we always knew about terrorist attacks. Through history there have always been terrorists involved in any fight in many countries. Today it is an international movement. So he's right that it has to be constant; we have to find who they are, where they are, cut their funds and so on, and in the case of al Qaeda, who were protected by the Taliban, we decided to launch an attack in Afghanistan and the Canadians participated.

PM: That's a good point, because just before Christmas, when you were talking about what our involvement would be in Afghanistan, you suggested that Canadian troops would be there to hand out food and clothing. They weren't looking for a big fight. Now we're clearly in a big fight—

JC: Successfully.

PM: And you're the first Canadian prime minister in fifty years to send ground troops into combat. How did you feel making that decision?

JC: It was our responsibility. Fighting terrorism is very important and we decided to take part. When we sent the troops in January, we said, "They will be there, we'll help with transportation, they will help with distribution of foods." But when the decision was made, we were involved in the security of Kandahar Airport, landmine problems and so on, and there was a need for our troops in Operation Harpoon.* They moved there and they were successful. When you're involved in a situation like that, you have to do your duty. I was very impressed by the quality of the work of our troops there, and everybody is very satisfied by the performance and their abilities to do the job quickly and effectively.

PM: You've been prime minister now through three majority governments. Halfway through the third one, what do you still want to do as prime minister?

JC: I want to do a good job. We still have our agenda that was in the Speech from the Throne and the program that is being implemented: innovation, productivity, investment in excellence, our agenda with children, our agenda with natives. A lot of things have to be done to improve the quality of life of Canadians and prepare Canada to be in a very good position to compete in this new century. We've come a long way. We were bankrupt in 1993 and now are in good financial shape, and we're very competitive.

PM: As you know, in a couple of days the Alliance party—the official Opposition—is going to pick its new leader. We all know your jokes about the number of opposition leaders you've faced over time and defeated. So let me ask you a more basic question about the Canadian political system. Is it good for Canadian politics and democracy that one party is so dominant in this country?

* Operation Harpoon was the 2002 Canadian contribution to the first major U.S.-led offensive in Afghanistan against the Taliban and al-Qaeda.

JC: Some will argue that it would be much easier in the country if we had only two parties fighting, as is the case in the United States. But we have to live with the reality that we have a British-type system of politics that leads to more parties, and some parties tend to be regional. For me, when you're at the national level, you have to be politically national. I paid a certain price in my own province for a while because I always thought Canada was my responsibility. Some nationalists back home didn't like me and apparently I made a comeback in Quebec, but that is my pre-occupation, because I always said that when you're in federal politics, you have to think of the whole nation. That is your duty. If you're in provincial politics, fine. But national politics has to have a national perspective to have the country work together.

PM: I appreciate that and respect everything you've said, but the question is, is it good for Canada that there is, in your view, only one party that speaks for the country at large?

JC: The NDP think nationally too. They don't have the support, but they think nationally. I think the Conservatives try to speak nationally, but we have a better recipe. In democracy it's not for the leader of the government to be too preoccupied about the problems of the opposition. I have to run the country and I have to run my party, which is a big coalition. I have people in my party who are to the left of the NDP and some who are to the right of the Alliance, but we debate and solve problems in a very active Wednesday-morning caucus meeting every week.

PM: You love this, don't you? You're not going anywhere, are you?

JC: Oh, you never know. Someday I will say that it is time to go. But it's not today and I'm still enjoying it, yes. But it's a tough job.

Paul Martin

I WAS IN A FOURSOME WITH PAUL MARTIN one summer at a charity golf event in Ottawa. He can hit the ball a mile but, like many of us who play the game, it's never clear which direction that mile will take. In some ways his time in office was like that; one was never sure which direction things were going to head.

Martin was prime minister for two years and two months—far from what he'd hoped for, even talked about, when I first interviewed him just two weeks after he took over the top office in the land. I find it fascinating to look back at some of these old interviews, knowing that what would happen later would turn out to be so different from the hopes and dreams of the moment.

2003-12-27

Peter Mansbridge: Prime Minister, I guess it's fair to say that you've coveted this job for some time now. Now you've been in it for almost two weeks, what's surprised you most about being prime minister?

Paul Martin: It's every bit as exciting as I really thought. The opportunities for the country are exactly as I thought. I have been able to maintain that kind of excitement, and it's just not going away.

PM: You talk in terms of what you'd like to achieve over a ten-year plan. Is it a ten-year timetable for you? Some people are wondering whether that's really appropriate—talking about a ten-year term in office and the changes that they would want to make. That's basically three elections.

Martin: I really believe that we are at the beginning of one of the most significant decades in this country's history. There are great changes taking place outside of our borders. The rise of China, the rise of India—these great tectonic plates clashing together. How does a rich country like Canada focus and play within that? That's why I wanted to be prime minister. I want to be prime minister because I really want to make sure we succeed. Is it going to take me five years, eight years, ten years? I don't really know. I suspect that when I step down, the new prime minister will look at the decade ahead of them. I'm not doing this to be prime minister for four months; I'm not doing it because I want to win an election. I'm doing this because I believe so strongly in the potential of this country and the potential of Canadians. And that's going to be manifested over a decade-long period.

2004-12-18

PM: Prime Minister, it's been one year on the job. People—journalists, academics—are making their assessment of just how you've done in the role. I want to probe how you assess your own performance. Which achievement are you most proud of in the past twelve months?

Martin: I think it's the health accord. For the first time in a very long time you had the ten provinces and the three territories all sign on the agreement to have national benchmarks set up by impartial third parties; provincial objectives against those benchmarks; the ability to hold governments, including ourselves, accountable.

PM: If that was the achievement you're most proud of, which one gives you the most pause, that you feel didn't work the way you wanted it to work?

Martin: Well, obviously there were the rough patches at the beginning of the year.

PM: The sponsorship scandal.

Martin: There's no doubt that that took a lot of time, and it did derail a certain amount of the things that we wanted to do.

PM: Like what? What did it derail?

Martin: There was so much time spent on that. I felt very, very strongly that when you have something like that—sponsorship—the only way to deal with it is to be as open and as transparent as you possibly can be. Simply, I think people are entitled to answers, and my way of governing is that you let it all out. Obviously that took a lot of time and there was a lot of concentration on that. That being said, I really do feel, certainly since the election, that we have hit our stride and that we are governing the way that we really want to.

PM: Was one of the things it derailed the hope for a majority government? Did the sponsorship scandal cost you a majority?

Martin: It certainly didn't help. I don't think there's any doubt about that, and obviously I would have preferred to have a majority government. We have a very ambitious agenda. I think there's a tremendous opportunity for Canada to seize its potential, to put our plan into place in terms of the economy and social programs and in terms of foreign policy.

PM: Can you do that with a minority?

Martin: Yes, we can, and I think that we're in the process of demonstrating that. It's not as easy, but the answer is yes.

PM: You're off on another series of foreign trips. What's the importance of these trips to you?

Martin: I think Canada can make a difference in the world, and I think a central part of our sovereignty is manifesting our sovereignty, whether it be in the Arctic or whether it be internationally.

I don't think Canadians want to see us turn inward among our-selves, to begin with. But second of all, in terms of our economy, we're an exporting nation; we live in the world. We can't put up barriers to the world and turn in on ourselves; you have to be pre-pared, then, to deal with the world's problems. And what are the world's problems? They are an election coming up in the Middle East and civil wars throughout Africa. There are massive environ-mental problems that the world has to deal with. I think, because of the nature of our country and where our popu-lations come from, the fact that we were not a former colonial power, and because we've effectively built the institutions of democracy, there are very few countries that have the role to play that we can play. That's one of the most optimistic things that the world has seen, and it's happening around the world. People are insist-ing that their democracies work. There's a real opportunity for Canada to make sure that those people can accomplish what they want to see happen.

Stephen Harper

EVERYONE SAYS STEPHEN HARPER hates the CBC. He wants it closed down, sold off, privatized, whatever. All I know is that as far back as I can remember, whether he was working with us as he did on an "At Issue"–like panel in the 1990s or being interviewed by me as Opposition leader and later as prime minister, he's always accepted the invitation and always acted pleasantly no matter how testy the exchanges have been—and some have been testy enough to draw the ire of his supporters. On that score he's no different, nor are his supporters, than most of the previous prime ministers I've questioned. (In fact, only Jean Chrétien ever turned me down for an interview, and he did that after receiving a rough ride during a Town Hall I moderated in the mid-1990s).

2007-12-22

Peter Mansbridge: Your party has spent some money in the past
year attacking the leadership abilities, or lack of them, of the
Opposition leader, Stephane Dion. In light of that focus on his
leadership ability, can I ask how you personally define leadership?

Stephen Harper: That's a very interesting question. I guess the
short way I would put it is, leadership is setting some goals, taking
some decision on actions, bringing a team along with that, and
ultimately getting the job done. And ultimately, of course, taking
responsibility whether those decisions are right or wrong. In that
sense we've had a pretty good record over the past couple of years.
We've been a decisive government. I think we've tackled a lot of
challenges in the last year. We've tried to focus a little more on
the long term, which isn't very easy in the context of this minority Parliament. I think ultimately leadership is getting things
done, and getting things done in a way so that people understand
what you're doing and your own people follow you.

PM: On that point, is leadership taking the country in the direction that you want it to go, or is it taking the country in the
direction you think the country wants to go? I ask that in light
of the news of the past week that your government is doing a lot
of polling, more so than previous governments, with various
panels established on a wide range of issues. It seems like you're
looking for what the country wants, as opposed to where you may
personally want it to go.

SH: When you're asking is it what we think, or what I think, or
what the public thinks, Peter, it's a judicious combination of these
things. I don't think I would consciously take the country in a
direction I believed would be wrong and damaging, even if public
opinion said I should go there. At the same time, I hope I'm not
so arrogant as to believe that I will simply impose my personal

views, or that even our cabinet would collectively impose its view on the judgment of Canadians, of stakeholders, of business, of those who are learned in a certain profession. We do consult. I travel a lot around this country. I've talked to a lot of people to get a better sense of what they think, because often they know more about this than I do or the people or our government know. In the end what I would say is this: whether it's informed by a committee or whether it's informed by public consultation or whether it's simply the government having a strong view that we should go in a certain direction, in the end the government has to be prepared to defend and to live with the decisions it takes. If we make the right calls, hopefully Canadians will judge us appropriately in the appropriate time period. And if we make the wrong calls, presumably we'll pay the price for them.

—

STEPHEN HARPER ALMOST PAID THAT PRICE a year later in December 2008 when his government was challenged by a coalition of opposition parties to a vote of confidence over the handling of the economy. Instead of risking likely defeat, he shut down Parliament for a month to regroup. We spoke *One on One* a few days later.

2008-12-09

PM: Last week, dramatic events—no doubt about it. I don't think any of us have seen anything quite like what happened on the Hill over those days. I went through a number of your speeches on the campaign not that long ago, and I centred on one you gave on September 17 in Welland, Ontario, because there are some interesting comments you made there: "Any government has to be able to command the confidence of the House on major financial and economic matters. That's a long-standing principle." And later in the speech: "I would rather lose a vote in Parliament than do something that I know would put the Canadian economy into deep jeopardy."

SH: Yeah.

PM: There was no vote last week, and no sense of confidence on the part of Parliament in your economic plan. There seems to be a difference between your words that you campaigned on not long ago and your actions last week.

SH: First of all, Peter, before we can reach that conclusion, let the government table the first full step, or the first next step, in its economic plan. I think that's important. I don't think we want to be in a position, and I don't think Canadians would expect Parliament to be in a position, to express judgment on an economic plan before the government has had a chance to put it into practice. The House of Commons only sat for two weeks. The government delivered an economic statement with a promise in the Throne Speech, which we had just delivered and Parliament had just passed, to produce a significant number of economic measures in a budget.

PM: But wouldn't put it to a confidence test.

SH: There'll be a confidence test as soon as we have a budget, and that's as soon as the House comes back. Look, the responsibility I have as prime minister—I was elected to act on the economy. I'm not there to play parliamentary games. We're elected to provide our economic plan. If Parliament rejects our economic plan, obviously there will be consequences, but let's first get everybody focusing on what those economic actions should be. The government will come forward and present a wide range of measures in January. In the meantime, what I would not just challenge but invite the opposition parties to do is lay down precisely what it is they want to see the government do. We have a right to that input. Some of the opposition parties are saying they want to run the

government. That's fine. Precisely what is it you want to do? Let
Canadians know that and maybe the government can decide
whether or not it considers those actions wise.

—

IN 1979, JUST DAYS AFTER BEING sworn in as the country's
sixteenth and, at thirty-nine, its youngest prime minister, Joe Clark
headed off to Japan to represent Canada at the G-7 economic
summit. It was his first test on the international stage, and the
media, including me, were at the ready to pass judgment on his
debut performance. There was one moment I will never forget—
nothing substantive about policy or international tensions, but
purely optics. The Japanese hosts had arranged a traditional
Japanese lunch, with chopsticks. Reporters and columnists gathered at the huge television screen delivering the "pool" feed, a
culinary photo opportunity for the international media. Some of
the more experienced leaders—Jimmy Carter from the United
States, Helmut Schmidt from West Germany, Valéry Giscard
d'Estaing of France—knew this routine and the unspoken rule
that governs it: do nothing until the cameras leave the room,
because why risk an embarrassing moment?

No one had mentioned that to Joe Clark, though. It felt like
slow motion as we watched Clark reach for his chopsticks and
venture them towards the food on the plate. You could feel the
anxiety in the press room. Some pretended to cover their eyes for
fear of the outcome. Then, the moment: Clark's chopsticks
squeezed around a tiny morsel of food, lifted it off the plate and,
with the "world" watching, slowly brought it towards his mouth.
Would it make it?

After a few agonizing seconds, the astonishing result: success!
The room of Canadian journalists suddenly erupted in a cheer.
"What was that about?" you may well ask. Well, I've come to
think that the cheer wasn't really for Joe Clark as much as it was,
in a silly kind of way, for Canada. In that moment I don't think
Clark was the leader of the Progressive Conservative Party; he

wasn't representing a political ideology or even himself. He was more than any of those—he was Canada. And as innocent and innocuous as this story is, it has made me think a little more deeply about what it must be like for these men and, so far, one woman who represent us. And what it must take to be one of them.

There's a lot of cynicism in politics and in political journalism. Neither field was made for people with delicate feelings, people who are easily bruised by below-the-belt attacks or blunt insults. The politicians who make it to the top are pretty tough customers. They have sturdy egos, and confidence in themselves and their policies. To use a hockey analogy, when elbows go up in the corners, they're the ones likely to come out with the puck. When you speak with them one on one, when you aren't fishing for just a ten-second sound bite, you can feel their energy. And you can feel that they truly believe what they're doing is what's best for the country.

While I'm proud of our Canadian traditions, there's at least one thing Americans do that I wish we did. It involves how we treat our former senior public servants such as prime ministers and premiers. I wish we'd continue to address them by those titles even after they've retired or been defeated. I think they've earned it. In fact, I almost always do just that, even though it's not the Canadian custom. When I see John Turner, I say "Hello, Prime Minister." Peter Lougheed, Bill Davis—they're still "Premier" to me. And always will be.

TED SORENSEN

IN THE OLD BLACK-AND-WHITE television broadcast we see Harry Truman and Dwight Eisenhower and Richard Nixon. Lyndon Johnson is there, and so is the Chief Justice of the United States, Warren Burger, and the famous poet Robert Frost. They're all in that January 1961 broadcast watching a new president taking the oath of office. It's the moment leading up to one of the most famous speeches given by any American, certainly in modern times. It lasted only fourteen minutes and contained 1,300 words, but it would define a man and a time.

When John F. Kennedy uttered the phrase "Ask not what your country can do for you; ask what you can do for your country," surely everyone there recognized that it was a great line. But did anyone know it would become one of the signature lines of a generation? Theodore Sorensen was listening to that phrase, and to every other word that day, because he had helped write the inauguration speech, as well as countless others Kennedy had given on the road to the White House. Few people know more about the architecture of a successful speech than Ted Sorensen. When we heard he was coming to Toronto for a business meeting, I leapt at the chance to talk with him. At a time when landmark speeches are few and far between, this was a chance to understand why great speech writing has become almost a lost art form.

The vast majority of speeches I've witnessed as a journalist have fallen well short of moving the room they were given in. Pierre Trudeau had a few special stage moments during his time, as did Brian Mulroney in his 1984 campaign, but some of the bad speeches I've witnessed have been really painful. I can remember one candidate for the leadership of a federal party, in front of a national television audience, actually losing his place and never finding it again. The crowd was horrified and he looked as if he simply wanted to vaporize—anything—just to get out of the hall.

Most speakers, it seems, ramble on too long or, worse, have nothing of any real merit to say. Many of the great speeches of the past, such as the Kennedy one, Lincoln at Gettysburg and Churchill in his radio talks during the Second World War, were very focused and quite short. We rarely see or hear that anymore. Interestingly, as you're about to see in our fall 2007 interview (keep that time frame in mind), Ted Sorensen claimed that there was someone new who he felt had the right touch, and that analysts were underestimating this person's ability to move a crowd, and perhaps a country, just as John Kennedy had so many years ago.

Sorensen was well into his senior years when he stopped by our studios, and his failing eyesight meant that we had to carefully manoeuvre him across the studio floor towards our *One on One* set. When the program opening came on the monitors in the studio it contained one of the JFK inauguration lines Sorensen had written: "Let every nation know, whether it wishes us well or ill, that we shall pay any price, bear any burden, meet any hardship, support any friend, oppose any foe, to ensure the survival and the success of liberty." I could see a distant look on Sorensen's face as he listened intently, almost as if, for him, it was that 1961 moment all over again.

2007-11-17

Peter Mansbridge: When you see that inauguration speech—

when you read it again or you listen to it—does it still excite you the way I'm sure it did the day that President Kennedy gave it?

Ted Sorensen: Yes. To be absolutely honest with you, just this minute I was moved and almost tearful, and a little chilled, because I don't see that speech, much less the moving image of that man, very often.

PM: Take us back to that day, because you were one of those who was very closely involved in that speech. I know that President Kennedy penned a number of the lines himself, but so did you. When he was walking up to the podium, did you have any idea that that speech was going to be something from which people could quote back any number of different paragraphs or sentences all these years later?

TS: No. We had worked hard on it over a period of time. He was worried because only a few weeks earlier he had given another great speech, the farewell to Massachusetts in Boston, and he was concerned and his parents were concerned—his mother even wrote me—that some of the lines used in that speech should have been saved for the inaugural. I reassured her, we still had some good lines for the inaugural.

PM: He wanted a short speech, didn't he?

TS: Yes, he asked me to find out how long the others were and to find out if his could be the shortest of the twentieth century. It turns out that Franklin Roosevelt's wartime 1940 inaugural was very short because the ceremony had to be abridged.

PM: But why short? What did he see in brevity that told him that was the way to go?

TS: That's the way he was. He kept his speeches shorter than some of our more recent presidents, who need not be named. And he liked short, precise, exact memoranda if I were briefing him on whether it was a major crisis or a minor one. But he thought that a short speech would be more likely to be remembered and not bore people.

PM: It certainly didn't do that.

TS: He hated to be bored himself, and he didn't want to ever bore others.

PM: But what I find amazing about that speech—I was thirteen when I saw it—is that all these years later there are so many phrases from it that have stuck in memory and that are repeated often. Of course, the "ask not" couple of lines, which is perhaps the most famous, but there are many others. I compare it to *Casablanca*, which was a movie of about—an hour and a half? Even today when you watch it, there's got to be twenty or thirty phrases or lines in that movie that one never forgets.

TS: That's true.

PM: And it's the same with that speech. Now you don't see that anymore. Speeches don't make that kind of an impact anymore. What's changed? What's happened?

TS: I think the age of eloquence has disappeared. Today television, the cool medium—for which you have some blame—is coming into their living room, or sometimes their bedroom. They don't want the old-fashioned eloquence because it seems so stately, pompous, out of date. Politicians today don't write their own speeches at all, and they want applause lines: one sentence that will catch the emotions and the politics of the moment and people will stand up and applaud. Kennedy didn't think in terms of applause lines. He wanted his speeches to convey values, and principles, and policy.

PM: It's a wonder they don't learn from that, because in so many ways the politicians of today still want to be John Kennedy. No matter what their ideology, they want to capture that same kind of spirit around them that he managed to capture.

TS: Yeah, well, I can only think of one that's close.

PM: Who's that?

TS: Obama.

PM: Well, we know you're an Obama man. But what else has changed? I watch politicians now, many of whom can speak well from the podium; you see them, especially at election time, going extemporaneously. Yet when they become the leader, they're wedded to their teleprompter—which sounds odd, I know, for a person who reads the news every night to criticize. Has that teleprompter changed the nature of the political speech?

TS: An interesting question. Kennedy didn't use teleprompters much. His first introduction to the teleprompter was his speech nominating Adlai Stevenson for Stevenson's second try at the presidency, in 1956 at the Chicago convention. They said, "We're putting it on teleprompter," and he even had to have a rehearsal to see what it was like to read it from the teleprompter. And the teleprompter broke.

PM: That's not a good thing to happen.

TS: He, fortunately, being of the old school, had a text of the speech in his pocket and took it out and read it.

PM: Did he change things on the fly?

TS: Of course. In fact, would you believe that a couple of years ago there were two books written about that inaugural address?

PM: Yeah.

TS: All these years later, books written about a speech! And when the *New York Times* interviewed me, I said, "Don't you think that it's more important to ask what's happened to the policies and principles enunciated in that speech instead of asking who wrote particular words?" In any event, one of those books said that, given the last reading copy that he had signed off on before the event, Kennedy made—I forget the number—twenty-three or more slight changes on the fly as he was reading.

PM: So . . . who *did* write it?

TS: (pauses) Ask not.

PM: (laughs) Are there too many speech writers today? Perhaps this is an odd question to ask a speech writer.

TS: Yes. No. Well, I don't want to say anything against the proud profession of speech writers. After all, Hamilton and Jefferson had their days as speech writers, and some other very distinguished people. The problem is too many speech writers on the same speech. I never had a collaborator except John F. Kennedy himself. I never had a team. Now they have speech writing departments in the White House. Maybe they do in the Prime Minister's Office in Canada, for all I know. There are six, seven, eight or nine speech writers in that office and at least three of them work on every speech. I don't think that's the way to get good, clear, precise, direct statements.

PM: And you probably end up with a speech that's too long as well.

TS: Too long. Not only wordy, but not as clear, not as direct, not as commanding.

PM: What is a good length for a speech?

TS: Time? JFK thought twenty, twenty-five minutes. Of course, if you're giving the State of the Union address, everybody has to get his program in there and it begins to sound like the budget or the telephone book after a while. So that can go on. His State of the Union addresses I'm sure went much longer than that. But certainly for an audience that's standing, or even sitting, he felt you can get across what you want to say in twenty-five minutes.

PM: How do you describe leadership?

TS: I think that of the key qualities of a leader, number one is judgment. A leader has to select a team. He has to select a strategy. He has to know timing. He makes so many decisions. To decide is to choose. To choose requires first-rate judgment. Some leaders have it and many do not. He also has to have the ability to mobilize by inspiring other people—not much point being the leader if he doesn't have followers.

PM: It does seem that generally the public feels they are bereft of good leaders, that the quality of leaders has somehow fallen considerably from the golden age of leaders, whether it was Churchill or Kennedy, although there's much debate about the leadership quality of Kennedy—

TS: Oh, I don't know about that. I think that in Kennedy's time, de Gaulle was president of France. Adenauer was chancellor of Germany. Macmillan was prime minister of England. There was an overlap with Trudeau as prime minister here. Those were giants, and we haven't had an age of giants since.

PM: But are they giants because we were growing up during that period and saw them that way? Do we now judge leaders much more harshly?

TS: I think it's in part because the times require giants. Internationally, the Cold War was a test for the very survival of Western civilization, and it required leaders who were strong and far-seeing. At home we had the civil rights crisis, and Kennedy was able to turn that around as no one had for hundreds of years. Even in science, it was under Kennedy's initiative that man finally left the moorings of Earth. Great times demand great men, or women.

PM: But are we not allowing the system to encourage potentially great men and women to get into it? Politics has somehow become a dirty word.

TS: Yes, not that everybody admired all politicians even back then. Kennedy used to joke about the woman in England who supposedly wrote to her son's headmaster, "Don't teach my boy poetry. He's going to stand for Parliament." (laughs) Again, I don't really want to keep pointing the finger at you, Peter, but the media has some responsibility.

PM: I agree with that.

TS: The "gotcha" kind of political attack has been fanned, indeed encouraged if not discovered, by the news media. A lot of very good people do not want to enter public service of any kind. They don't want to run for office at any level because their lives, their personal lives, will be investigated, scrutinized, publicized. Their pay is not much compared to what they can make in the private sector, so they say, "Who needs it?" Sure, lots of people are running for president in both parties in the United States this year, but very few of them are deserving of the "outstanding leader" title we're talking about here today. Good people seem to be driven out by the vicissitudes of the profession.

PM: What is it about Barack Obama that you find so appealing?

TS: Ah, well, this is only a half-hour show.

PM: If you'd point to his leadership quality—because if there's a knock on him it's that he doesn't have the broad national experience. He was a state senator and—

TS: Oh, that's true—(mockingly) like Cheney and Rumsfeld. That's true, he doesn't. He doesn't have experience in Washington. He has experience at the state level, like Franklin D. Roosevelt did. He has experience at the grassroots level as a community organizer in South Chicago. He has experience as a civil rights law professor. He has experience in living abroad, which as noted in this morning's *New York Times*—if I may invoke that bit of cultural imperialism—gives him a perception of the role of the United States in the world that those who have never lived abroad simply don't have. I think Obama's experience is a unique experience that uniquely qualifies him for high leadership in our government, and I think enough people will recognize that that he'll win. As a Democrat, I'm tired of losing. Above all, he has that quality I mentioned before: judgment. He opposed the war in Iraq even before it started. None of the other candidates can say that.

PM: You know, we all tend to think—certainly those of us who grew up during that time—that we know everything that we need to know, possibly could know, about John Kennedy. Tell me something that will surprise me about that man.

TS: You're going to have to wait until next May, when my book comes out. (smiles) My memoirs, which took me six years to write because I can't see anymore, are going to have lots of new information, anecdotes, my relationship with him over eleven years. I think you may be surprised at what a marvellous sense of humour he had. I think you may be surprised at the depth of the relationship between him and his wonderful wife. I think you may be surprised at how cool he was during the worst crisis facing our country. And in that connection, everybody's going to be surprised at the extent to which the man who spoke those words—"pay any price, bear any burden"—was actually a man of peace. He was determined not to go to war, and there were several opportunities where with that enormous military it would have been so easy to go to war. But he had been through a war in the South Pacific, lost two of his best friends. And as he said in his best speech, the American University commencement, "The world knows America will never start a war. This country has seen enough of war. This generation of Americans," he said, "has seen enough of war."

—

IN 2008 TED SORENSEN WROTE about his time with John Kennedy, and later with his brother Robert, in the book *Counselor: A Life at the Edge of History*. There are a few nuggets of new information about the two assassinated brothers, but the Sorensen line that struck me most about a man who made a career out of advising and writing for others, is when he observed, "When the Kennedy brothers died, it robbed me of my future."

BARACK OBAMA

PEOPLE OFTEN ASK ME IF I GET NERVOUS before a big interview. Often they claim I don't look nervous, but I know appearances can be deceiving. The truth is that I usually feel butterflies before every interview. And I'm glad I do, for one simple reason: it helps get my energy up.

So I was surprised that morning in February 2009 when I woke up in a Washington hotel room feeling extremely calm, even though I knew that in a few hours I would be sitting in the White House interviewing Barack Obama. It was to be the CBC's first one-on-one interview with a sitting U.S. president that anyone could remember. I got up, did a few sit-ups and stretching exercises, and showered. Then I picked up my razor and shaved, always a dangerous proposition when you're pumped and about to go before the cameras, but no blood-dripping cuts ensued. I put on a clean, nicely pressed white shirt and decided on a blue tie, knowing the odds were he'd be wearing red. Reached into the closet for my suit pants and slipped into them. Put on my shoes and gave them a quick polish. Read the *Washington Post* and the *Wall Street Journal*, ate some fresh fruit and washed it down with some decaf coffee. Put on my suit jacket and headed for the door. I was so relaxed that I said to myself, "President of the United States? White House? What's the big deal?"

So imagine my surprise when I got off the elevator, walked across the hotel lobby and caught my reflection in a mirror—my suit jacket and pants were two very different colours. I'd put on the wrong pants. As I raced back up to my room I was almost relieved, because this little embarrassment proved of course that the interview was a big deal, and an appropriate amount of nervous energy can be a constructive thing.

It's a short three-block walk from the Willard Hotel, where I was staying, to the White House, and I've made it many times over the years, usually just to record a stand-up in front of the most famous residence in America. I'd been inside the White House only once before, during the Reagan years, as part of one of those media scrums let in for a few staged comments and then quickly ushered out. This was a lot different. For almost a quarter of an hour I would be effectively "alone" with the President of the United States.

I was escorted through White House security at the main gate on Pennsylvania Avenue, ushered along the driveway where the correspondents do their nightly "hits" for U.S. network newscasts, and then through a service entrance and down a red-carpeted hallway towards the first-floor room where the interview would take place. "The President will be here at 9:13. Please be ready," said one of his communications people as I arrived shortly after eight o'clock. "Sure," I thought, "9:13. I bet no one is that precise."

At 9:13 Barack Hussein Obama bounded along the hallway, turned the corner into our room, hand outstretched, and said loudly and warmly, "Good morning, Peter. It's great to have you here." I wanted to think, "Hey, he actually knows me!" but common sense prevailed. I assumed that the last thing whispered into his ear before entering the room was, "Hey, the guy's name is Peter."

So there we were, the former Transair baggage handler and the most powerful man in the world, small-talking the seconds away before the conversation was to begin. The set-up in what's called the Map Room (for its storage of historic U.S. military maps) had been monitored and approved every step of the way by the Secret Service and the President's communications staff. But just as we were about to start, his press secretary, Robert Gibbs, declared, "Wait, the lighting isn't right." Everything was delayed one or two minutes as the lighting was adjusted.

I looked across at the person who one assumes is busier than anyone else you'll ever meet and said, "Sorry about this, Mr. President." He smiled and almost with resignation responded, "Don't worry about it. This happens all the time. It's the 'shine' police at it again." It was a light moment, a reference to the gaggle of image people who follow him around trying to ensure that every time he's caught on camera, nothing looks bad. They should have relaxed. Our main camera that day was operated by Doug Husby, one of the CBC's best. He's someone who over the years has captured some of the most famous people in the world on camera, and no one has ever complained about how they looked. Neither, as it turned out, would Barack Obama.

The President's people had made it clear that the interview was to last ten minutes, not a second longer. And while you can't see them when you watch the *One on One* conversation, among the dozen or so people hugging the walls off-camera were a few of his staffers literally counting down the seconds. I went into the interview with half a dozen issues I wanted to raise but knowing I'd be lucky to get to three or four. Ten minutes goes by very quickly, and you have to know where to start, when to move on and what to drop. This is not a perfect science, but you make decisions, usually on the fly, and hope for the best.

My first decision was not to allow the opening minutes to be chewed up on softer stuff but to get right to the substantive issues: trade, the economy, energy and Afghanistan. Before I knew it, producers Leslie Stojsic and Samira Hussain (the two people who had worked hardest on getting the interview) were relaying the "one minute left" signal. I could sense the President's staff pacing. Outside over the White House lawn, his helicopter, *Marine One*, was circling, waiting to pick him up for a shuttle to *Air Force One* and a flight to Denver. The chopper was circling because the press people had told it to stay aloft to prevent the noise of its landing from disrupting the interview.

My next move would determine how long that helicopter kept hovering. With about fifty seconds remaining I said, "I've only got a minute left," made a quick crack about his famous BlackBerry addiction by saying that he carried a bit of Canada on his belt, and then asked, "What's your sense of Canada?" In doing so I'd punted the last time cue to him, and control of the interview's length was now in his hands. It was up to Barack Obama if this baby was going to end on time. He gave a great answer. Counting a brief final exchange and the thank-yous, it went more than two minutes, putting the interview well past the ten-minute barrier dictated by his staff. Hey, not my fault.

2009-02-19

Peter Mansbridge: Mr. President, thank you for doing this. Canadians are very excited about your trip.

Barack Obama: Thank you.

PM: When they watch you sign your recovery bill into law today, how concerned should they be that the "Buy America" clause is still there? Even though you've given assurances that international trade agreements will be respected, how concerned should they be?

BO: I don't think they should be too concerned. If you look at history, one of the most important things during a worldwide recession of the sort we're seeing now is that each country does not resort to "beggar thy neighbour" policies, protectionist policies. They can end up further contracting world trade. And my administration is committed to making sure that, even as we take steps to strengthen the U.S. economy, we are doing so in a way that actually over time will enhance the ability of trading partners like Canada to work within our boundaries. My expectation is that where you have strong U.S. competitors who can sell products and services, a lot of governors and mayors are going to want to try to find U.S. equipment or services, but that we are going to abide by our World Trade Organization and NAFTA obligations just as we always have.

PM: You mentioned NAFTA. A year ago you were pretty critical of NAFTA. In fact, you even suggested at one point that the U.S. opt out if it couldn't renegotiate. Do you think it's the time now to be making that case or is it something that's set aside now?

BO: I think there are a lot of sensitivities right now because of the huge decline in world trade. As I've said before, NAFTA—the basic framework of the agreement—has environmental and labour protections as side agreements. My argument has always been that we might as well incorporate them into the full agreement so that they're fully enforceable. But what I've also said is that Canada is one of our most important trading partners. We rely on them heavily; there's $1.5 billion worth of trade going back and forth every day between the two countries, and it is not in anybody's interest to see that trade diminish.

PM: Especially now?

BO: Absolutely.

PM: Part of that trade involves the energy sector. A lot of oil and gas comes to the United States from Canada, and even more in the future, with oil sands development. Now there are some in your country—and Canada as well—who feel the oil sands is dirty oil because of the extraction process. What do you think? Is it dirty oil?

BO: What we know is that the oil sands creates a big carbon footprint. So the dilemma that Canada faces, the United States faces and China and the entire world face is how do we obtain the energy that we need to grow our economies in a way that is not rapidly

accelerating climate change. That's one of the reasons why the stim-
ulus bill that I'll be signing today contains billions of dollars towards
clean energy development. I think, to the extent that Canada and
the United States can collaborate on ways that we can sequester
carbon, capture greenhouse gases before they're emitted into the
atmosphere, that's going to be good for everybody. Because if we
don't, then we're going to have a ceiling at some point in terms of
our ability to expand our economies and maintain the standard of
living that's so important, particularly when you've got countries
like China and India that are obviously interested in catching up.

PM: So are you drawing a link, then, in terms of the future, of
tar sands oil coming into the U.S., contingent on a sense of a continental environment policy on cap-and-trade?

BO: What I'm suggesting is that no country in isolation is going
to be able to solve this problem. So Canada, the United States,
China, India, the European Union—all of us are going to have
to work together in an effective way to figure out how we balance
the imperatives of economic growth with very real concerns about
the effect we're having on our planet. And ultimately I think this
can be solved by technology. I think that it is possible for us to
create a set of clean energy mechanisms that allow us to use things
not just like oil sands, but also coal. The United States is the
Saudi Arabia of coal; we have our own homegrown problems in
terms of dealing with a cheap energy source that creates a big
carbon footprint. So we're not going to be able to deal with any
of these issues in isolation. The more we can develop technologies
that tap alternative sources of energy but also contain the environmental damage of fossil fuels, the better off we're going to be.

PM: I know you're looking at it as a global situation, in terms of
global partners, but there are some who argue that this is the
time. If there was ever going to be a continental energy policy
and a continental environmental policy, this would be it. Would
you agree with that thinking?

BO: I think one of the promising areas for not just bilateral but also trilateral co-operation is around this issue. I met with President Calderón here in the United States, and Mexico actually has taken some of the boldest steps around the issues of alternative energy and carbon reductions of any country out there. It's very rare for a country that's still involved in developing and trying to raise its standard of living to stay as focused on this issue as President Calderón's administration has. What I think that offers is the possibility of a template that we can create between Canada, the United States and Mexico that is moving forcefully around these issues. But as I said, it's going to be important for us to make sure that countries like China and India, with enormous populations and huge energy needs, are brought into this process as well.

PM: Afghanistan. As you know, Canada has been there from the beginning, since the fall of 2001, and has suffered extreme casualties in its combat missions there. And the Canadian Parliament has decided that we will be out of combat by the year 2011. When you get to Ottawa, will you have any suggestions to Canada that it should reconsider its role in Afghanistan?

BO: First of all, I think the Canadian contribution has been extraordinary, and for all the families who have borne the burden in Canada, we all have a heartfelt thanks. I'm in the process of a strategic review of our approach in Afghanistan. Very soon we will be releasing some initial plans in terms of how we are going to approach the military side of the equation in Afghanistan. But I am absolutely convinced that you cannot solve the problem of Afghanistan, the Taliban, the spread of extremism in that region solely through military means. We're going to have to use diplomacy; we're going to have to use development. My hope is that in conversations that I have with Prime Minister Harper, he and I end up seeing the importance of a comprehensive strategy, and one that ultimately the people of Canada can support, as well as the people of the United States can support. Because obviously, here as well, there are a lot of concerns about a conflict that has lasted quite a long time now and actually appears to be deteriorating at this point.

PM: But are you saying that you will or you won't ask Canada to remain in a combat role?

BO: We've got until 2011, according to the Canadian legislature. I think it's important for the Canadian legislature and the people of Canada to get a sense that what they're doing is productive. So what I will be communicating is the approach that we intend to take. Obviously I'm going to be continuing to ask other countries to help think through how we approach this very difficult problem, but I don't have a specific "ask" in my pocket that I intend to bring out in our meetings.

PM: Is Afghanistan still winnable?

BO: I think Afghanistan is still winnable in the sense of our ability to ensure that it is not a launching pad for attacks against North America. I think it's still possible for us to stamp out al Qaeda, to make sure that extremism is not expanding but rather is contracting. I think all those goals are still possible but that as a consequence to the war on Iraq, we took our eye off the ball. We have not been as focused as we need to be on all the various steps that are needed in order to deal with Afghanistan. If you've got narco-trafficking that is funding the Taliban, if there is a perception that there's no rule of law in Afghanistan, if we don't solve the issue of the border between Afghanistan and Pakistan, then we're probably not going to solve the problem.

PM: I'm down to my last minute. A couple of quickies on Canada. As you may know, you carry Canada on your belt—that BlackBerry is a Canadian invention.

BO: (smiles) Absolutely.

PM: You've been to Canada. What's your sense of the country?

BO: I've been to Canada a couple of times. Most recently it was to visit my brother-in-law's family, who's from Burlington, right outside of Toronto. I think that Canada is one of the most impressive countries in the world, the way it has managed a diverse population, a migrant economy. The natural beauty of Canada is extraordinary. Obviously there is enormous kinship between the United States and Canada, and the ties that bind our two countries together are things that are very important to us.

　　One of the things that I think has been striking about Canada is that in the midst of this enormous economic crisis, Canada has shown itself to be a pretty good manager of the financial system and the economy in ways that we haven't always been here in the United States. That's important for us to take note of—that it's possible for us to have a vibrant banking sector, for example, without taking some of the wild risks that have resulted in so much trouble on Wall Street.

PM: We appreciate this very much. You still haven't seen your first hockey game.

BO: I'm looking forward to making it happen at some point.

PM: Mr. President, thank you very much.

BO: Thank you so much. Appreciate it.

—

AS SOON AS THE INTERVIEW WAS OVER he was generous with his handshakes, and then he disappeared out the door with Secret Service agents at his side and his entourage rushing off after him. It was helicopter time, or so I thought. As Samira, Leslie and I were doing a quick post-mortem there was a commotion at the door, and guess who barged back in? The President, with a big smile and a hearty, "Peter, you gotta meet this guy. He's from Victoria!" The guy was Marvin Nicholson, Barack Obama's national trip director, a giant of a fellow who clearly is also part of that group of friends who play basketball with the nation's number-one basketball fan. "He's a pal of Steve Nash," said the President, talking about the great Canadian-born NBA player, "but he's got no game!" "No game" Nicholson moved towards me, hand outstretched, saying, "Wow, Peter Mansbridge—my mother loves you." Never thought I'd hear that one while standing next to the President of the United States. And then finally, to the relief of his travelling entourage, he was off towards the helicopter, laughing all the way.

FINAL THOUGHTS

A FEW WEEKS BEFORE OUR INTERVIEW and shortly after
his inauguration, Barack Obama had made headlines around the
world by saying "I screwed up." He was talking about his choice
for a particular cabinet officer who later had to withdraw his
name from nomination because of a perceived wrongdoing.
Saying he had "screwed up" was unprecedented for a United
States president, but it was candour that was welcomed around
the world. It was the kind of thing that had made Obama the
most popular political figure anywhere at that time.

But we all know that times change, and it was that possibility that had framed the question I never got to ask that day in
the White House: "Mr. President, how many times can you reach
for one of those 'I screwed up' excuses before the people lose their
affection for you?" But I ran out of time, which is a shame because
I'm sure his answer would have been interesting. That's the nature
of interviewing with a fixed end time: there will always be questions you are never able to ask and wished you had.

I often give speeches about current events and the challenges
we face in journalism trying to cover them, and when I do, I
invite questions from the audience when I'm finished. Perhaps
the most frequent one I get is this: "Who from the past do you

wish you could go one-on-one with today?" It's a fantasy of course, but it's one that's fun to ponder. Some nights I'll lie awake thinking about the possibilities. Christ, Muhammad, Caesar, Hitler, Elizabeth I, Einstein, Gandhi, Mao, Galileo, Mozart and, for Canadian content, Sir John A. Macdonald—they all figure prominently in a list that can be as long as your imagination. But for me it almost always comes down to one person—Sir Winston Churchill—because I have for so long been fascinated by his life, his decisions and his times.

But when I wake in the morning, it's the list of the living I consider. A list that seems to only grow longer with people who can stimulate our minds, challenge our assumptions and fascinate us with their experiences. My hope for the future is that we'll continue to see many of them sitting in that chair right across from me.

PETER MANSBRIDGE IS THE CHIEF CORRESPONDENT of CBC News. He anchors CBC's flagship nightly news program, *The National*, and all CBC News specials. He is also the host of CBC Newsworld's *Mansbridge One on One*. During a decorated career, he has received twelve Gemini Awards for excellence in broadcast journalism. In the summer of 2008, Governor General Michaëlle Jean named him an Officer of the Order of Canada, Canada's highest civilian honour.

BIBLIO RPL Ltée

G – JAN. 2010